Wingless Butterfly
Healing the Broken Child Within

Casi McLean

Copyright © 2017 Casi McLean
All rights reserved.
ISBN: 978-0-9912029-8-0

Introduction

*"You don't want to know him;
He's the kind of man who pulls wings off of butterflies."*

Her mother's warning haunted her through a childhood steeped in mystery, and sparked a domino effect reflecting what she perceived was true. Until she uncovered secrets and lies in her past that changed everything.

A TRANSFORMATIONAL SELF-HELP MEMOIR

Wingless Butterfly shares a lifetime of secrets like whispers from a best friend and unveils the metamorphosis of a broken child, her struggle to escape a silken chrysalis cocooning her heart, and her desperation to find love, validation, and self-worth. When the mist of a new dawn settled, the fragmented little girl emerged confident and secure with wings to fly in a whole new world--**that child was me**.

Intimate stories linger within each of us; a unique saga that is ours alone with twists, turns, hopes, and dreams. Some people thrive on messages perceived through childhood; others splinter. But as different as each individual may seem, we all love, hurt, and bleed the same. The distinctiveness of our past develops who we become.

So can we change and, if so, is it possible to erase a lifetime of beliefs? Perspective is reality. When I shattered the broken reflection in the mirror of my past, I finally healed and followed my dreams. This is my story.

Dedication

For my mother who spent her life trying to protect me, my dad--my hero--and the millions of lonely souls who lost the passion to live their dreams.

Part I
Reflections

Chapter 1

*Our self-image, strongly held,
essentially determines what we become.*
Maxwell Maltz

Her warning still echoed in my mind. "He's the kind of man who pulls wings off of butterflies." The faceless man haunted me for as long as I could remember. I shuddered, clenched my eyes as tightly as I could, but the admonition refused to be silenced. My life was drenched in betrayal, a virtual revolving door of insincere men. I married two of them, but one autumn morning in 1989, as I sat sipping coffee in my kitchen, I decided I wanted—no, needed to know why...

A week passed since the adoring voice on our answering machine confirmed Zack's affair. My husband called repeatedly begging me to listen to his lame excuses, but the scenario was all too familiar and I wasn't ready to endure that drama again. The soft whir of a distant train murmured a somber song shooting a sudden chill rippling through me. As I reached for the sweater draped across the desk chair, I noticed a book peeking from beneath the crumpled letter that forewarned his illicit relationship. "I guess the wife really is the last one to know." I grumbled, reaching for the book then flipped through the pages.

Someone had highlighted the final words of the novel and the florescent yellow caught my attention. *"I still believe, in spite of everything, that people are truly good at heart."* Anne Frank lived through hell, but despite her suffering, she remained adamant that people were innately good. Her diary, a solace for her, ultimately inspired hope in millions of people who faced their own demons. I closed the book, laid it back on the desk and wandered toward the kitchen. My struggles paled in comparison, but I shared her passion and kindred spirit. Still, when it came to trusting people, I wasn't so sure. Not anymore.

Drawn to the refrigerator, I opened the door and stared at the jumble of food and drinks. I wasn't hungry, but the fridge held an irresistible attraction when my mind searched for answers. "What's wrong with me?" I shook my head in disgust. "I'm educated, thoughtful, honest, kind—" I closed the fridge door empty handed. My self-assessment sounded like a girl scout.

Perfect--a 37-year-old girl scout. Surely I possessed more substance than that. I was so tired of feeling used, betrayed, and tossed aside like some disposable nothing. Why did I choose men who cheated then fabricated elaborate lies to cover their trail, lies I believed? I drew in a deep breath, held it then sighed as the air rushed from my lungs. They say the first sign of going crazy is talking to yourself. My warped relationships were pushing me over the edge. Why did my decisions regarding men always end in disaster?

I reached for my empty coffee cup, filled it, and wrapped my hands around the steaming mug. The rich aroma of the strong, nutty brew filled my senses, the hot liquid slipped down my throat and radiated, comforting me like a warm blanket. Ambling back toward my chair, I paused at the somber image looking back at me in the mirror. My God, how did I turn into this person? I barely recognized the frumpy figure staring back at me.

"Pathetic," I whispered, pulling my long, stringy, dark hair from my face. I grimaced at my reflection. My eyes, swollen and red from a week of wallowing in self-pity drooped into brownish-gray bags, and my coffee stained robe clearly bore signs of having been my only attire for several days. I looked pitiful--and old. No wonder he had an affair. I wouldn't want me. I hated who I'd become. My life had slipped into oblivion--no passion, no excitement, no love. I walked through life on autopilot. Damn, what happened to the determined, vivacious young girl who dreamed of conquering the world?

Collapsing into the chair, I noticed the empty journal on the table beside me. Mother gave the diary to me a few months earlier in an attempt to encourage me to write again. I used to love writing. I used to love a lot of things, before life devoured my passion, drained my energy and swallowed my dreams. Mom's insightful gift lured me. Opening the cover, I stared down at the blank pages and ran my finger across the pen attached to the binding. Who knows, maybe writing could help.

The wind whistled, sweeping around the chimney and I shivered, feeling the chill of the autumn morning as it stole through the open flue into the room. Curled up in my favorite overstuffed chair, I tugged at my robe and tucked it neatly around my feet. I picked up the pen and my mind began to unveil forgotten memories.

Journal entry, October 1989

I am--me. I can't change who or what I am any more than I can move the moon or touch the stars. I feel deeply, think far too much, and dream of passion and love beyond the scope or fantasies of typical people. I was society's child, daring to dream, but only in the solitude of my bedroom in the dark of night. Something deep inside held me hostage, sabotaged my ardent ambition. Mama told me endless stories of my childhood, but I have little to no memory of those days. I can't recall playing with my sister, Brianna or my brother, Alex, no birthday parties, holidays or special events. I can't even remember my mother shopping with me, fussing over my hair or taking me to the park, but, Mother's stories are seared in my mind.

My thoughts drifted through a portal in time to Mother's tales of my early childhood...

****

Mama said even as a child, I was introspective, inquisitive, with innocent eyes and steadfast hope. Not a classic, curious three-year old who asked why the sky was blue, I had a tendency to catch people off guard with deeper questions, a trait that never failed to astonish my parents. How could they explain to their toddler why *blue* was blue?

Mother delighted in recounting *Casi* stories. She said I was perpetually happy, a little Pollyanna who always saw a silver lining and insisted on happy endings. From the moment I jumped out of bed until I drifted into slumber, my vivid imagination and cheerful outlook flourished. I skipped down sidewalks singing songs and complete strangers often approached us to offer me a piece of candy or comment on how lighthearted they felt to see such a happy child. Constantly energized, I only stopped to question some minor detail that caught my attention before I flitted off again.

Strikingly animated at times as well, I amazed Mama and Daddy, like the time she took me to visit him at work. Daddy teased her about his new secretary and described the woman as an *absolute doll*. In front of several coworkers, I innocently chimed in, "When you lay her down, Daddy, does she close her eyes?" That naive comment brought laughter to Daddy's office parties for years to come.

My spontaneous enthusiasm did not impress everyone, however. The first time I went to the *big* church, I felt frustrated because I didn't know words to their songs, so when everyone bowed their heads in silence, I belted out my version of "It's Howdy Doody Time." The pastor, donned in his long black robe, glared down disapprovingly from his pulpit, while my mortified mother whisked me out the back of the church to the nursery.

Mama told me of times I embarrassed her with my innocent jargon. Once, when I accompanied her to the dry cleaners, my visit caused quite a ruckus. As we walked through the door, my eyes lit up at rows of hanging clothes stretched back as far as I could see and soft mist hovering above racks. Mama, unimpressed with rising steam and vast array of clothing, spoke to the clerk and attempted to hand him several pairs of Daddy's trousers. Each time she put a pair of pants on the counter, one by one I pulled them off and held them tightly in my arms. Frustrated at my behavior, she paused her conversation to attend to her misbehaving child.

"Why don't you want the man to clean Daddy's clothes, Casi?"

With a wrinkled brow and thrust out lower lip, I whimpered. "Mr. Man might lose them."

"You don't have to worry about that, honey. Now please leave them on the counter."

She turned back to the clerk while I leaned against the wall and sulked. A few moments later, I happily twirled around in circles. Mama patted me on the back.

"Now that's my good girl." She grabbed my hand and turned to leave the shop.

I paused with a big smile stretched across my face, looked up at the clerk and announced, "I know you won't lose my daddy's pants. They're the only ones with a zipper in front."

In those days, my entire frame of reference consisted of girls—except for Daddy, of course, and zippers on girl's clothing always appeared on the side. I may not have come to the right conclusion, but even at three, I had an analytical mind.

Mama called me energetic, inspired and self-confident, and destined for a significant and successful future. As a young woman, I recognized my potential, but dark shadows lurked in my soul and held it captive. Escaping their grip required battling my demons face-to-face.

For the first few years of my life, our family moved constantly. Whenever I began to feel comfortable with my surroundings, I'd awaken one morning to stacks of packed boxes and suitcases. I grew to dread the empty feeling in my stomach as I peered out the back window of our old, black Packard, and waved goodbye to yet another home.

On several occasions I stayed with my grandparents in Decatur, Illinois, while my mother settled us into a new house. When we moved to Decatur, Georgia, a suburb of Atlanta, the idea of two different places with the same name confused my immature mind, and I didn't understand why Mommy wouldn't take me to see Grandma.

A deep need to connect to someone or something familiar overwhelmed me, so I stuffed a few treasures into an old, brown, paper bag and, with teddy in hand, took off down the road in search of Grandma's house. Hours later, tired and disheartened, I sat on the curb of a distant street feeling lost and alone. Knowing what I know now, I can't imagine the anguish my mother must have felt after hours of searching for her precious little daughter gone missing.

As the police car approached me and hovered by the side of a road, Mother scarcely waited for the vehicle to come to a stop before she leaped from the car, collapsed to her knees and scooped me up in her arms. Elated to find her little girl, she held me tightly to her chest, sobbing tears of relief.

"Casi, what were you thinking?" She scolded me through tears. "You frightened Mommy. I was so afraid someone took you."

I was so upset by her reaction I never brought up Grandma again, and Mama never mentioned punishing me either. Continually uprooting a child in her formative years obviously makes it difficult for her to feel like she truly belongs anywhere. In all our moving around, I never questioned my hazy memories. A few recollections, mostly those attached to traumas, managed to seep through the fog though, like the distant train that whistled through the woods behind our house. I never actually saw that train, but the faint whir comforted me and lulled me to sleep on many occasions.

One evening Daddy took my puppy, Lucky, out for a walk in the woods, but he came back home with only her leash in his hand. He looked at Mommy with serious eyes and shook his head.

"Lucky is gone." He gazed down at me.

My eyes welled with tears. "Daddy, where is she?" I sobbed frantically, yanking at his pant leg. "Did my puppy get lost like I did?"

"Lucky wanted to run and play, Casi." He began to explain. "You know how much fun she has chasing squirrels." He wrapped his arms around me lovingly and wiped a tear from my cheek. "She ran onto the railroad track as a train approached and froze like a deer, hypnotized by headlights. She couldn't hear me whistling or yelling for her. I tried everything I could think of to get her attention, but when the last car faded into the distance, there was no trace of Lucky. The train took her to heaven, Sweetie."

I was inconsolable. That train carried my friend's daddy away too, and at four years old, I couldn't understand why he parked his car so close to the tracks that the engine was able to grab him and take him to heaven. The once comforting whistle no longer soothed me at night. Instead, like a tarnished knight of death, the droning sound made me feel alone and abandoned.

I do recall one happy memory from my childhood, feeling safe and secure sitting in Mama's lap, my head on her shoulder as she read to me. An insatiable audience of one, I dreamed of faraway fantasylands always with happy endings. I longed to be able to put words together like those in the books I adored, and as time moved forward, I did. Writing in my diary from my own memories and experiences was the best way to start.

My first clear recollections came from Langley, Virginia, a small town on the outskirts of Washington, D.C. populated predominantly by upper middle class and saturated with political figures. Daddy, a struggling CPA, was far from rich, and I considered myself fortunate to grow up in such a prosperous area surrounded by wealthy families whose pulse focused on the heartbeat of the nation. Supported by affluence, the public education was unparalleled. Our young lives were sheltered and pampered. Passing the CIA or Robert Kennedy's home and sharing classes with the sons and daughters of prominent politicians became routine.

My sister Brianna and I were not best friends or confidants. We squabbled from time to time, as most siblings do, but five years my senior she showed little patience for her annoying baby sister. In fact, she went to great lengths to avoid me, but I adored her anyway. So did Mama who spent many Saturday mornings shopping with Brie and often returned with bags of beautiful new clothes for her. True, I eventually became the beneficiary of all of her outfits, but only after my sister grew tired of them.

Brie was flawless; I was not. Her enviable figure and beauty inspired me. She could do so many things I wanted to do, always with elegance and perfection. She came home from summer camp with the most incredible stories of fantastic adventures. She rode horses, ice skated beautifully, and was athletically talented at every sport she chose to play, yet she could be graceful and polished when necessary.

So, no matter where we lived, my sister befriended an unending stream of girlfriends, and boys on the phone or by her side whenever the notion suited her. I used to tiptoe to the family room door and peek around the corner, hoping to catch a glimpse of Brie with her suitor-du-jour, secretly wrapped in his arms in a passionate kiss. I wanted to be like my sister and tried to emulate everything about her.

My relationship with Alex, four years my junior, was another matter entirely. He was the baby of the family. My paternal grandma doted on him, always showering him with little gifts for no apparent reason, but somehow she forgot about the girls. Still, I felt a motherly affection for him and would defend and protect him whenever he needed the help, which was often. Because he was their only son, my parents coddled him. Though Brie and I enjoyed exceptional public education, Alex attended the finest private schools. He was given every advantage my parents could afford to ensure his successful future.

Sandwiched between the two of them, I accepted that I didn't merit new clothes or special treatment. I wasn't jealous. I just acknowledged the situation as fact, but inferiority silently seeped into my soul. No one ever explained the reasons behind decisions my parents made, so I naturally put my own spin on things. I had no idea my brother's private education was influenced by the social revolution of the sixties, not by parental favoritism.

When Mama put cardboard into the toes of my shoes or clothed me in hand-me-downs, the thought never occurred to me that my parents struggled to make ends meet. Brie got new clothes, most of which were secondhand, or gifts from neighbors, because she constantly grew out of her clothing and, as the oldest, there were no family hand-me-downs for her.

Daddy discovered my fractured self-image after he received a small bonus from work. He decided to take me to the store to buy some new pajamas, a novel experience for me. Mother held a nightie up against me to check the size while tears squeezed from my eyes and trickled down my cheeks. I ran to hide behind Daddy, grabbed on to his leg and peered back whimpering.

"I don't need a nightie." I softly tugged his pants and pleaded with him. "Lets go home Daddy, please, tell Mommy it's time to go home."

"Okay Sweetie." He picked me up and held me close. "It's all right. We'll go home."

Santa brought me new pajamas that year and Daddy resolved to always set aside money to ensure that all three of his children received new clothes from time to time.

Daddy was my hero. His job took him out of town often, but I knew he would always be there if we needed him. Mommy insisted he would battle dragons for me, regardless of his silent nature and the demands of his growing career. When he traveled, I imagined myself a princess tucked safely in my bed while Daddy, fully clad in shining, knightly armor, slew dragons and protected me in a faraway land. He worked hard to provide the best life for us. I adored him and always tried to be his perfect little angel.

I never saw my parents argue, but I often heard them late at night when they thought I was asleep. I sensed concern in their secret discussions. My mother's voice, drenched in desperation, trembled as she spoke words that confused me. Anxiety ripped through my body when I heard her say things I didn't understand. I pulled the blanket over my head and hid, as if from a horrible monster lurking in the bedroom, and I listened intently while my stomach churned with apprehension.

****

..In those moments I visualized a faceless knight with vacant eyes leering at me from behind a mysterious mask, his armor tarnished and damaged. He frightened me. Determined to make things okay, I resolved to become Daddy's best princess, prettier and smarter so he would be happy. Then, curled safely under my covers until the voices silenced, I eventually drifted off to sleep. The light of day always found my mother cheerily preparing breakfast and the visions of the eerie midnight sessions faded into the stockpile of forgotten dreams...

I twiddled my pen between my fingers as I read over my newly composed journal entry. I'm no therapist, but even I could analyze my early childhood. From the outside, no one would have guessed my internal anguish. My cheery disposition was my disguise, a defense developed deep and early. I felt I needed to earn my daddy's love, so I tried to be perfect—like Brie. I created a Pollyanna outlook because I believed my family's happiness depended upon me. My responsibility required me to make sure everyone stayed happy.

I've heard perspective is the key to what we believe. Self-confidence creates a strong ally, but I think self-doubt can be an equally strong adversary. A poor self-image stole my childhood hopes and ambitions, but I wondered if my self-worth developed from my broken belief system. Could I rebuild my self-image and find my dreams again?

I stood and walked back to the daunting mirror. "You are in there somewhere Casi," I whispered to my reflection, "It may take time, but I will find you. I'll determine where my life wandered off track and why my choices derailed my future.

My memories drifted through the cast of men in my past and the melodrama of broken promises--then to Zack. He would be home soon and I needed to pull myself together. A sudden shiver swept over me as the faceless man flashed through my mind again, followed by a surge of desperation, rejection, and fear. I couldn't shake the feeling that something bad, maybe traumatic, happened in my early childhood. Were the memories lost somewhere my mind? The late night whispers silenced, trapped inside a protective fortress. If only I could recall details, I might unravel my elusive past and maybe find the destiny that faded into forgotten dreams.

Chapter 2

As novices, we think we are entirely responsible for the way people treat us. I have learned that we are responsible only for the way we treat people.
Rose Lane

He grabbed me from behind, locked his arms around my waist. I screamed, but he easily overpowered me.

"I brought you into this world and I can take you out."

"Ha." My son laughed and twirled me around. "I'm sorry Mom, you're right." His sarcastic tone emphasized his cocky attitude. "What was I thinking?" He straightened my disheveled hair.

At ten years old, Josh was already taller than me, but regardless of his height, he still looked up to me. When he was small, he would run through the door to tell me some exciting news and I would sweep him off his feet and swing him around in a loving embrace. Now the tides changed. I could no longer twirl my little boy around, but he had no trouble picking me up and would often catch me totally off guard.

"I really like the new 'do,' Mom." He inspected my hair more closely.

"Thanks, buddy." My skeptical reply urged him to elaborate.

"No, I mean it. Sorry I messed your hair. Really, I like your new cut and it's nice to see you wearing outfits that actually fit instead of your usual baggy clothes. Who would have thought there was a woman under all that?" He teased again. "What's come over you lately? Never mind, I don't want to know, but whatever it is, it suits you. Keep it up." He grabbed a coke from the fridge and ran upstairs to Nintendo and his little brother Jace, leaving the room as quickly as he entered.

I yelled up the stairs after him. "Thanks, I think."

Turning back toward the kitchen, the corner of my eye caught a glimpse of my image in the mirror and caused me to pause. I did look a bit younger or thinner these days. Maybe I just felt better about life in general, but something definitely changed. I gazed through the reflection to the room beyond where my diary sat on the side table. The transformation started with that journal. The first moment I began to write, I felt different, as if the words drained my angst and exposed a submerged soul, but the demands of my two children took precedence. Super-mom's busy life left little time for self-indulgence, and the lure of my diary faded to the background.

While my inner child slept in the pages of my memories, Zack managed to soothe my ruffled ego enough for me to settle back into my daily routine. I rarely thought about my diary for over a year, until Josh discovered the notebook in the attic one afternoon. Shortly afterward, the journal began to surface in obvious places around the house. My intuitive son found my writing intriguing, and I had to admit exposing my inner thoughts in writing provided a solace for me. Like sharing secrets with a close friend, writing clarified my perception.

The allure enticed me and I wandered toward my diary. Moments later, with book in hand, I headed toward the screened porch and solitude. A late afternoon sun glistened through the trees and the warmth caressed my face. I lost myself in memories. The smell of burning leaves triggered an isolated but pleasant childhood memory that took me back to autumns past when I used to help Daddy rake blankets of crisp foliage into mounds before he burned them. I played more than helped, jumping into huge heaps and rolling around as they scattered beneath me. Autumn leaves provided a great source of entertainment for an imaginative child. My boys loved to play in leaf piles too and I knew the experiences seared wonderful memories in their minds.

Curled into the porch swing, I closed my eyes, inviting visions of Josh and Jace's childhood to interlace with mine, as pleasant thoughts shifted through time together. Suppressed memories still haunted me. My children would not have that legacy. We always talked of their past and volumes of videotapes filled with events of their lives lined shelves of our TV room. The boys chose to watch movies of themselves over Sesame Street or cartoons. Tapes not only reinforced their memories of birthdays and holidays, but also routine daily occurrences, a reminder of how we worked, played, and laughed together.

We built an incredible relationship. Josh and Jace knew they could talk to me about anything. I don't remember ever having that kind of connection with my Mom or Dad. Damn, why couldn't I recall my childhood? I had no problem with high school. That I remembered all too well. I opened my journal and began to write as forgotten moments materialized with vivid clarity.

Journal entry, November 1993
As an authority, Mom always deferred to Dad. He was the rock, patient, firm and the core of the family. His word was gold and I never questioned his influence or purpose.
Mom was artistic and talented. She read, played piano, sculpted and wrote stories and poetry that would never be offered for publication. She rarely socialized and had no close friends that I knew of. Her whole life entwined with family. The "Stepford Wives" robotic perfection had nothing on my mother. She kept an immaculate home and always made sure dinner was ready, children bathed, and homework done before Dad got home from work. A typical teenager, I wasn't quite so accommodating.

As a teen during the sixties, I discovered adolescence changes everything...

****

Before puberty took over my body, mind and soul, people saw me as predominately carefree. Mom said almost everyone found me to be charismatic and endearing, but she knew I was also expressive and strong willed. Moving around helped me to adapt well to new environments, a sunny outlook attracted friends, and my creative nature provided endless activities to feed childhood imaginations.

The move to Virginia stabilized my life. It was the first time friendships had a chance to grow and for three years, innocent giggles and fun took root. EJ, Missy, Beth, and Anna, my new neighborhood brimmed with little girls my age. Summer days filled my world with playmates, secrets, and adventures. When school started, I met more friends and for the first time I could remember, I felt like I belonged. From hide-and-seek and Barbie Dolls to realizing boys no longer had cooties, our bonds deepened, but when puberty began to transform our bodies, my friends changed as well.

EJ and Missy were the first to desert me. They whispered whenever I came near them, and it didn't take a genius to figure out I was no longer welcome in their company of friends. I couldn't figure out what I did to upset them and I began to feel increasingly self-conscious. They huddled together at the bus stop, told secrets, laughed and moved away whenever I came close, so I was left to connect with the boys, like Richard and Billy who at least seemed interested in my thoughts or opinions.

I never found out what I did to push my friends away. In hindsight, I'm pretty sure the wedge between us evolved when I was the first to develop boobs. But boys were friendly, so I hid my insecurities and tried to find balance in my unbalanced world.

Mother tried to comfort me. "When God closes a door, Casi, he generally opens a window and life changes." She was right as usual, and it took little time to discover that hanging out with boys could be truly — stimulating.

Richard lived down the street from me and had since we were twelve. He was always charming, cute, witty and a great distraction from the girls who betrayed me. We talked, laughed and hung out from time to time and, at one point, he touched me like no one ever had before, and I mean that literally. One minute we were just two kids leaning against a fence talking and laughing, and a moment later, I knew I was a woman.

When something beside me caught Richard's eye he reached over to grab it and slightly lost his balance. His body leaned in, pushed against mine and as he fell against me while a surge of hormonal bliss ignited sparks inside of me. It was a physical sensation I'd never experienced — exciting and marvelous. I'm sure he has no recollection of the event, but I'll never forget that moment. Most people have memories of their first love or their first time, but I recall the first moment my intimate awareness awakened. Many boys crossed my path over the years, but Richard was my first infatuation and to this day, I still remember the thrill of that touch.

Becoming a teenager came with perks, but the sixties were trying years for an insecure teen. My mother thought me a radical, but in truth, I felt inhibited and hesitant. Maybe my caution grew from the fact that my dad, a struggling CPA, wasn't as affluent as most of the parents of my peers, or perhaps because my mother's Quaker upbringing resided on the opposite end of the spectrum from the *hippy* era.

It's possible my inherent prudence kept me from living on the edge, or maybe I had more sense than I give myself credit, but whatever the reason, I generally erred on the side of caution, especially when it came to experimenting with drugs or sex. Growing up in the 1960s was wondrous and challenging.

The Vietnam War fought in full throttle. Rock and roll swept the country, filling our young minds with lofty dreams and influenced our belief system. Love, peace and freedom driven by the hippy movement were not merely issues relevant in the news, but the agenda of our daily lives. Washington, D.C. was an incredible place for a teen during that era. Georgetown was as close as our high school football stadium and frequented more often.

The drinking age was eighteen, but fake IDs were simple to get, so, at sixteen, most of us were well known at area beer stores, bars and clubs. Drugs were as common as dime store candy, on the news as well as on the streets, and whoever wanted to get high had little trouble finding grass, hash or hallucinogens like LSD. The freedom we enjoyed, coupled with the availability of drugs and alcohol made it easy to fall victim, and too many teens indulged for recreation or to calm their inner fears.

I suppose as a rite of passage teenagers relish in an insatiable desire for excitement. Curiosity, passion, and an indestructible sense of self guide their daily lives and often-reckless decisions. For us, rampant affluence and scant adult supervision added to the mix and created a dangerous, volatile cocktail.

It was a unique era. We experienced, first hand, the birth and evolution of rock and roll and felt its strong influence in our lives. The music inspired a sense of freedom scarcely felt by previous generations, offset by the very real threat of a faraway war, too close to home.

The Vietnam War, a clear and present danger lurking in our immediate future, overshadowed our innocence with a fear that crept into our dreams. The newly implemented military draft was a constant reminder of our vulnerability. It ripped boys full of youthful ambition from the solace and security of their homes and loved ones to drudge through rice fields on other side of the world. Then to stand battle and die for a cause they didn't even understand.

Every day they saw the horrifying reality of death and destruction while they fought their own battle to survive. The lucky ones came home, but never escaped the untold horrors that would haunt them forever. Not even the affluence of our parents could buy peace into our minds from the real fear that awaited boys at the end of our senior year, and the birthday draft-lottery told us exactly which of our friends would be the first to go.

I don't know how I would have reacted if I was a guy, and the stark reality of newspaper photos and TV clips reminded me the draft affected not only boys, but girls as well. When junior-high girls ditched me, boys stood by me and now they were my best friends. It scared me to think of them crawling through the trenches of Vietnam.

Many people may look back on their high school years with fond memories. I am not one of them. My grades were acceptable, but not too good. I knew I could do better, maybe make A's, but I wanted to fit into with the crowd. I thought if my grades were too high, I'd be singled out again as a nerd or egghead. I wanted to have girlfriends and be popular. I tried to fit in, but girls can be so petty and competitive at that age, manipulative and even devious. I didn't know which ones were worse: the blatantly stuck-up snobs or the girls who were sickeningly sweet to my face yet sabotaged me behind my back.

I guess even as a teen, I had trust issues. So, when competitive female hormones increased, my circle of girlfriends correspondingly decreased, and the majority of my high school friends edged closer to males. Guys were straightforward, uncomplicated and never in competition with me. They kept me grounded and, though their motives weren't always completely honorable, I got them and knew where I stood.

Boys were great friends and as long as they stayed just friends, I felt comfortable around them. We talked, partied, drank beer, sneaked out late at night, skipped school, and created what we believed to be eternal bonds, while we searched for the comfort zone that would determine our destiny.

My closest friend felt more like a brother. We met on the first day of high school, during French class. Tiny balls of paper hit me in the face and my expert investigative skills soon discovered the source of the barrage. Behind me, sitting one row over and three back, sat an attractive boy dressed in a light blue, long sleeve, button-down oxford shirt and dark pants. His short-cropped, reddish-brown hair and impish grin triggered the beginning of an incredible friendship.

To this day, the sight of a spitball makes me smile. Adam was cute, animated, full of adventure, and from the first moment our eyes met, I felt at ease around him. His endearing personality had me pretty confused at first, but I soon discovered he had an identical brother. The twins took great pleasure in switching places from time to time and laughed at the resulting confusion. Most people couldn't tell them apart, but I had no problem. I learned to know Adam from the inside out, and though Andrew had his face, to me they were totally different.

We became close friends and it was nice to have someone I could finally depend on. If we weren't going *steady* with someone else, we hung out together at football games, parties and hip Georgetown nightclubs.

Swept away on many occasions by the cute boys in my life, I usually ended up with a broken heart and Adam was always there, waiting in the shadows to pick up the pieces of my shattered dreams and help me find my way again. A friend over years and distance, Adam was there long after others became faded memories.

Richard infatuated me throughout high school, but he was popular, the president of the school, and involved in so many activities. He gravitated toward drama and was a remarkable actor. We hung out around the neighborhood, but I never had enough confidence to let him know how he made me feel every time he stood close to me. So, I watched him from afar, excited for him and filled with pride each time he succeeded. Richard touched my heart. For years to come through distance and time, I would hear his voice or see his smile and the spark I felt by the fence that day so many years before would always flutter.

Nash's friendship touched me too. He was sweet, honest, and talented, wrote beautifully, and possessed a sense of humor beyond his years. We took classes together with mutual friends so he was always around, but whenever I walked by, he got quiet and kind of shy, so I never thought about dating him. Knowing him as I do now, Nash could have been the one person who might have changed the course of my life and kept me from succumbing to the emotional baggage that enslaved me for decades, but that wasn't our destiny.

God's design is far beyond the realm of my comprehension, and He works in his own time. As it was, my fate followed my own jagged path before the mystical connection between Nash and me surfaced, a path created by my own choices in spite of my tentative nature. Cautious and inhibited, I still managed to make my share of mistakes, which focused primarily on the guys I chose to date.

I think my idea of relationships sprung from the lyrics of songs. Music was such an incredible force in our lives during the late sixties. Its influence not only stimulated a revolution, lyrics infused an image of love in innocent, impressionable minds, particularly those of teenage girls. From Jefferson Airplane, to Tommy James and everything in-between, The Buckinghams, Frankie Valli, The Association, BJ Thomas, the songs inflated naive expectations with visions of undying love, romance and passion. A cocktail of raging hormones and sixties love songs on the rocks of a childhood fairytale happily-ever-after foundation easily distorted the notion of what love should be, especially for me. For some reason, my impressionable psyche manifested more dreams than the average teenage girl.

Typically attracted to the wrong attributes, I was swept away by handsome, popular or athletic guys, visual Adonis' whom I envisioned would bring romance into my life, a vision firmly planted in my head by the music I adored. The reality was, those ended up being the very boys who lived shallow, self-absorbed lives. Simple qualities like honesty or depth beyond that of a Neanderthal would have been refreshing but instead, I was attracted to boys who exuded confidence and egocentric entitlement, who prioritized their own desires regardless of the people they walked over to attain their goals. What stupefies the teenage male species, causing their raging hormones to dominate their existence, totally taking over their brains and replacing them with the blind instincts of a dog in heat?

I didn't feel like a beauty by any of my own standards, but my long, dark hair, green eyes, slender figure, and bulging breasts, definitely seemed to be a catalyst for male hormonal spontaneous combustion. Proving to me at an early age that testosterone was the driving force of masculinity. At thirteen, my femininity flourished and paired with my slender frame, it was apparently difficult for a boy to meet me with his eyes focused on my face.

I wanted to be appreciated for who I was inside, pursued by a boy who was sensitive enough to see something in me beyond my obvious physical attributes, but I was a *pretty girl*, a physical stimulus, and I quickly learned that my brain and personality held little significance when compared to other qualities I possessed. For girls like me, the wrapping interested guys, not the gift.

I felt like the focus of a child in a candy store, whose favorite piece was the one he happened to have his eye on at the moment. The object of fleeting surges of passion, guys briefly romanced me with dreamy gestures and promises, but when my old-fashioned morals got in the way, the candy store patron soon turned his affections to other sources for satisfaction.

A strict, moral upbringing convinced me to protect my virginity, so I endured names like Prudence and was regarded as a tease, which made me a challenge to many of the handsome, overconfident males I endearingly called face-men. To them dating me presented a conquest, a trophy to be won or lost but in either case, cast aside, as they moved forward toward their next encounter. More bluntly stated, they dumped me when I didn't put out.

I wasn't a prude or a tease. Naive, innocent, trusting, and gullible in an era influenced by free love and self-indulgence, I was an anachronism, with dreams that I would one day find my soul mate and forever love, to whom I would surrender my virginity and ride into the sunset happily ever after. My childhood fantasy of a knight in shining armor shaped my expectations and high school boys had a hard time living up to the image in my mind. Relationships, male and female, validated my weakening self-worth, inflated by the phantom who hid deep within my soul, constantly whispering his secret song—a song that guided me down a perilous path.

Over time, high school dates turned to male friends rather than love, as I forged my self-fulfilling prophecy of an unfulfilled dream. Note to self: If you don't take steps to change weaknesses in your life, you destine yourself to failure. Bottom line: males comprised the majority of my friends with very few exceptions.

But the few girls who befriended me bonded like sisters and remained close throughout my life, despite some tense moments. When we first met, Jenny, Kirsten, Sandy, Kendall and I were so in sync we became inseparable. Excited to have new girlfriends again, I loved to spend time with them. My mother referred to us as the five musketeers.

Jenny was beautiful with golden brown hair and deep green eyes, elegant and exceptionally talented. She had long legs and danced like an angel. Completely absorbed in drama and performing arts, she planned her future and we never doubted she would one day be a star. Still, she was a typical teenager. We shared secrets, talked about boys, and hung out together when our studies or her training didn't get in the way. Truth be told, I yearned for Jen's spirit. Her confidence and an inner harmony reached beyond our petty adolescent status quo.

Kirsten's Scandinavian ancestry beamed through her long blond hair and ivory skin. She lived in a blended family with four biological siblings and three new stepsisters, so she learned to get along or take a back seat when tension arose. A devoted friend, she would hurt herself before anyone else. Most people saw her as the quietest of the five, but one-on-one she was more spirited than any of us. I knew I could always depend on her and she on me, which was fully put to the test on several occasions, but that's another story.

Sandy's cute, bubbly energetic soul made her the kind of girl you just loved to be around. Always happy, she exuded an infectious smile. Sandy saw the silver lining in any storm cloud.

Medium ash-brown hair, soft features and slender, her petite stature and nature entwined inherent beauty and effervescent personality, and she always had a boyfriend. Still, her friends were important to her and never cast aside.

Kendall was one of a kind. Her long, blond, naturally straight hair glistened and mixed with her striking features; she was beautiful. Outgoing, daring, goal driven and dynamic, Kendall seemed to enjoy living on the edge and was definitely the bold one of the group. Hanging out with her gave me a taste of the wild side that was not my nature. She was fun and brought excitement into our lives. When she set her sights on something, she usually got it, which tested our friendship more than a few times.

The five of us created incredible dynamics together, and each of my girlfriends possessed traits I found deficient in myself. Regardless of friendly competition, for the first year of high school, we did almost everything together. Kendall was usually the trendsetter, while Kirsten and Sandy merely join in. Jenny's interests focused on the future and I longed to be like her. She knew what she wanted and was centered and driven. I had incredible dreams, but an inner voice haunted my spirit, fueling self-doubt and apprehension.

Our freshman year social calendar kept us busy. No matter what the venue, if one of us attended, it was a good bet all of us would be there unless our parents' authority or practical matters, like my job, took precedence. My dad worked to make ends meet and I knew if I wanted to actually drive when I got my license, I needed to make my own money. I took a job as a salesgirl in a chic local boutique, which provided a great way to put cash in my pocket as well as buy trendy cloths at discount prices.

But the owner insisted her employees participate in fashion shows from time to time. The limelight and runway experience should have been fun and exciting, but modeling placed me at the center of attention, which always felt uncomfortable to me.

So I tried to concentrate on the important issues, making enough money to spend some on clothes, save, and go out with my friends as well, all subject to Mom's approval, of course. Having a Quaker mother sometimes put a dampener on my activities.

Overprotective, conservative parents in the late 1960s were not conducive to becoming a social butterfly. My curfew was 11:00 P.M. with few exceptions, while my friends enjoyed the freedom of staying out as late as 2:00 AM. Countless times friends or dates returned to parties after they took me home. Mortified at the reigns imposed upon me, I rebelled, but my mother remained firm so I had little choice but to accept her rules. The only way to side step her authority was through sleepovers, which I planned as often as I could.

I respected my parents, but my tenacity nurtured a resourceful mind, and it frustrated me that they didn't trust my decisions. On several occasions I came home, only to sneak back out after Mom and Dad went to bed. I never got caught, but I always left a note on my pillow to explain where I was, a provision made in an attempt to minimize mother's fear and anger in the event she discovered my empty bed. I hoped the gesture would reduce consequences of my defiant decisions. I tried to please my parents and my friends, an impossible task doomed from the start, and outside influences made my attempts even more difficult.

Any time teenage girls band together, jealousy can rear its ugly head, and we occasionally saw Kendall's flirtatious nature as a threat. Was it Lyndon Baines Johnson, Sun-tzu, or Michael Corleone that said: "Keep your friends close and your enemies closer?" No matter who said the quote first, Kendall exemplified the statement. Thankfully she was never an enemy, but our friendship still shuddered from a few bruising blows. I went steady only three times in four years of high school, and Nick was the first. Attention from an upperclassman excited me, but a senior interested in me, a mere sophomore, boosted my ego and enticed me.

Nick seemed to see an elusive me I couldn't summon in the mirror. His soft, warm kisses sent tingles down my back, and his intense passion convinced me he reciprocated the emotions. His attention enveloped me, warm, comfortable. Nick respected me, at least at first, because he didn't see me as a sex object or a trophy to be won and I adored feeling appreciated. But peer pressure and high school intertwined in those days, influencing boys as well as girls, and Nick reacted in kind.

The sweet, tender boy who stole my heart inflated his testosterone around his friends and, like most hot guys, his eyes wandered. I accepted some lusting after other girls as typical behavior, until his attention drifted toward Kendall. We broke up--and a few days later her requited response deflated me. Protecting my heart moved to the forefront.

During our sophomore year, our high school social sorority invited Kirsten, Sandy and Kendall into their group. Sandy wasn't interested in the club. Her boyfriend and friends satisfied her, and she was secure enough to know it. I wasn't. The sorority considered me for membership on several occasions, but each time they held a secret vote, one black ball always surfaced among the whites, banning me from the clique.

Rejection is always hard regardless of the circumstances, and I felt ostracized, but the rejection hit a chord deep inside of me. On the outside, I shrugged off the blackballing and acted as if the vote didn't bother me, but in truth I felt inadequate and discarded, the teenage version of the confused little girl who hid her feelings so well.

To vent my insecurity, I wrote in my diary, a journal I always kept hidden under lock and key. I wore a façade, but wrestled with an inner turmoil I didn't understand. Flashes of hazy memories and daunting dreams continued to haunt me, and the girls of Alpha Pi just validated my self-doubt.

The sorority monopolized much of Kirsten and Kendall's time and, as the years passed, I felt a distance grow between us. Sandy's boyfriend kept her occupied, and Jenny's dancing and acting held her focus, so I often felt left behind, alone. I liked some other girls in school and tried to befriend them, but a deep-seated fear of rejection kept them at arms length, and my male friends couldn't fill the sense of inequality evoked by the group of girls I longed to be a part of.

A few years later, Adam explained his viewpoint on my rejection from the club. "Casi, it wasn't you." He smiled his mischievous grin and leaned back against a huge old oak tree. "Missy was just jealous. A lot of guys buzzed around you and seeing all your boyfriends, they —" I cut him off.

"Not boyfriends, Adam, boy 'friends' and what's wrong with that?"

"That's just it, those girls didn't see them as friends. They felt threatened. Especially when one of *your* friends was *their* boyfriend, like Missy's."

"Missy? You have to be kidding. I barely even knew Bruce."

"Maybe so." He cocked his head, raising an eyebrow. "But Bruce said hi to you every time he saw you in the halls, and you smiled and said hi right back to him. It drove Missy crazy. As the President of Alpha Pi she influenced the sorority girls. Bruce kept her in line, for lack of better terminology, by flirting with you. Whenever she upset the status quo, he threatened to move on.

'I could date other girls you know, like Casi. She's cute, and I bet she'd go out with me.' Missy's claws came out. She couldn't stand him to think about other girls, and she blamed you for flirting with him."

"I never flirted with him. I wouldn't have done that. And besides, Missy doesn't even know me. She hasn't said two words to me since elementary school aside from a snide remark now and then." My defenses flared. "Why did she choose me to be her enemy?"

"I don't think she thought through the situation. But hell hath no fury like a woman scorned, or possibly even a girl who fears being scorned."

I was quiet for a moment and thought about Adam's explanation. "It's funny, Bruce was the school's big football star. I never imagined he'd date me, I guess I believed he was totally out of my league. I don't think I ever had a single conversation with him."

"That didn't matter, Casi. You were a threat to Missy — end of story."

Adam's perspective may or may not have been right. The reason for my exclusion from the sorority was really irrelevant. Only my perception of why they blackballed me held significance. I saw that I was unsuitable and valueless. So, feeling rejected by the girls, my male friends became even more important to me, which apparently created an ongoing dilemma.

****

I considered myself a dreamer. My childhood love for the written word evolved over time and I learned to write eloquently. Writing was my Shangri-La, providing a vessel to express my fears and feelings of inadequacy through poetry and journal entries meant for no one's eyes but my own. It was my perfect way to experience my fantasies and let go of anguish.

When I wrote, I expressed dreams held captive in the corners of my mind, followed the allure of far away places and sailed on oceans rolling out to unknown eternity. I responded to enticing whispers of deep and passionate love. My imagination flew to distant shores and opened up a world where I could be or do anything my heart desired. An escape, writing linked my deepest passions to the key to my soul.

I took a deep breath after lingering in those painful high school years. Okay Casi, it's time to put those analytical skills to work. Hindsight is always 20/20.

A persisting need to be Daddy's perfect daughter competed with social pressures from my peers in a battleground that loomed over me throughout my whole life, like the image of conscience—the devil on one shoulder and the angel on the other. A struggle to maintain balance and conform to both worlds left me feeling I belonged to neither, while my dark knight stood guard, trapping the strong, dynamic woman deep inside for decades to come. I didn't have the desire to be a rebel or the courage to follow my heart. Instead, I continued with my Pollyanna attempts to make everyone around me happy and often neglected my own needs.

Little girls dream of being a princess or falling in love with *Prince Charming,* but my dreams evolved into more than childhood fantasies. A naive vision of my shining knight left me increasingly vulnerable. I realized something was missing that should have been there and by the time I reached high school, a burning desire to feel wanted, treasured, roared inside of me with an eternal flame. What was that about?

I had friends, but they rejected me when the sorority lured them away, which reinforced my disintegrating self-image. There was a barrier, real or imagined, that I couldn't penetrate and it trapped me on the outside. Kids can be cruel, oblivious to the damage they inflict, and my injured self-worth fortified. The need to be accepted strengthened my childhood defense strategy, which already held my sense of self-worth in a death grip. The only choice I saw convinced me to re-mold myself into someone more captivating.

My love life was a disaster. When puberty hit boys surrounded me, which in theory seems ideal. But male friends and boyfriends didn't mix, and when I managed to choose a guy who made my heart flip-flop, the sweet talk faded when my moral upbringing bound my passion. A lack of interested boys wasn't my problem, but a *pretty girl* gets only lustful attention, not adoration, and I was an unwilling target.

So the emptiness inside me grew into a gaping black hole, a vacuum for emotional love. I tried to change my pattern of dysfunctional relationships, but the adjustments were not for the better. When I turned to boys for friendship, my inner fears kept them at arms length.

So, in essence, I gave up. High school reinforced my inferiority and I accepted the sentence, a single acknowledgement that destined me to spend most of my life convinced I was unworthy of real and honest love. I set in motion a life-altering trend. My future relationships would have little to do with trusting my heart. I would date boys and ultimately men whom I believed would accept the unworthy me I saw in the mirror — I began to hate that mirror.

The faceless man flashed through my mind again, along with a more recent memory and I cringed at the thought. I did emotionally connect with my mother — once — but it was several years after high school. The one time I was able to truly communicate with her led to a profound discovery. The deep emptiness that shrouded my heart was a suppressed memory. I learned my knight in shining armor grew from an internal manifestation created at conception, the outcry of stolen innocence.

Chapter 3

By your thoughts, you are daily, even hourly building your life; you are carving your destiny.
Ruth Barrick Golden

    Molested by her next-door neighbor and ultimately raped, Nicole lost her childhood when she was eleven. My niece struggled in silence to cope with the trauma, ashamed and afraid to tell her mother. The thought of his aging hands touching her body made her physically ill, and every time she saw him, she relived the attack.

    My sister's marriage ended in divorce and she blamed herself for her daughter's sudden behavior change, but the divorce had little to do with her oldest daughter's torment. Brie found it increasingly difficult to deal with Nicole's defiant, reckless attitude and begged for my help. So, my niece came to live with me in the middle of her eighth grade year, desperate to find someone to validate her self-worth.

    As a cry for attention she found comfort in food and sex, both of which inflicted a devastating effect on her. At 235 pounds, severely overweight and depressed, she conceded free reign to her sexual hormones, living the lifestyle of a sexually active young woman, with the experience and maturity of a thirteen-year-old.

    Brie couldn't understand why her oldest daughter was so self-destructive, and it took me months to break through Nicole's defenses enough for her to confide in me. When I finally learned what happened, I tried to persuade her to get counseling and did what I could to help her overcome the emotional aftermath of her rape. The year she lived with me, she worked out almost every day, ate healthy foods and gained self-confidence in proportion to her weight loss, but the trauma still haunted her.

Nicole worked hard to overcome her nightmare. Now, eight years later, I felt a deep sense of satisfaction when I received her college graduation announcement. I taped the invitation on the fridge door next to Jace's baseball picture. There was no way I could make a trip to Virginia for the ceremony, but I would send her a gift.

Nicole survived her trauma. But Kathleen, her younger sister, now drained Brie's energy. Kathy was a handful since her freshman year in high school when she begun to experiment with drugs and alcohol. Luckily she'd be graduating soon and peer pressure would be less threatening. I remembered all too well how difficult those years were for me. It seemed no one in our family was immune to childhood anguish. We all struggled with inner demons.

I glanced across the room toward my journal and recalled my own high school graduation. I got into an argument with my mother and told her not to even bother coming to the ceremony. It's funny, I don't even remember what the argument was about, but I'm certain I hurt Mom with my sarcastic comments. I was so relieved to see her, smiling proudly, sitting front and center as I walked across the stage to receive my diploma. Graduation represented a whole new beginning for me, but it made little difference. I was broken inside, and no matter where I went or what I did, I still managed to find a way to sabotage my life. Reaching for my journal, I snuggled into my favorite chair with memories reaching beyond my high school years.

Journal entry, May 1994:
Graduation came with the usual pomp and circumstance and filled our young minds with hopes and tears. On June 6, 1970, we discarded our naïveté, or so we thought, to embark on life's journey, each going in our own directions, with only memories of treasured experiences and friendships to carry us forward. Some of the boys were drafted and found themselves in the rice fields and jungles of Vietnam, but the majority of my classmates, like me, were off to colleges scattered across the country. Best friends separated and eventually lost touch, forging forward to build their lives and fulfill their dreams...

College is a turning point for most people, but living in lies can trap you in the past, unable to really enjoy the moments of your life...

****

I left Langley, Virginia in the fall of 1970, headed for school and eager to embrace my exciting future. College enchanted me with football games, sororities, frat parties, and all night study sessions. It was a universal equalizer where students with diverse backgrounds from scattered geographic locations all met together on common ground. Not having our parents to question our decisions created a wonderful sense of freedom and, for me, an unfamiliar feeling of self-confidence. I had a clean slate and new friends were easier to make — and keep.

Sororities and fraternities were dominating forces on campus and almost everyone joined in some capacity, be it social or academic. Several social sororities rushed me and the feeling of being not only accepted, but actually desired, was new and exhilarating. So, when I received the invitation to join Alpha Delta PI, I accepted without hesitation.

My sorority sisters were loyal friends and I began to rebuild some of the damage to my self-worth that was twisted by my childhood and reinforced by unpleasant high school experiences. At times I felt uncomfortable and guarded about being accepted into a sorority. I worried the situation was only temporary. Something would surely happen to enlighten my new sisters of their momentary lapse in judgment. They were, of course, oblivious to my concerns, but self-doubt had me determined to prove myself by becoming the perfect pledge. My sorority was like family. We lived, partied, and ate together, helped each other study, and I always had someone to go with me to football games and frat functions.

Unlike high school parties, fraternity bashes hosted kegs of beer, live bands, and incredibly hot guys. The 1970s' music still fed my soul and the bands introduced more ballads, which continued to skew my vision of love, but confiding in girlfriends helped me to realize I wasn't so different, and my self-perception found some balance.

My roommate, Drema, and I became instant friends. I felt completely comfortable around her, a unique experience for me. We were polar opposites in appearance. Her long, blond hair and fair skin next to my flowing, dark brown locks and olive complexion turned heads as we walked across campus side by side, like sunshine and moonlight strolling together. Our exteriors may have been different, but on the inside, we were just alike.

We agreed on almost everything and our thoughts were so in line we completed each other's sentences. It felt good to finally have a girlfriend as close as a sister, but I still tended to conform to her needs or ideas, suppressing my own individuality. Drema's boyfriend, Bobby, was a first-string football player. Tall, blond, and ripped, he hung out with jocks from the same mold, so I was destined to be surrounded by athletic hunks, the type of guys who always held an addictive allure to me.

Bobby and Drema were high school sweethearts and planned to marry one day—an interesting concept to me, a self-proclaimed bachelorette, but his friends were hot. They were nothing like the high school boys I remembered. These were fully developed men, and one of them totally took my breath away.

To this day, Brad remains one of the major regrets in my life. I'm not sorry I got involved with him. To the contrary, he was kind, thoughtful, smart, talented, and handsome. He played first-string defensive end on the college football team, and his athletic physique was strong and sexy. Despite my experience with athletes in the past, I could tell that Brad was different. Though tall, dark and charming, he treated me like a princess. His dreamy eyes melted my heart and his firm musculature wrapped around my body made me feel safe—and lustful.

From the first moment our eyes met, the chemistry between us was undeniable. He touched my heart and I was off-balance and shaken. We could talk for hours, amazed at where the time went. I remember sitting in the car out in front of my dorm deep in conversation, not realizing hours slipped by until the dawn began to lighten the night sky.

For months, we dated and spent most of our free time together. When he came to Virginia during Christmas break to spend a few days with me, the connection between us blossomed and I knew I was falling in love with him. The truth is I dreamed of Brad since I was a child. He was the embodiment of my knight in shining armor, but it was hard to trust my feelings and even harder to believe in Brad's.

Internal convictions whispered their subtle warnings. I was unlovable and it was only a matter of time before Brad would discover the truth and walk out of my life. I would inevitably disappoint him somehow, do or say the wrong thing and show him the "me" I had come to see in that evil mirror.

I dreamed of hearing, "Casi, I love you," but at the same time, feared the confession. It's not like I hadn't heard the words before from lustful high school boys, but in those days, my armor was securely in place. I knew the game and played it with style and expertise. The forged wall around my heart was a successful fortress that no one penetrated — until Brad.

I'll never forget the day I lost that dream. It was an unusually warm spring afternoon. The aroma of flowers floated on the air and the warmth of the sun felt incredible as the rays beat down on my face. The cold, winter dreariness finally behind us, I couldn't bare the idea of spending that amazing spring day listening to a lecture in a drab, windowless auditorium, so Brad easily persuaded me to skip the rest of my classes. He must have been confident I would blow off school and spend the day with him because he prepared a picnic basket brimming with all of my favorites.

We found the perfect place to spend the afternoon, a beautiful secluded meadow, close to campus with a little stream that trickled softly as it flowed over rocks below. We spread a blanket and stretched out with our faces toward the sun, talked, ate, tossed grapes at each other, and enjoyed the flawless afternoon.

As the sun began to sink into the evening sky, we both fell back onto the blanket in quiet contentment. Brad stared at me and smiled, but I pretended not to notice. He reached his hand out and softly stroked my cheek with the back of his fingers, then ran them through my hair and drew me close. Excitement rushed through my entire body.

He gently pushed against me, his kiss hot and moist. A ripple of delight surged through my veins as his hand slipped under my long dark hair and caressed my bare neck. He pulled me closer, kissed my cheek and soft lips traveled down my neck, licking and softly biting along their path.

Our passion ignited. He fumbled with the buttons of my shirt then reached under it and I trembled as his strong hands gently ran down my stomach and legs. I tugged at his shirt and grappled with his belt. I wanted him and knew he wanted me. The heat between us was like nothing I'd ever imagined as we groped each other wrapped in blissful foreplay. Our bodies entwined, and I responded to the contact with his virile bare chest.

Overcome with emotion and passion I craved his touch—his body, as if addicted to his aura. I wanted him to make love to me, needed to surrender and melt into him. The whole afternoon was a dream come true and I felt completely elated, a feeling so foreign to me, but when his strong hand touched the inside of my thigh--suddenly I couldn't breathe.

A shot of anxiety rushed through my body and an inner conflict jerked me back to reality. It was the moment-of-truth, and panic consumed me. I pushed Brad back from me and swallowed the lump caught in my throat then turned and rolled to my side, still lying next to him--still feeling his passion. My heart pounded. He touched my cheek as if remorseful for moving too fast, but I pulled away.

Confused at my unexpected rejection, he began to apologize for his advances, but I held my hand up and gestured for him to stop then silently turned my head away and stared blankly at the stream. Brad sat up and wrapped his arms around his knees. My mind raced frantically in search of some logical reason for my strange behavior.

I wasn't afraid to make love to him, and though my mother's conservative influence forbid premarital sex, I decided years earlier that if the right man held out his hand, I wouldn't let my moralistic rearing influence my decision to be intimate.

God, I wanted him with everything I was, but panic snaked around my body and squeezed, tighter and tighter, draining every ounce of oxygen from my lungs. How could he understand? I didn't understand myself. What could I say to explain my sudden rejection of him?

Overcome with emotion, I wiped away the tear that rolled down my cheek. I felt like a child and shuddered at the thought of what he was thinking. He reached across and touched my hand. The silence was deafening, and I needed to say something. Without further thought, I blurted out the first thing that entered my head.

"I can't do this. I'm—uh..." I struggled for something—anything to say to explain my moment of insanity. Then it came to me. The one thing I knew he'd believe. "I'm involved with someone else, Brad, someone from home, so this can't happen. I'm so attracted to you. The last few months have been amazing but—" Silent again, I scrambled to come up with more to say. "I just can't go this far."

Obviously stunned, Brad finally spoke, "What are you talking about, Casi?"

My creative instincts took over as the fabricated yarn continued to roll from my lips. "It's been great hanging out together and fun. I love being with you. It's just—"

"This doesn't make any sense." He reached over and pulled me close again. "I know you, Casi, and there is something else going on here. Something is wrong. Just talk to me. If you're not ready, it's okay. I shouldn't have assumed—I mean—if you want me to slow down, I'm fine with that. I'm sorry I got carried away. You're just so—"

"Stop, Brad." I blurted out. "You're not helping. Hanging out is one thing, but I can't do this. I have to be—faithful." Faithful? The words echoed in my mind as I spoke them, faithful to what, a life of loneliness and unfulfilled dreams? God, why was I so damn self-destructive?

I prayed the words were only in my head—that he hadn't heard me or at least that he would declare his love and fight for me. After all, that's what knights do. Instead, he silently stood up, refastened his clothes, looked back at me with a blank stare, and then walked stoically away, without saying a word.

My anxiety reached a crescendo. I felt physically ill, but fear and childish pride prevented me from running to him, confessing my fleeting moment of stupidity. Falling back onto the blanket, I lay there alone until the sun set, bringing a chill back to the air. Stunned at myself, what I just did, I moved in slow motion and mindlessly gathered my belongings, attempting to process the impact of my naivety.

My gentle knight now had a face, Brad's face, and I stabbed him in the heart. He gallantly bowed out of my life and left me to my imaginary lover. I was alone again—and totally baffled. In one fleeting moment I inadvertently destined myself to someone more deserving of the inept, unworthy woman I had come to believe I was. Brad and I never even talked after that day. I couldn't blame him. Even I would have walked out on me. I'm sure he must have thought I was a head case—and I guess I was.

Throughout my life, Brad would remain my lost fantasy, the path not traveled, the image of love I didn't deserve. That evening I imprisoned my heart and turned down an alternate road, a detour to a parallel life guided by fear.

True to my past form, I began to reject guys who showed an honest interest toward me and ended up with the usual suspects. Always a magnet for insincere men, I attracted and was drawn to the exact sort of males who would hurt me—and did. Instead of following my dreams, I reinforced my protective walls every time my heart shattered, then continued with the same pattern in a rinse and repeat cycle. I started dating only men whom I believed couldn't hurt me, guys I felt little or no attraction too, or those I saw as friends, and I locked up my passion because love always resulted in pain.

Dillon epitomized my warped revelation. He was sarcastic, brash—the complete opposite of Brad. Popular and well dressed, he was average in stature and appearance, cocky as hell and though not physically abusive, he couldn't pass up an opportunity to tease, prod or degrade my friends or me.

The first time I saw him, he was telling off one of my sorority sisters. I could feel the heat rise from the base of my spine to the top of my neck as I listened to him berate her until I finally flew into a rage and spoke up in her defense. I couldn't stand Dillon when we first met. His egotistical, narcissistic attitude appalled me. I'm quite sure he had no use for me either and thought of me as an outspoken bitch, stunned at my interruption of his arrogant tongue-lashing.

Whenever we saw each other, we bantered back and forth and though I was quite articulate, I was truly no match for his accomplished skill. Our eloquent exchanges must have intrigued him though, and me as well, because we found ourselves running into each other on a regular basis. Dillon was the first man I chose to date who I couldn't see marrying.

****

On some level I thought I deserved Dillon's abusive nature, but cognitively I believed he couldn't hurt me. I knew I would never marry him, thus I protected my heart. I looked at the bright side, he provided tender moments, which fed my need for romance so, in a perverted way, I found myself drawn to him. It wouldn't be difficult to break things off whenever I felt the need to move on. His pompous nature gave me endless opportunities.

For the next few years, I focused primarily on classes. Dillon provided a date for football games, parties and other school functions, and I fell back into old patterns. I accepted my destiny based on my twisted perception, molded my own self-fulfilling prophecy, and deliberately walked away from love. But in doing so, I unintentionally morphed into an easy mark, a vulnerable, empty vacuum, desperate for a man to declare undying love, which pushed me straight into the arms of a classic player.

Closing my journal, I stared down at the book as if it were a crystal ball, a glimpse into the past of my future. It was all so clear, now. Afraid of trusting, of loving Brad, I spiraled out of control. I convinced myself I was unlovable and was sure Brad would, at some point, abandon me. What was I thinking?

Why was it so hard for me to trust, to take a chance with a man whom I really desired? The fear that lurked inside haunted me. Oblivious that I set myself up for failure, I crouched behind the walls of an inner fortress created brick by brick for self-preservation, and imprisoned my heart. From that point on, I gullibly believed I entered relationships with hope, but my protective walls actually pushed me toward snakes, and it wasn't just my love life that faced imminent peril. My entire future fell into jeopardy. The patterns I created literally prevented me from pursuing my dreams.

My thoughts turned to Nicole. She went through a horrible trauma, but by all indications, she moved past the trauma. I wondered, though, what long-term effect her rape might have on her. I knew from experience that past pain could cause a dangerous obsession--a desperate need to feel loved that skews your sense of self. Protection from harm is an instinctive human response, and it truly doesn't matter if the pain is real or merely perceived.

Part II: Sins of the Father

Chapter 4

Don't compare your insides to other people's outsides.
Anonymous

From the moment of impact there was no doubt what the outcome would be. The crowd roared as the ball flew over the fence and was lost in the trees beyond. As he trotted across home plate, Jace's teammates rushed the field and raised him high in the air, then waltzed around with my son on their shoulders. They won the championship, and Jace hit the winning home run.

Elated fans spent the next half hour recounting the details of the game and reveling in their victory. In all the excitement, I didn't even notice Christine. As she sulked toward me, her eyes were fixed on Jace. They were best friends for years, but somewhere between pigtails and party dresses, her feelings deepened, and my son became more than a friend. It was obvious to me, but Jace remained in the dark.

I glanced in the direction of Christine's attention and saw Jace hugging a new friend, Brittany, as he savored his moment of glory.

"He'll be needing this." Christine stood in front of me, her arm stretched out with Jace's glove tightly grasped in her hand. She wiped a conspicuous tear from her cheek.

"Great game," she managed to squeak out.

"Thanks, it was a close one." I took the glove from her hand. "Tell him congrats for me." She stammered then turned and walked back across the field, still eying Jace and Brittany. I knew all too well the hurt she was going through and I hated that my son was the reason for her pain.

The whole drive home I thought about Christine. Broken hearts are a part of life. It was her first, but I knew it wouldn't be her last, or her worst. I unlocked the door, threw Jace's baseball glove on the sofa, and grabbed my journal from its familiar resting place.

Journal entry, April 1996:
Broken hearts are a rite of passage as we grow up and my ticket was well worn. The summer before my senior year in college I met Bryan, a musician playing at **The Bayou***, a local nightclub located under the Whitehurst Freeway in Georgetown. It was in an eclectic, funky section of Washington, D.C. that attracted the hip, younger generation with its quaint little shops, charming restaurants and trendy nightspots, the perfect venue for an aspiring young talent. Bryan's nightly routine typically involved targeting some young woman in the audience who sat close to the stage. She would be his focus for the evening and he directed his romantic repertoire to her. One summer evening that woman was me. Bryan's performance lured me into a web of deception, but that snare was only the beginning...*

No one can protect you with secrets and lies. They only make things worse—a fact I discovered in the mid 1970s...

****

Though routine to Bryan, I was drawn in by the spotlight centered on me while he looked directly in my eyes and sang: *"I Want to Make it With You."* The song, originally recorded by Bread, lured me into Bryan's cunning web with a romantic gesture, which opened the door for him to approach me during his break and sweep me off my feet. He saw the longing in my eyes as he sang, and played into my weakness. A player knows exactly what to look for, what to say, and how to say it--and, knowing what I know now, Brian fit the player image perfectly.

His band placed him in the limelight, an ideal position to provide an endless flow of groupies, most of whom were cute, young girls. He was handsome and muscular with slightly long hair typical of musicians, and the women swooned when he strummed his guitar and sang romantic ballads. I was the perfect target—an insecure *pretty girl*, brainwashed by lyrics of romantic love songs, and starved for the focus his expertise could provide.

Dreamy and romantic, I wanted to believe that Bryan hung the moon. He wasn't at all like Brad, but he singled me out and put me on a pedestal in front of an audience, then reeled me in with his tender words and romantic moves. A pawn in his hands, I felt a Zen-like inner peace--for a while anyway.

A whirlwind romance left me feeling I'd truly found the love of my life. I wasn't going to succumb to my internal conflict this time, I was older now—more worldly. I had no reason not to trust him. More importantly, I needed to start trusting myself...but I was still naïve.

That whole summer was magical. My days were filled with sunshine, friends, laughter, swimming pools and the smell of Coppertone, and nights were spent serenaded and romanced by an Adonis who loved me. Life was good. I was young, happy and infatuated. Bryan was an expert at getting what he wanted, and for some reason, he wanted me. I didn't question his affection. Instead I drank it all in and remained intoxicated by the nectar of love.

In the fall of 1973, I reluctantly returned to college to complete my senior year. Bryan wrote love letters almost daily and we talked by phone on a regular basis. He occasionally flew down on a Friday night, only to be gone in the blink of an eye by Sunday afternoon. Between the letters, phone calls and brief visits, I felt like I knew him completely but, in reality, I only scratched the surface.

In those days there were no cell phones, texting, email or Internet so communication limited long-distance relationships, but Bryan's romantic charm was seductive, especially for someone young and hungry to find their soul mate. When he asked me to marry him, I wasn't surprised. It was a romantic proposal made during winter break and, on Christmas Eve, 1973, I surrendered my heart to him, and my virginity.

For the next eight months we wrote letters and talked long distance while we planned an elegant wedding. In June of 1974, I graduated from college with a design degree, and minors in English and education. Eager to return to Virginia to put finishing touches on our fairy tale wedding and honeymoon, I left before the graduation ceremony.

Two months later, on August 10th, I married Bryan believing he was the man of my dreams. I was sure I'd caught the brass ring, so when my fiancé was late to the wedding, I rationalized his delay to an accident or some equally devastating event.

His groomsmen searched feverishly for him and finally found him asleep, naked and wrapped in the arms of a girl they didn't even know. They whisked Bryan off to the church, while he dressed in the back seat of the car. When Brie learned what happened, she assured me my fiancé was on his way and explained that his bachelor party lasted into the early morning hours and he simply overslept. My sister wanted to warn me, tell me the truth, but seeing me with hopeful eyes standing in front of her in my wedding dress, she just couldn't destroy my dreams.

My parents were never fond of Bryan. His compliments and eloquence reminded them of Eddie Haskell, the cunning troublemaker on the old sitcom "Leave it to Beaver" who turned on the charm when adults were around. They questioned Bryan's sincerity and motives for marrying me. When they learned he was late for the ceremony, they were told the same story as me.

But Dad, already convinced my fiancé was a scoundrel, found Bryan's irresponsible behavior a confirmation of his analysis.

"I have no problem paying for a canceled wedding." Dad put his hands on my shoulders and turned me around to stare at him face-to-face. "Your future is far more important to me than money. Think about what you're doing, Casi. This marriage will only end up in disaster. You can walk out now and no one will ever question your decision."

"But I love Bryan, Daddy." The prospects of even postponing the wedding, the humiliation and expense, was too overwhelming to think about. "And he loves me too. Four hundred people are waiting for a wedding in the sanctuary. My friends flew in from all over to be here. How could I ever face them again?"

I'm sure my tears broke his heart as he wiped a stream from my cheek.

"Look Daddy." I spoke in my best adult voice. "A last fling bachelor party is completely normal, especially for a self-proclaimed bachelor. But Bryan chose me. He loves me. I can't walk away from him."

So despite parental warnings, I convinced myself life with Bryan would be a dream come true. The wedding continued without further incident and the guests never learned why the ceremony was delayed. In hindsight, I'm pretty sure the pastor knew, or at least suspected why the groom was a late arrival. He performed the ceremony, but not without making an adamant point strongly emphasizing a husband's commitment and responsibilities in marriage, as if he was reprimanding Bryan.

Some of my friends and family later learned of the indiscretion, but they never shared the lurid details with me, a pattern that would follow in the months to come with my husband's future promiscuous behavior. Matrimony wasn't an obstacle to Bryan, and it didn't stop him from having sex with a parade of other women.

Six months into our marriage my husband's infidelity devastated me when his affairs were exposed. I received a surprise phone call from Becky, his fiancé—and I crashed and burned.

Becky was shocked when she learned Bryan married me. She confronted him, but the inconsistencies in his story persuaded her to find out the truth for herself. She broke down, cried inconsolable tears, while she stuttered a dialogue drenched in desperation. Had I not been so upset myself, I might have felt sorry for her, but my focus was on my own situation. As she spoke, I listened intently, while a hole burned into the pit of my stomach.

"Bryan told me that he *had* to marry you"--She took a deep breath--"because you are pregnant and all, and I feel bad for you but—"

"Because I'm what?" I shrieked into the phone. "You've got to be kidding. I am not, nor have I ever been pregnant."

I could hear Becky collapse emotionally. She went on through her tears and confessed her entire relationship with my husband. Our long-distance relationship made it easy for Bryan to keep up a dual life. He was ingenious really, and so deceptive, down to the most minuscule details. The gifts Bryan gave to Becky, jewelry to flowers, were duplicates of those he gave to me, less chance for confusion on his part. He had his techniques of deceit down to a science.

That's what players do, though. It's all a game to them, a balancing act. Apparently, he was engaged to both of us at the same time and for some reason he chose me. He probably just flipped a coin to decide which one of us he would marry. Ha, and I lost.

When Bryan arrived home that night, I confronted him. His response was as rehearsed as an Academy Award actor's acceptance speech.

"Casi, you have to believe me." He cried and begged for forgiveness. "I never meant to hurt you. This is about me, not you. There's something wrong inside of me."

The audacity of his arrogance blew me away. He expected me to actually believe that *he* was the victim.

"How could you do this to me, to Becky?" Tears of anger and betrayal welled in my eyes until they burst into a stream down my cheeks. "You said you loved me, took vows, and the whole time you were engaged to her. Nothing you could say could explain that. My God, what an idiot I was. I fell right into your arms and believed everything you said."

"Please, just listen to me, Casi." He sat down beside me and continued his performance. "You know you've asked me so many times about my past, and I always side-stepped you. Well, here it is: I dated a girl in high school I truly loved and when she died in a car accident, the loss destroyed me. Ever since that day I haven't been able to trust loving anyone." He sobbed as he revealed insecurities and his inability to believe in happy endings. "Ever since Amanda died, I needed a backup. I couldn't bear the thought of losing someone I loved again and ending up alone with all of that pain."

His pitiful explanation almost convinced me he was damaged, but it didn't explain his lies. Tears gushed down my face, and my stomach retched as I mustered the courage to ask him to leave. I felt used, insignificant, and could almost feel the walls harden around my heart again. I lost all trust in my husband that day, but worse than that, I lost complete trust in my own judgment.

I've never been able to understand why Bryan actually married me in the first place, unless I was a conquest he had yet to achieve. I'm sure Amanda never even existed. Bryan fabricated the tragic story to back up his flagrant lies. His rock star image fed his ego. He was hot, talented, romantic, and his aura as addictive as it was mesmerizing, fed into the perfect storm to breed a player. I was only one in a long line of his victims.

When my world imploded, I needed the comfort and guidance of my parents, but how could I go to them, especially after my dad's insistent warnings. How could my parents understand?

Divorce was not an option in my family. You made your choices and lived with the consequences. My parents' marriage was perfect. I'm not sure I ever saw them so much as disagree. Daddy tried to open my eyes, but I was too stubborn. What is it about parents? Do they have some sixth sense vision of the future? How could they possibly know Bryan would devastate my life, and how could I ever admit they were right?

My quiet behavior spoke volumes to them making obvious something was bothering me. As hard as I tried to convince them I was just tired, they didn't buy it. I was never good at concealing my emotions, so I wasn't surprised they knew something was seriously wrong. It's not that I was trying to hide anything. I just had no clue how to tell them their perfectly imperfect daughter was about to confirm her inadequacies.

Divorce wasn't something I could just slide under the carpet. Everyone would find out eventually, but I needed to prepare Mom and Dad to soften the blow. They made so many sacrifices for me and gave me a future filled with promise. Now, I had to look into their eyes and admit that my strong will and stupidity destroyed their dreams for me.

I took a deep breath before spilling my guts.

"Mom, Dad, we need to talk."

"Here it comes, Laura." Dad looked over at my mom and hitched his chin suggesting she sit down. "Okay, Casi. Let's have it. What's goin' on?"

Now, Mother was never vocal in troubling situations. She sat quiet as usual, while I struggled through my story, my face drenched in tears. Each word echoed in my head and fell silently on the chill of the evening.

The expected "I told you so" was never spoken. Daddy touched my shoulder before sitting down, and my submissive mother uncharacteristically took the foreground, softly comforting me. Does history truly repeat itself or is it a cynical twist of fate? Mom understood exactly what I was going through. At twenty-three I learned my entire life—was a lie.

"If you think hard Casi, you'll remember and you'll know what I'm saying is true." Mom embraced me as I sobbed uncontrollably. "Your dad is not your biological father."

I couldn't speak. My dad, my rock, the man whom I adored and looked up to my entire life, was not really my dad?

"Your dreams sweetie." Mom tried so hard to nudge my memories. "Remember your dreams and how scared you were. You had nightmares for years. We moved so many times just to keep you girls safe...and when you disappeared looking for Grandma's house, I was sure Matthew took you. I constantly looked over my shoulder terrified he'd find us—until I met your Daddy. Try, Casi, you'll remember."

"But you lied to me. Why didn't you tell me the truth?" I leaned back, broke loose from her arms and pulled away as the reality set in. "You knew I forgot, or blocked my father out. Why the secrets and lies? How could you have done that to me?"

"It's not easy to explain, sweetie. Your sister is the one who blocked out your biological *father*, not you, and the doctor said she would remember when she could emotionally handle it. He said to let her discover the truth in her own time, which meant we hid the truth from you, for her sake. Over time, you just forgot. Your memories turned into scary dreams, and we thought it best to keep it that way." Her face wore the angst of drama she had yet to divulge. "You would have told your sister, Casi, even if you didn't mean to. A secret like this is too heavy for a child to carry. We just wanted to protect you both. Please understand. Dear God, I've had this discussion with you a million times in my mind. Just know we did what we thought was best. Your Dad and I love you so much."

"And what about my *real* dad? What—"

My mother cut me off, her demeanor shifting from sympathetic to inflexible.

"Your real dad is right here. This man sitting in front of you is your dad in every sense of the word. He raised you, loved you, and was always there for you. Don't ever doubt that."

My mother's compliant behavior made so much sense now. She adored this man and felt eternally grateful to him because he not only loved her, but also embraced her two little girls as his own. I had no idea of the anguish and fear Mom went through. From the outside she led a carefree and happy life. No one would have ever guessed she suffered.

My paternal grandmother's attitude toward my sister and me made perfect sense too. Alex was her grandchild. Brie and I were merely the offspring of the recycled wife her son chose. Obviously she never approved of my mother or her pre-existing family.

Secrets and lies were the foundation for my entire belief system. How do you deal with that? I was so angry, but everything began to fall in place and finally made sense. I coaxed Mom more deeply for answers. There was so much I wanted to know, but when her explanation was over, she would say nothing more.

I was given minimal information about the past. Mom's youthful escape from her strict upbringing sent her right into the arms of a handsome, self- absorbed cheater. He married her, but abused her--abused Brie and me too. Mom finally took her two daughters and ran.

The man I knew as my dad appeared on the scene some time later and picked up the pieces of her shattered life. Daddy married Mom, adopted Brie and me, and my mother was devoted to him. My sister and I were young, so young our fragile minds blocked out the abuse from our biological father. Our memories shifted to hide painful visions of our violent past. "Father" by definition, is the one man in a child's life who should always provide a safe haven of unconditional love.

Perhaps it was a blessing we had no conscious recollection of those turbulent years, but the anguish in our subconscious injured our spirit. Our hearts searched for love and acceptance to fill the emptiness left by our absentee father.

Yes, it all made perfect sense, the muted late night discussions my parents secretly held when they thought I slept. They discussed Matthew Stafford, my biological father, not Daddy, and my innocent confusion between Daddy and Matthew explained the tarnished black knight as well. I was suddenly overwhelmed with a deep retching feeling of betrayal and abandonment.

I wanted to know more about this man, my father. Mom was clearly uneasy when I broached the subject, and she made me promise to never hurt Daddy by searching for Matthew. She insisted Daddy was my father in every way that mattered, and DNA was irrelevant. That night I vowed to never hurt my dad by flaunting my birth father in his face, but I needed to know more. As much as I begged her to tell me about Matthew, Mother refused any further explanation except to say:

"You wouldn't want to know him, Casi. He's the kind of man who pulls wings off of butterflies."

I wasn't sure what her comment meant, but I knew it was supposed to satisfy my curiosity. Instead, the words haunted me. They didn't quench my thirst for knowledge. Pulling wings off of butterflies was sadistic, left the insect powerless and fated to live a tortured life or suffer a cruel death. The description sounded a bit extreme, but my mother was probably bitter and hurt.

It was such an interesting analogy. Mom was intelligent and always put a lot of thought into what she said. I couldn't help but wonder why she used that metaphor. A butterfly never meets its parents. It's destined to survive on its own, independent and alone. A beautiful, delicate masterpiece of nature, doomed to go through life as a stranger to affection. A sudden chill ran through my body. I shivered to cast off the uncomfortable sensation.

****

How could any father abandon his own child? There was a lot more to the story and my questions mounted. Perhaps my "parents" fought or maybe Matthew wasn't the perfect husband, but I was still his daughter, his own flesh and blood. It couldn't be that difficult to track Brie and me down. In my mind, he never made a single attempt to find us or cared enough to know who we had become.

I was flooded with feelings of inadequacy. God, this was the ultimate rejection. I was oblivious to the fact we were constantly moving because my mother lived in fear — fear our father would find her, or worse, would find us. Ironically, despite her best attempts, Mother's secrets and lies actually hurt her precious children whom she was so frantic to protect. Whatever happened between Matthew Stafford and my mother was the root of my deep-seated need for––and fear of––love. Why I walked away from Brad and into the arms of users. My father's rejection and abandonment pierced my heart, making me the perfect vulnerable mark for players.

Bryan's infidelity and my broken marriage took a back seat to the devastating realization that my whole life was a lie. My biological father was the initial villain in my life. He was the first in a string of men to throw me away — dispose of me without so much as a glance backward. Bryan just continued the pattern and I was the only one who could break it...

I closed my journal, laid it back down on the table and walked to the window. A soft rain began to fall and the raindrops pelted the water in my backyard pond causing ripples to roll like waves to the edges. A ripple effect plagued my life as well. The whispers I heard as a child in the dead of night did not fall on deaf ears. I heard the tragic stories of my *father* as my mother poured out her heart to Daddy.

Matthew forged the foundation for my deep feelings of abandonment. He discarded me and ever since his departure, I felt unworthy of anyone's love. He was the reason for the emptiness I felt throughout my life and the cause of my desperate need to be loved and treasured.

Mom was right about one thing, Matthew may have been my *father*, but he wasn't my *dad*. Robert Gordon McLean was the only *Dad* I would ever have. I needed to find a way to come to terms with Matthew's decision. Children are resilient. If they are traumatized in their youth, they can bounce right back and move forward unscathed — right? Knowledge is half the battle, so I should be able to turn things around. I felt abandoned by Matthew, but from what Mom said he didn't choose to leave me. It was my mother who chose that path. So if I wasn't abandoned, all I needed to do was tuck that knowledge into the back of my brain and start over with a fresh perspective. In my mind, that made all the sense in the world, but I believe we are also a product of our direct environment, and we learn what we are programmed to know.

I glanced at my watch and realized it was close to dinnertime. Christine's broken heart jarred many memories. I would have a heart-to-heart talk with Jace after dinner and make him aware of her feelings. He didn't have to love her, but if he was aware of the situation, maybe he could be more sensitive to her or even help her. As an adult, I could see that Christine was hurting, but Jace had no idea. I think that's how it is with most people. We compare what we feel inside of us to what we see on the outside of others.

I never imagined the trauma my mother experienced. From all indications she was happy. My frame of reference was unique to my own thoughts, and I really had no idea of what was inside of the people around me--their struggles or pain. Maybe if we could see people from the inside out, we would be a lot more tolerant and compassionate toward each other.

My mind focused on the past, I decided to prepare one of my favorite childhood meals. I rarely ate comfort foods anymore. My body was noticeably more slender than it had been in years, and my more active lifestyle made me feel so much better. Still, my boys loved fried chicken, and I hadn't prepared it in a long time.

I opened the fridge and pulled out a package. I would only have one piece for dinner. Moderation, not denial was working for my physical transformation. Changing my outside appearance wasn't complicated. I became more active and dropped a few pounds, which inspired me to buy some new, trendier clothes and get an updated hairstyle. I started to recognize and even like my mirror image again, but changing myself on the inside would be a lot more difficult and would take more time. As I began to prepare dinner, the question nagged at me. Secrets and lies dictated who I became. How could I find the woman I was meant to be?

Chapter 5

Never be afraid to give up the good to go for the great.
Kenny Rogers

"Please help me Casi, we have to look for him." Brie's voice was tinged with desperation. She dreamed about Matthew Stafford and was hell bent to find him, but my mother's warning was seared in my mind. I was torn between an inherent curiosity and keeping peace with my sister. What if mom was right? If we *were* able to successfully track down our *father*, we might regret finding him. Our *father* might even be dangerous.

I slept fitfully all night, tormented by the prospects of a lengthy search, but ultimately curiosity won the battle. We really needed to learn more about Matthew--at least for our medical background, and Daddy didn't have to find out about our search. He wouldn't be hurt if he didn't know. If we discovered anything treacherous, we could simply back off and discontinue our quest. My rationalization seemed valid and, after being cooped up all winter, I was ready to take on a new adventure.

Spring always held an allure for me. It was a time for new beginnings, and I was so ready for that. I walked out to the screened porch to drink in the crisp morning air. It was late April and the azaleas were in full bloom. They only lasted for a week or two, but every spring they turned my back yard into a botanical wonderland. The birds flitted back and forth from my multiple feeders, singing their morning greetings. Springtime gave me a sense of rejuvenation. Nature regenerated with new birth. The idea of starting over with a fresh slate invigorated me.

My journal propped up against a pillow on the porch swing. The book mysteriously appeared in my secret havens, no doubt my intuitive son at work again. He sensed my metamorphosis was somehow connected to my journal. I loved to sit on the porch swing with a cup of coffee in hand and greet a warm April morning. The aroma of freshly mown grass and spring flowers floated on the air and I took in a deep breath as I sat.

Zack loved this time of year, but not for the same reasons. His life was baseball from the moment he could hold a bat and spring brought the opening day of a new season. Picking up my diary, my mind drifted back to the first time I met my husband.

Journal entry, April 1997:

My mother's admission changed my perspective of my childhood and the years that ensued should have been filled with self-discovery to renew my confidence and buoyancy. After all, my dilemma was solved, so it only stood to reason I would be able to move forward and let go of my broken childhood shattered self-image. I thought I could simply start over, but self-doubt proved to be a formidable adversary. I now understood how I romanticized love and distorted the role of men in my life. My warped ideas spun fairytale expectations into reality. I just needed to clear those visions out and reboot my assessment. So for the next few years, I decided to focus on my inner self. I vowed to swear off men completely and concentrate instead, on more significant issues like my career and future. I resolved to close the book on fantasies, try to discover what I wanted in life, and throw myself into that vision.

It's not enough to want to change your life. First you have to figure out what went wrong, then work like hell to escape the quicksand of your past...

****

"If you reach for the moon and miss, you are still among the stars." I taped the quote to my bathroom mirror and the inspiration reflected back at me every morning and night. I wanted to reach for the moon, to make a difference for having lived on this earth, but unforeseen obstacles pushed me off-track. How could I find my way back? There was no doubt I would survive. My determination and tenacity would see to that. I simply hit a speed bump along my path. I needed to chart an alternate course and tuck my dreams and passions neatly away where they would be overshadowed by daily events.

Since childhood, my cheery façade masked an insecure, abandoned little girl. Inside I felt devastated Matthew deserted me. Didn't he at least wonder what became of his little girl? I wanted to be able to see his face when I closed my eyes, to know if he smiled when he looked at me or sneered with disgust. But my memory was a blank page––a blank page that yearned to be filled.

I tried to rationalize, convince myself it was *his* loss, and not mine. I tried to prove, maybe more to myself than to him, that I was a worthy, valuable woman, not a disposable nothing that could be discarded without so much as a backward glance. I wanted to throw my father away too, to bury the sense of insignificance he instilled in me, but the harder I tried to dismiss my feelings, the more Matthew haunted me. The faceless, impassive knight was always there, taunting me.

Afraid of failure, or worse, of success, I lacked the self-assurance I needed to pursue my dreams or begin a significant career. I was well educated and experienced, primed to become a successful professional, but instead I accepted lesser, more transient jobs like waitressing.

Depressed by wasting my time and energy in a dead end job, I dreaded spending every night in a hole-in-the-wall bar filled with lonely people whose dreams already faded into the canyons of their minds. I prayed I would never become one of them, but I felt myself slipping into their mold.

You have to be tough skinned to serve drinks in a bar. I still remember the stench of stale cigarettes and the alcohol breath of the sleaze-bags snatching a feel of my butt as I walked by. The insidious men who frequented that place made me want to scrub myself raw every night before bed. Enduring their brazen advances and lewd remarks disgusted me.

"Come here sweetie, you're ignoring me." He slurred his speech as he grabbed my ass, his eyes fixated on my breasts. "I need another drink, and you've left me all alone over here."

The tips weren't bad, but the suggestive comments and roving hands motivated my daily search for a more significant position. I finally landed a job as a salesgirl selling rental contracts at an upscale apartment complex in Alexandria, Virginia, but the new environment didn't really change anything. At first I was surprised I got hired, having no experience in sales, but it didn't take a mental genius to discover my experience wasn't the required prerequisite. I worked there for less than a week before my boss called me into his office.

"Close the door, please." He looked up from his paperwork.

"You asked to see me, sir?"

He slid his glasses down, perched them on the end of his nose and stared at me for a moment before he placed them carefully on his paperwork. "You're a smart woman, Casi. You could go far in this company." He stood and leaned against the front of his over sized desk.

"Thank you Mr. Miller, just let me know what you need and I'll take care of it." That was apparently the wrong thing to say, because moments later as he sung my praises, he backed me against the wall and braced his arms on each side of my body, trapping me. After several moments of carefully choosing my words and eluding his advances, I managed to duck under his left arm.

"I'd better get back to work." I quickly scooted out the door.

Sexual harassment ran rampant in those days, at least for me, and after six months of my boss' hands and erotic innuendo, I possessed enough sales experience and self-respect to look for employment elsewhere. The jobs changed, but there always seemed to be someone who made unsolicited advances. I felt like I had a neon message tattooed across my forehead that said: "play me." Why did I attract an endless stream of men who felt obliged to make passes?

Disillusioned at every turn, I wanted to be done, finished with men once and for all. What if I made a conscious decision to give up on the species all together? No, the fairytale life I dreamed of included children, and though men failed to live up to my gallant expectations, my strong maternal instincts lured me back into the dating field. At the ripe old age of 24, I felt my biological clock ticking and since, to date, it was a physical impossibility to have a baby without the assistance of a sperm donor, I decided to adjust my impossible standards. Giving up on men was never a real option. In truth, I ached to be in the arms of a man I loved, one who truly loved me.

Over time, I learned how to deal with men in a work situation, but relationships still eluded me. I changed my game plan into a strategy that seemed logical. I'd protect my heart by stopping myself from falling in love. I'd only get involved if someone put me first, cherished and loved me and, as long as I felt some chemistry, maybe I didn't need love.

The plan sounded reasonable enough, so I tried to bury my passions even deeper and accepted that my childhood dreams of a soul mate were created as a result of my volatile past and the secrets and lies of my parents. An honest, loving man who had eyes for *only* me could work, as long as I could keep him from breaking my heart. He didn't have to be my knight, but I could still live the "American dream."

My job experience over the past few years taught me a lot more than what could be listed on my resume. I possessed attributes that gave me distinct advantages and I learned to capitalize on them. In the summer of 1977 I was hired as a token female in a male dominated business. Since I was the only woman in the entire company, the other employees swarmed around me like bees on honey, but my newfound skills managed to disarm their stingers.

I kept everyone at arms length, but Wes, the group manager, saw right through my defenses and took every opportunity to probe into my personal life. Wes was happily married, which to me was a mystery, and he was determined to restore my faith in men, so it didn't surprise me when he insisted I meet his best friend.

"Zack is a great guy, Casi." He stood up from his chair, walked around to the front of the desk and plopped down on the edge of it. "He's a total gentleman and the most honest man I've ever known. You really should give him a chance. Just have lunch with him and get to know him."

His comments were interesting, since Zack was the one man in the office who consciously ignored me. He was always there, but whenever I glanced at him, he'd look away and appeared uninterested in the swarming beehive. Unfortunately, that intrigued me. Wes convinced me Zack was an honest guy. Virtually every man in my life lied to me, so honesty became the most important virtue to me. After weeks of less than subtle nudging and against my better judgment, I succumbed to Wes' pestering and agreed to meet his friend over lunch.

As he reflected on his past, I found Zack to be totally likable.

"I was an athlete most of my life." The little boy in him exuded pride, laced with humility. "You know, the football and baseball star in high school. Went to college on a scholarship and was really lucky. When I graduated, I was drafted by a major league baseball team and played AAA. I was living every little boy's dream—until I slid into third base during a practice game and tore my rotator cuff. Everything changed after that."

The injury destroyed Zack's shoulder and took away his dream as well. Three years after the accident ended his career, his musculature wasn't what I'd call athletic. He was tall and quite handsome, but as my dad put it, a bit portly. His image didn't fit the Adonis stature of buff hunks I typically dated, with bulging muscles and strong features, but I saw that as a positive. He was cute, an odd choice of words since he towered over me, but that's how I felt about him.

I wasn't drawn to Zack by instant chemistry. It was more of a process, from intrigue, to empathy, to allure. We had common interests and he made me laugh, an attribute that was missing in my life. He put me at ease right away with his jovial attitude and fun-loving personality, and I could be myself instead of hiding behind my perfect façade.

Zack and I had fun together and connected on multiple levels, but he also had a compassionate side that caught me off guard. As we got to know each other, I sensed his attraction and sincerity and I finally felt comfortable enough to open up to him about my past relationships and apprehension toward marriage. His sympathetic reactions to my history dropped my defenses even further. I thought about Daddy and how he embraced Brie and me along with my mother, and wondered how Zack would respond to a built-in family. I impulsively threw out a question.

"It's easy to accept my marriage to Bryan, but how would you feel if I had children in tow?" His response melted my heart with his first mention of love.

"I would stretch my arms to wrap around all of you." He smiled a boyish grin. "Your children would be a part of you, and I would love them as much as I love you. I can't believe what Bryan did to you. I would never hurt you, Casi, I swear. If you ever give me a chance, I promise you will never regret it." Zack disarmed me and I believed him. "You leave me breathless, Casi. When I leave you, I can't wait until we're together again."

He brought me flowers for no reason except that he wanted to see me smile. He understood the damage my past inflicted and swore...no, he vowed to never be the source of any pain in my life. That pierced my armor. I believed he truly loved me and, more important, that he would always be faithful and honest.

A year after we met, Zack and I were married in an intimate evening ceremony with family and close friends, followed by a small gathering at my parent's home. Wes was Zack's best man, a fitting tribute to the man who brought us together. Brie planned the whole ceremony and made an elaborate cake for the reception. She liked Zack, but was not totally convinced I should marry him. Her protective manner felt as cool as the crisp November air. I loved Zack, but Brie's gut instinct bothered me and I had trouble shaking her reluctance to be all in with my decision.

The ceremony went off without a hitch, thank God. We exchanged vows and the reception faded any misgivings I may have felt. Around midnight, we ducked a cascade of rice and waving hands as we ran toward the car and our future. We drove away from our friends and family, the rattle of tin cans and old shoes clattering over the road echoed against the silent night. Once out of sight of the house, Zack pulled over to detach the array from the back of my ornately decorated Datsun 240SL. While he was busy making our ride a little less conspicuous, my thoughts drifted back to Brie's cautious concern.

A soft snow began to fall as we pulled away and the hypnotic flurries swirled around the car and dusted the street. Glad Zack was driving instead of me I stared out the windshield, mesmerized by the snowflakes. A sudden ripple of anxiety crawled up my arms and chewed at the base of my neck, overwhelming me with emotion. The stark reality began to set in. I pledged my life to this man, but the idea of marriage again still terrified me. All of my trust issues flooded to the surface and my stomach lurched.

I needed Zack to reassure me, but I couldn't explain my feelings. I didn't understand the sudden surge of silent tears myself. I couldn't let him see me crying, so I turned my head and stared out the window at the frozen world enveloping us, while my stomach clenched as if a chard of ice cut twisted into my core.

By the time we reached our hotel room in downtown Washington D.C., we were both totally spent. We dragged ourselves to our room and collapsed into the plush comforter that welcomed us. We fell asleep in each other's arms, snuggling together and whispering about our future...leaving our first night as husband and wife unconsummated.

Morning brought a whirlwind of anticipation as we rushed to catch our flight and begin our lives together. The daunting emotion of the prior night faded into hidden corners of my mind. We spent the second night of our honeymoon in the penthouse of the Miami Hilton. The room overlooked a spectacular view of Miami Beach in three directions and we felt like royalty gazing down at the ocean below as waves rolled to the shore. The next morning we sailed for a week on an extravagant cruise ship, followed by a few days at Disney World. The whole trip was carefree and fun, so it was easy for me to dismiss my wedding night nerves as a momentary rush of cold feet. In hindsight, I'm not so sure.

****

As hard as I tried to deny my feelings initially, I loved Zack. He was the right choice for me at the time. He didn't take my breath away the first time I saw him — or when I kissed him, but marriage takes more than passion to succeed. Our relationship had substance, unlike some built purely out of chemical lust that dissipates over time, leaving the couple to wake up one day and look at each other aghast in wonder what they ever saw in each other. Zack and I connected on so many levels and with real compassion and love that grew stronger every day.

As I look back, I can't say I made a mistake when I married him. If I hadn't, Josh and Jace would not have been born, and they were the lights of my life. Despite what the future brought us, Zack and I were meant to be.

I put my pen down and drank in the aroma of the freshly mown grass. Spring was a time of rebirth, of new beginnings and that's what I needed. I just wasn't sure how to set my life back on track. My warped ideas directed me down a path to Zack, but I couldn't shake the feeling that somewhere inside of me I harbored a deep conflicting turmoil.

My thoughts drifted back to Mom. I wondered how she felt about Matthew when they married and what really happened between them. I wanted to help Brie find our father. We both needed to know who this man was and why he coldly dismissed us. Finding Matthew Stafford was the key to a door I needed to open.

Chapter 6

Never fear shadows. They simply mean that there's a light somewhere nearby.
Ruth E. Renkei

Stunned at what Sandy told me, I collapsed into the overstuffed chair and the phone slid off my hand to the floor. From the first moment I met her, she was the essence of happiness and optimism, but I guess a lot happened in twelve years. Even though our lives took us in different directions, my high school friend and I kept in touch. She was always so happy and carefree. It was hard to visualize Sandy struggling with anything, least of all panic attacks. Her external exuberance totally masked the stress and anxiety she experienced. I shuddered as I realized how familiar that sounded.

I walked across the family room toward the fireplace and glanced out the window into the back yard. The snow had been falling for hours creating a crystalline fantasyland that evoked silent serenity. I rubbed my hands together briskly and spread them above the blazing fire. Tranquility felt totally elusive when I struggled with my own panic attacks and I cherished quiet moments of calmness.

A corner of my diary peeked out from a soft throw draped over my overstuffed chair, triggering a familiar allure. Sandy's trauma drew me back into the most difficult battle of my life. I knew exactly what she would face in her immediate future and the fear she would need to overcome. Dealing with anxiety disorder was the most daunting obstacle I ever faced.

Even now, chills ran through my body when I thought of the debilitating surges of adrenalin that siphoned my energy and paralyzed my life. Anxiety attacks threw the ultimate blow to my self-confidence—a setback I wasn't sure I could overcome. Unsettling visions flooded my mind and took me back to the dark trauma that triggered the onset of my harrowing battle.

Journal entry, winter—November 1997:
In the fall of 1980, Zack made the decision to move to Atlanta, Georgia. He thought the job market might prove more lucrative there, so we packed our belongings and left our home and family to embark on a new chapter in our lives. Atlanta was beautiful. We bought a house in Marietta, a suburb northwest of the city. Zack found a job he really liked, but the position required him to travel quite a bit, so I was left alone to fend for myself in unfamiliar surroundings.

My neighbor Kelly and her husband, Todd, moved in across the street a few months earlier. Kelly and I became instant friends. So while Zack was away, I searched for a teaching job, hung out with Kelly, and exercised to lose the few extra pounds I'd put on since the wedding. The move was stressful and the process of settling in to a new town took a lot of time and energy. I was exhausted, but excited to pioneer our new adventure—until the day I stumbled upon a gruesome discovery.

Memories of the early 1980s will always be hard to revisit. They epitomize one of my mother's favorite quotes: "What doesn't kill you, makes you stronger..."

****

We lived in Atlanta only a few months when Kelly decided to take a brief trip out of town to visit her parents. She called me one evening frantic to get in touch with Todd.

"I've tried to reach Todd so many times today." Her voice trembled. "He just won't pick up the phone. It's not like him to ignore me. I'm really starting to worry something happened to him."

"It's probably nothing, Kel." I tried to comfort her. "Please Casi, go see if he's at the house."

Fortunately, Zack was home that afternoon. He motioned for me to give him the phone.

"Kelly, I'm sure Todd is just tied up. Maybe he worked in the yard all day and couldn't hear the phone ringing. Just try to relax." His tone conveyed an air of strength as he attempted to calm her worries. "Casi and I will go over and see if he's home. If not, we'll keep an eye out and catch him when he gets back and tell him to call you. We'll call you back and let you know what's up, okay?"

Zack and I strolled across the street to her house, rang the bell and knocked on the door several times, but there was no response. We peered in the windows then walked around to the back to look for anything unusual. Zack grabbed the doorknob. Surprised to find it unlocked, he called out for Todd as we entered the house and began a systematic search of each room. We checked the entire house and I was about to go back outside when Zack grabbed my arm.

"Hold up, Casi." He reached for the garage door. "Let's see if his car is here." When he peered inside, my husband froze, gasped, and sputtered. "Oh--my--God."

I peeked around his arm and there was Todd, sitting in the driver's seat of his car, his head tipped forward, his face blue and still, with a tiny drip of blood at the base of his nose. The burgundy colored Oldsmobile Cutlass was silent, having run out of gas at some point. Three of the windows were rolled up tight, but the driver's side window was rolled down completely and replaced by a piece of cardboard taped securely to the frame.

A circle was cut into the center of the makeshift window with a flexible dryer hose duck-taped to the hole. The hose stretched down to the floor through a cooling system Todd improvised with a cooler filled with water now, but obviously contained ice to cool the car exhaust before it reached the interior of the car. The other end of the hose was taped tightly to the tailpipe and tied off with an old T-shirt. Business shirts were meticulously stuffed between the base of the garage door and the cement floor. Todd apparently wanted to make sure the garage was completely sealed off from outside oxygen to ensure his suicide attempt was successful. There was no note, but Todd still clung to two pictures of Kelly, obviously his last thoughts as his life slipped away.

The smell of stale exhaust fumes and death was too much to bear and I retched as I ran from the house with Zack following close behind. Shaken, we returned home and called the police as well as the pastor of our church. Kelly called repeatedly to see if we talked to her husband, but we didn't answer the phone. We didn't know what to say. How could we tell her the husband she adored took his own life?

When the pastor arrived, he offered to talk to Kelly the next time she called and I gladly accepted. I stood beside him, listening intently and couldn't believe how coldly he explained the situation to her over the phone. My heart ached for Kelly as he uttered each word.

I couldn't imagine how she felt, and when I heard her shriek through the phone when she realized what the pastor was saying, I felt the blood drain from own face. How could Todd do that to her? His own pain must have been inconceivable.

During the weeks that followed, Kelly was inconsolable and I felt helpless and beyond sorrow for her. She completely fell apart and withdrew from her friends, so distraught that she put her house on the market and returned to her parents' home after the funeral in an attempt to heal and regain some sense of normality in her life.

Her house quickly sold and we eventually lost touch, but the vivid memories were etched in my mind forever. It was months before the vivid images of the eerie scene began to fade, but the aftermath of Kelly's trauma was far from over for either of us.

Todd's death spun through my thoughts constantly, and on top of the stress I already endured, anxiety began to take a toll I never dreamed possible. In only a few months time, I moved, lost twenty pounds, started a new job and discovered a dead friend's body. Physical stress and fatigue would be normal for anyone in that situation, and apart from Kelly's horrible tragedy, the stress was positive. Zack and I were happy, excited about our future and we were trying to get pregnant. Unfortunately, my body didn't respond to the emotional strain in the same positive manner.

One afternoon, out of the blue, a shot of adrenalin rushed over me for no apparent reason and it wasn't an isolated event. At first the sensations were sporadic and brief, lasting only a minute or so. It was easy to attribute them to fatigue, but over the course of a few weeks, the intensity and duration increased, and the feelings began to scare me. They always subsided, but left me feeling nervous, similar to the feeling of a caffeine buzz. The low flux allowed me to carry on with my daily routine, but I dreaded the onset of the next surge.

When my anxiety attacks evolved into full-fledged panic attacks, my heart would race and my chest would tighten as I trembled and gasped for breath. Beads of sweat rolled down the back of my neck. Adrenalin rushed through my body, followed by a surge of nausea, and my muscles stiffened. Strange feelings of impending doom crept over me with a desperate urge to run somewhere—anywhere.

When an attack came over me, I could almost feel the flow of blood running through my veins, and this irrational fear felt as real as if I were standing in the headlights of an oncoming car, too paralyzed to move. After a few weeks of dealing with these exhausting sensations, I began to stay as close to home as possible to avoid experiencing a panic attack in public.

The dread became so intense I could barely force myself to go to the new job I adored. How could I teach children when the sensation of high-octane fuel shooting though my cardio-vascular system debilitated me? To top the devastating physical effects, Zack suddenly became MIA. I needed my husband for strength and confidence--that's marriage, right--in sickness or health, for better or worse, we vowed to support, honor and be by each other's side? Zack all but vanished with an unrelenting schedule. Maybe his own problems took precedence, or perhaps he just didn't want to deal with mine, but whatever the reason, he came home late and traveled more often, leaving me to fight my demons on my own.

I couldn't predict the onset of the panic any more than I could determine what it was, or why it was happening to me, so I finally decided I needed help. Anxiety disorder, though quite familiar today, was not a commonly treated ailment in the early 1980s. Specialists, treatment options and anti-anxiety medications like Prozac®, Paxil®, and Xanax® were not yet available to the public at large. The first doctor I visited asked if I was upset or depressed and suggested I go home and try to relax.

That made no sense to me at all. I wasn't depressed. In fact, I was excited and optimistic about my life. I had a new job, a beautiful home, and Zack and I just decided to have a baby. Frustrated, I went to another doctor, who called my ailment, *Post-Traumatic Stress Disorder* and he prescribed medication for the debilitating symptoms, but the drug didn't stop my attacks, and the side affects made me feel worse — confused and sluggish. I was sure the doctor misdiagnosed my problem.

I hated the affect of the drugs, and I convinced myself that my symptoms were from a chemical imbalance. Nothing I tried was working. Sleep deprivation left me even more exhausted, and on top of that, visions of Todd's suicide periodically crept into my tired mind and induced even more adrenaline into my body.

Determined to take back control of my life, I weaned myself from the meds and searched every source available for information about anxiety attacks. There wasn't an Internet back then, and despite all the books and articles I read, nothing gave me the insight I needed or provided any hope—until I made a freak discovery.

In late November 1982, Zack and I planned to drive to Virginia to spend the holidays with our families. As usual, he was out of town on business and arrived home on Wednesday evening, the night before Thanksgiving, so we were forced to drive through the night. I offered to take the wheel first, while he slept. By 1:00 a.m. as we approached the Virginia border I began to feel anxious. The welcome center was just ahead, so I pulled in, to relax for a moment and calm myself down. I parked the car and walked inside to the restroom to throw some cold water on my face.

The chilling night air easily pierced my jeans and T-shirt, and I realized how much warmer it was in Atlanta. By the time I returned to the car, I was freezing. I started the engine and adjusted the heater to warm my arms.

The radio station I was listening to faded, so I scanned the selections, hoping to find some music that would take my mind off of my anxiety. My options were limited, so I settled for a station that came in the clearest—a talk show. I reclined the seat, adjusted my body and closed my eyes. My focus shifted to the show, an interview with a woman who was explaining her debilitating ailment—a constant state of anxiety. I sat straight up with a jolt, my eyes opened wide, and I listened intently. Excited by the interview, I nudged my husband.

"That's me, Zack." I shook him again, this time more exuberantly. "That woman is describing what's happening to me."

For the next thirty minutes, at 1:00 a.m. on Thanksgiving morning 1982, we listened and discovered the answers that would help me begin to take back control of my life. How that radio station out of Charlotte, North Carolina, found its way to my ears on a cold November morning truly mystified me, but I have always believed that things happen for a reason.

Lou Owensby hosted the discussion. She and her guests, Faison Covington and Ann Seagrave, were the founders of *CHAANGE*, a help center for anxiety and agoraphobia. They put together a series of tapes and literature designed to help people who suffered with anxiety disorder. I grabbed a napkin left over from our fast-food dinner, searched for a pen and managed to scribble down the phone number. On that Friday after Thanksgiving, I ordered their program, which for me was a Godsend.

The tapes helped me realize panic attacks were a physical reaction to an overload of stress. Dreading the surge of adrenalin fueled the disorder, and the more fear I built up, the more intense the attacks became. Anticipatory fear and worry created a physical and emotional spiral that fed on itself. I unconsciously empowered a physical reaction to drain my energy, and the only way to escape the grip of the disorder was to break the spiral.

Finally my ailment had a name, but my cognitive reasoning needed to convince my emotional brain that the rush of adrenaline was merely a reactive sensation I began to fear. If I learned to relax and allow myself to feel anxiety without fear, the sensations would become insignificant, dissipate, and ultimately disappear. Simple right? Not even close.

Panic attacks shot adrenalin through me with terrifying sensations, and fear generated more anxiety. The spiral sucked me into a whirlpool of dread and adrenalin day and night, stealing the regenerative sleep necessary to build the strength I needed. Each fed upon the other, fueling the intensity of the attacks and siphoning my energy. My exhausted mind struggled to survive.

In his first inaugural address, Franklin D. Roosevelt said: "Let me assert my firm belief that the only thing we have to fear is fear itself, nameless, unreasoning, unjustified terror which paralyzes needed efforts to convert retreat into advance." He was referring, of course, to the pessimistic economic conditions during the Great Depression, but his reasoning was the perfect description of panic disorder. This ailment literally caused me to fear "fear." It destroyed what was left of my self-confidence and paralyzed my life. The spiral thrived on my terrifying dread of the disabling attacks, loomed over my every move and the only way to recover was to stop the cycle.

Overcoming anxiety disorder was the most difficult challenge of my life. I survived by focusing on one day at a time, and sometimes one moment at a time. When I felt the onset of an anxiety attack, I repeated a chant to myself over and over:

"I'm calm and relaxed. I'm calm and relaxed. I'm calm and relaxed." Of course, I was anything but calm or relaxed at the time, but eventually I reprogramed my computer-like brain and my anxiety began to fade.

****

"The butterfly only emerges after struggling with the cocoon." Like a butterfly, isolated and alone, I scratched my way out of my anxiety chrysalis and transformed into a stronger woman. Mother was right, "What doesn't kill you makes you stronger." I forged new resolve after my bout with anxiety that convinced me I could do almost anything if I set my mind to it.

Discovering a dead friend was enough to send anyone into a tale spin, but on top of other stress, my emotions flew into overdrive. The excess trauma triggered a debilitating anxiety disorder and my comfort zone evaporated. That's what fear does, slithers into your life, coils into a death grip hold that crushes the breath from your soul, squeezing tighter and tighter until it cocoons your existence. I needed to break free, escape the clutches suffocating me.

As I closed my journal and placed it beside my computer, I thought about the traumas life can throw in our paths and how devastating they can be. Kelly and I lost touch after Todd's death, but I wondered if she recovered from his suicide. He didn't even leave her a note to say goodbye. I couldn't imagine what she must have gone through to get through her ordeal.

My mind drifted to Sandy and the uphill battle she faced with anxiety disorder. Maybe she would have an easier bout than I experienced. Sandy was strong, with such a positive outlook on life. Her incredible family would support her too. She would be okay, but I didn't envy the next few months of her life.

To conquer anxiety, I reprogramed the software of my mind. Like a computer, it spat out only what was programmed into it. I learned to change my thoughts, actions and viewpoints, and believed in myself again—maybe for the first time ever. After a lifetime of a poor self-image, that was a huge obstacle. My anxiety subsided when I learned to let go of past anxious feelings.

I couldn't help but think of the movie "Rocky" when the boxer, Rocky Balboa, bloody and exhausted and beaten to a pulp, finally won. He yelled out to his wife, "Yo, Adrian, I did it." I did it too. I won the battle of my life and would never look at a challenge the same way again. If I could beat anxiety disorder, I knew I could overcome almost anything, including whatever my mind blocked from my past. I finally possessed the strength to find the woman I was meant to be.

Chapter 7

The Grand essentials of happiness are: something to do, something to love, and something to hope for.
Allan K. Chalmers

Every muscle in my body tightened. I held my breath and watched as he glided above the water, leaving almost no wake. He had a slight lead over one other boy and they were ahead of all the other swimmers by at least half a pool length. As they touched the wall underwater, it was impossible to tell who won the race.

My eyes tried to focus on the electronic timer positioned on the back wall, but Josh was already out of the water, racing toward me as fast as he could with his bare, wet feet. Convinced he touched out his opponent, he glanced at the timer for confirmation. There was only six one hundredths of a second difference from first to second place, but Josh won. Tears rolled down my face as I made my way through the crowd toward my son. It took years to reach his goal, but Josh was goal driven and his tenacity finally paid off.

Our ride to the hotel was filled with recollections of past swim meets and competitions. When we arrived, I checked in and we made our way to the elevator. My mind drifted back to Josh's birth. From the moment he was born, his determination flourished. It wasn't an easy delivery. My labor was exhausting and having made the decision to forgo drugs, I wasn't prepared for the excruciating pain of childbirth. The first contractions began over twelve hours before Josh's head crowned and, at one point, I remembered yelling out, "I changed my mind.

Having a baby was a bad idea." It wasn't, though. When the nurse put my perfect little baby in my arms, all of the pain and anxiety evaporated. No feeling in the world could compare to the moment you look into the eyes of your newborn for the first time. When I saw my son's tiny face, I fell in love.

A bell brought me back to the present as we arrived on the eighteenth floor. The doors of the elevator flew open and I tugged at our luggage, wishing a bellhop had assisted us or at least offered a baggage cart. Josh found our room and opened the door. I grabbed my big, black purse to keep it from falling to the floor and reached deep inside, searching for my journal. Relieved, I pulled it out, dumped the luggage by the dresser and plopped down on one of the double beds, while my son turned on the TV. Lost in the past, I began to write, to make sure I got the events and emotions on paper before they all slipped away.

Journal entry, October 1998:
Zack and I were not only husband and wife, we were lovers and best friends. He gave me the stability I needed and our love grew into a deep and abiding relationship. I was a dutiful wife, determined to be perfect and completely devoted to him both emotionally and physically. We both loved being married and couldn't wait to have a big family to fulfill Zack's dream, a houseful of sons--his own baseball team...

Something to do, something to love and something to hope for — the 1980s showed me that the loss of any of those three ideals can wreak havoc in your life...

****

My panic attacks began to subside, but I still suffered some lingering anxiety. Instead of focusing on my angst, I concentrated on teaching school and getting pregnant. Zack and I practiced making a baby constantly.

Every month our hopes surged as we waited in eager anticipation for a pregnancy test, only to be ultimately disappointed again. At first, we enjoyed the practice, but over time, we found ourselves timing sex with ovulation, and the intimacy began to lose spontaneity and romance. When my temperature dictated the time was right, my husband would rush home to provide the second half of the equation.

Zack, still unsure of his career direction, worked for my dad at that time and we often laughed at the irony of the brief breaks he took from work. He finally just came forward and stated the obvious.

"Well, I need to go home and have sex with your daughter." He joked to my dad, his boss. "Is it okay if I leave for a while?"

Over time though, it wasn't quite so amusing. Our attempts at parenthood failed for a year before we reluctantly admitted we needed help from an infertility specialist. After multiple visits and months of invasive and sometimes embarrassing testing, our doctor discovered my endometriosis. In 1982 the best treatment was a new drug called Danazol, which was extremely expensive and carried no guarantees. After considering all the alternatives, I began a six-month regimen of the treatment. The month later, I was pregnant and my attention shifted. No longer worried about panic attacks, or anything else for that matter, I concentrated on my unborn child, and my anxiety attacks totally disappeared.

The long process of endless doctors and tests was frustrating, but on July 19, 1983, Joshua Thomas burst our world. At 7 pounds 11 ounces this tiny baby stole our hearts and I could hardly bear let him out of my sight when the nurses scooped him up and whisked him off to neonatal.

Josh appeared to be perfect at birth, but within a few hours, he became increasingly jaundiced, and his doctors frantically searched for a cause. After extensive tests, they determined he was suffering from ABO incompatibility. My O-blood seeped into his B-bloodstream, and his immature liver wasn't yet capable of cleansing the invasion from his system.

Josh was placed in an incubator under special lighting to help absorb the impurities from his tiny body. If the lights failed to produce the desired results, he would have to undergo a complete blood transfusion. Under normal circumstances that was frightening enough, but this was 1983. AIDS was the latest medical bogyman and was recently linked to tainted blood in hospitals. For two weeks we were terrified our newborn baby might need the very thing that could put his life in jeopardy, but from day one Joshua was a fighter, and my tiny baby soon conquered his illness and was allowed to go home.

Zack and I decided to have a second child right away to increase our chances of success, but in spite of our plan, we endured two more years of tests and fertility treatments that ultimately frustrated the natural joy of making love. To combat the waning intimacy between us, my husband suggested wild, erotic scenarios that made me feel extremely uncomfortable. They were meant to entice me, but unfortunately had the opposite affect. I never considered ménage-a-trios before, and my strict moral upbringing put the idea to rest. With a toddler, a full-time job, and infertility issues, my plate overflowed and risqué trysts were too exhausting and illicit to consider. For a time, sex lost its passion and became a chore overshadowing our past pleasurable experiences.

After two more years of frustrating tests, I underwent laser surgery, the newest technology for the treatment of endometriosis, and a few weeks later, I was pregnant with our second child.

Even though my pregnancy was considered high risk, the doctor assured us that sexual intimacy would not endanger our unborn child, but the mere mention of risk must have triggered some concern for Zack. His apprehension grew with the size of my stomach. He pushed me away at intimate moments claiming he didn't want to put the baby in jeopardy.

The rejection struck a deep chord inside of me and the feelings of being unlovable were all too familiar. The mirror provided a constant reminder of my bulging, unattractive body and, coupled with my husband's rejection, old doubts crept back into my thoughts. Infertility strained our sexual intimacy, but this pregnancy erased it.

Finally, on November 18, 1986, Jacob Richard burst into our lives. At 9 pounds 5 ounces, Jace was all-boy. The doctors knew my small frame couldn't handle a normal delivery so I underwent a C-section and Jace entered the world with blatant enthusiasm. Like his older brother, he battled ABO incompatibility, but this time the doctors anticipated the crisis and prepared to treat him in advance of his arrival. Despite the invasive delivery, they released us to go home a few days after his birth.

The unconditional love of a child fills your heart, and the boys truly blessed my life. It was an incredible feeling to suddenly have these tiny boys who were entirely dependent upon me. Every decision I made and everything I did would affect their lives forever. I vowed to make sure they would have every opportunity in life.

I loved them with all of my heart and I was *in love* with them too. Not the romantic kind of love I sought after my whole life, but a deep, honest love that transcends everything. My husband and I were back on track too, intimately and emotionally. Josh and Jace became the core of everything we did, and we were their world, at least until their teenager years. One child was easy. We took Josh everywhere, but two children required a lot more time, energy and money.

The daycare expenses alone put a strain on our income. The cost was almost equivalent to my entire teaching salary, so Zack decided I should quit my job and stay home with the boys. Our total income would decrease slightly, but in the long run, the children would have a full-time parent to nurture, guide and teach them during their formative years. The decision wasn't a difficult one, and staying with the children zeroed in on my goal of becoming a perfect mom.

I loved being their mother and was involved in every aspect of their lives. I woke up early and fell into bed exhausted every night but the rewards far outweighed the fatigue. Zack traveled constantly to support us leaving me to the role of a single parent. I was consumed with the usual daily responsibilities of two toddlers as well as demands and upkeep of our home, so hardly noticed the gradual transformation in my husband's behavior, as his career monopolized more and more of his time. Over time, he slipped away somehow, disinterested, apathetic, basically absent from our lives, but caring for the boys overshadowed my awareness of his distant behavior. I felt secure in the knowledge that Zack and I could weather any storm.

By 1988, Jace was one and Josh was four. Caring for the boys took more energy than my old full time job. Zack's work whisked him away, especially when the children demanded attention. His out-of-town trips now lasted four to five days each week. Besides missing his arms around me, I needed my husband's help to keep our home and family afloat.

The children needed their daddy too, they asked non-stop when he would be home. Zack insisted our financial demands were too critical to cut back on his traveling, and finally decided to move us back to Virginia and close to our families so they could help me if necessary. His request seemed logical and the boys would be a part of their extended family with grandparents, aunts, and uncles near by.

Still, our financial situation remained tight and, for the life of me, I could never understand why. Zack's income approached six figures and living quite frugally came easily to me, but my husband was the man of the family and, as such, insisted on handling all of our finances personally, keeping me totally in the dark. I wasn't privy to financial details, but I grew up working for everything I owned, in a home with few luxuries. I knew how to make a dollar stretch. So, to decrease the financial burden, I cut back on spending and did what I could to help.

The majority of the children's clothing and toys I bought at garage sales. I clipped coupons or bought groceries at a warehouse club where bulk items cost far less than those at traditional grocery stores. I managed all house and yard work myself, including tiling, planting and maintaining an elaborate garden to provide fresh vegetables in the warm months and canned goods for winter.

An entrepreneur at heart, I started a children's consignment shop in our basement to supplement our income, offering seventy percent profit to the suppliers while I kept thirty percent for myself. The idea exploded so big I had to move the shop to a nearby clubhouse to compensate growth. Still, Zack insisted money was tight, and he worked long hours, with consistent traveling. I implored him to spend more time at home, but his reasoning, commissions increased when he met face-to-face with clients, sounded plausible and was left to raise the boys alone most of the time.

I missed my husband when he traveled, especially at night when the children were asleep. I longed for the strength of arms around me, the intimacy we once enjoyed, but at least he came home most weekends, and the boys kept me busy during the week.

When Zack was home, he played with them and taught the fundamentals of football kicks and bat swings. He loved our boys, but had little patience for the day-to-day demands of two little ones. I knew traveling exhausted him by his frequent outbursts of anger.

As I look back, I don't think Zack ever recovered from the loss of his childhood dream. His heart beat for sports and nothing replaced the emptiness he endured from his unfulfilled dream. I tried to encourage him to look for work in the sports field, saying even if he took a pay cut we would survive, but he convinced himself he was too old for dreams.

Becoming a professional baseball star was Zack's childhood fantasy and when he was home, he shared that dream with his children, but they missed their daddy when he traveled, especially in the quiet times. Josh wanted to run into Zack's arms at night to show off his latest accomplishment, like a picture or play dough sculpture. Jace begged his daddy come home so he could cuddle with him and listen to bedtime stories or ride on his back and play horsey...

****

The boys missed sitting on their daddy's lap, while they told him about their imaginary jungle expedition or their flight on the wings of a magical dragon. They longed for his laugh, his touch, and his strength, but his presence was rarely there. I comforted them and tried to explain why Daddy couldn't be home, but the concept was hard for their little minds to understand what could be more important to him than we were. In truth, it was hard for me too.

Well, Casi, you are beginning to see a pattern here, I whispered to myself. As I studied my journal entries, a significant word screamed at me. Perfection. My whole life I felt an incredible need to be perfect at whatever I did. The perfect daughter, friend, pledge, girlfriend, wife and mother, but perfection was an impossible goal to achieve. Internally I longed to prove my worth, not just to others, but to myself. Everything I did projected outward from the damage in my heart. The pain of my *father's* abandonment was always there—taunting me. He walked out of my life by choice, disappeared. But I still clung firmly to him and the emptiness he left behind haunted me.

Then there was Zack. As I closed my journal, I knew exactly when I lost my husband. I glanced over at Josh on the other hotel bed. He was on the phone with his girlfriend, preoccupied with the events of the day's swim meet and the details of winning his big race. I stuffed my diary into my purse and motioned to my son, to let him know I was headed down to the hotel lobby. The truth was, I was going to the lounge. A stiff drink was the only thing I could think of to ease the tension of my sudden insight.

I strolled into the bar and sat at a high top table near the back. The room wasn't crowded and the people, mostly executives, were involved in their own worlds. That was good. I hated being hit on by lonely men in hotel bars. I thought of Zack again and wondered how often he was one of those men.

The bartender walked over to my table.
"What will it be, Ma'am?"
"A vodka martini—dirty, and make it Kettle One,"
"You've got it, Ma'am."

Ma'am, I repeated under my breath. God, I felt old, and where did the martini come from? Had I ever ordered a vodka martini in my life before, dirty or otherwise? No. I rarely drank at all. I remembered martinis from my waitress days and knew they were strong, but I wasn't sure why I just blurted out the request.

The bartender shuffled back with my drink and I wrapped my hand around the glass, swirling the olive before sliding it off the toothpick into my mouth. I almost gagged with the first sip, but before long the liquid easily slipped down my throat, radiating a calming, warmth through my body.

After a few swallows, I felt as if I chugged two glasses of wine. My mind flooded with conflicting memories. I managed to mess up my life on numerous occasions in the past, but this time was different. This was the big one — the slap you up the side of the head, stomp on your face, knock you off your feet--tsunami.

The one person in my life who vowed to never hurt me set in motion years of anguish, deception, and betrayal. The big one--that was on Zack.

Chapter 8

Love never dies a natural death. It dies of blindness, errors and betrayals, of illness, wounds, weariness, withering, and tarnish.
Anais Nin

The first martini anesthetized my body, but the second soothed my mind. The lounge was dim and comfortable, and the 1970s music shifted me to a different era, perfect for my frame of mind, and each song triggered a faded memory of my past. I sipped on the almost straight vodka and continued to write.

Journal entry, winter 1998:
Shortly after we moved back to Virginia, I received a letter in the mail bearing no return address. I opened the missive and read a poignant and direct note:
"You should know where your husband is when he says he's out of town."
Zack was away on business again, as usual, but called to say he was on his way home. I had no clue what I would say to him when he walked through the door. It wasn't the first time I was betrayed, but Zack? I never expected Zack to cheat. When I confronted him, he responded defensively, but assured me the letter was sent by a disgruntled employee who, after being dismissed, swore revenge. In my infinite wisdom, I dismissed the note and took my husband at his word, at least until a few weeks later...

Betrayal is the most devastating deception, and the moment duplicity occurs, the damage can never be erased...

****

My hands were immersed in meatloaf when the phone rang, I yelled upstairs to Zack.

"Can you grab the phone, Babe? I'm stuck in meatloaf."

He did so, but not before the answering machine picked up the call. In 1989, answering machines were not technically advanced, so unbeknownst to Zack, his conversation was not only being taped, but also broadcast in the kitchen. Over the course of the next few minutes, the woman on the other end of the phone shattered my life.

"I need to see you, Zack, I miss you so much." Her voice was drenched with passion.

"I can't believe you called me on my home phone." Zack whispered. I heard him walk across the bedroom and close the door. "What were you thinking? Casi is just downstairs. What if she answered the phone?"

"I would have hung up," the voice assured him.

"Not again. She's already wondering why we keep getting hang up calls. You can't phone me here again. I told you, that."

"I'm sorry, Zack, I just wanted to hear your voice."

"I know, I miss you, too, and I can't wait to have you in my arms again, but we'll be together soon. You just have to be patient."

I froze as a knot fisted in my chest. I could hardly breathe. The meatloaf bowl dropped from my hands, sending glass mixed with raw hamburger everywhere. I fell back against the wall and slowly slid down to the floor. The sound of the crash brought the call to an abrupt end.

"I've got to go, something just happened downstairs. I'll call you when I can." Moments later Zack stood at the top of the stairs, calling down to me.

"Casi, you okay? What happened?"

Somehow I managed to speak, "It's nothing, Zack."

I sat there trying to focus on what I heard, still dazed and confused. Moments later I walked to the recorder, pulled out the tape and held the recording tightly.

After taking a few deep breaths, I walked up the stairs and stood at our bedroom door, staring at my husband in disbelief as he watched TV as if nothing happened. Thankfully the boys were both down the street at a friend's house.

"Hey Snowy." His lighthearted use of one of the many pet names he created for me cause a shiver to rush down my spine. "What was that crash downstairs? Do you need any help?"

I didn't reply. I just stood and stared at him.

"What's wrong, Snow?"

I held out my hand revealing the cassette.

"What's that? You're acting a little strange, Casi. What's going on?"

For several moments I continued to stare in disbelief, then calmly spoke. "Leave."

"What are you talking about, Snowy?" He gazed at me with vacant eyes, totally unaware I heard the entire conversation he just had with his lover.

Again I repeated, "Leave." Then I stared directly into his eyes and added, "The phone call, Zack. The answering machine picked up on speaker. I heard your entire conversation. This"—I shook the recording in my hand, my grip so strong the plastic began to crack--"this is the tape of your conversation with your mistress, Zack."

Caught off guard, he slowly stood. "I can explain that, Casi. Please, don't overreact."

"Overreact." I repeated his description. "What? Are you kidding me? How could you, Zack? After everything I've been through—what we've been through?" I sat down on the side of the bed and pulled a pillow to my chest. "You promised you would never do what Bryan did to me, and I believed you. Why Zack? How could you?"

"Babe, give me a chance to explain. You've got to understand, it's not what you think. Come here." He pulled me close, tried to hug me, but I pushed him away.

"Don't. Don't touch me. Just leave me alone. I need to think—to make sense of this."

Zack tried to explain, but I interrupted him before he completed his first sentence. "No, I can't do this now. Please, just leave." I stood up, grabbed an overnight bag from the closet, threw the duffle on the bed and tossed clothes from his top drawer at the opening.

"I'll do that." He grabbed the suitcase and packed while he attempted to explain again. "In spite of what you *thought* you heard, Casi, you don't know the facts and you clearly misunderstood the conversation."

"I heard—what I heard, Zack. There's nothing to misunderstand. You're involved with another woman. You can't sugar coat that or manipulate the truth to make me believe you're not having an affair."

"I know you're upset."

"How insightful," I snapped back at him.

"Look, I'll spend the night in a motel room so you can calm down, but I don't believe for a moment that you want me to leave. You have to listen to me, Casi. I love you, and what you heard wasn't what it sounded like. I promise." Grabbing the packed suitcase, he marched down the stairs and walked out the door.

My anger overtook my devastation, and I reached for a laundry basket filled with his clean clothes and flung the contents out the door onto the driveway.

"I'll come back in the morning so we can discuss this calmly." He picked up the laundry clothes and tossed them in the passenger seat. "Just try to relax. If you need me—need to talk, Casi, please page me." He stepped into his car and yelled out the window as he drove away. "I love you, Snow-Jo. Only you."

As his Ford Taurus disappeared into the evening mist, my eyes welled up with tears; the emotion overwhelmed me until I could do nothing but collapse to the ground.

I couldn't understand what I did to men that chased them into the arms of other women. After all, the one constant in every relationship I ever had was me. I was the common denominator so I had to be doing something wrong. Something within *me* caused all my relationships to end in betrayal. The one belief I held throughout my marriage was I could trust Zack.

He loved me and would always be honest and faithful. There was that word again, *trust*. I apparently held some faulty wiring when it came to choosing people who were trustworthy. The concept totally baffled me. Considering my past with men, honesty remained the most important quality a man could possess, but I couldn't seem to escape the consistent reoccurring theme of betrayal.

When the boys came home, they sensed Mommy was upset and became overly affectionate. Thank God for their innocent concern. I tried to regain my composure for the sake of my children and focus on them instead of the traumatic situation, but for seven days, I wallowed in self-pity.

Zack was gone and I refused to let him come back that entire week. He left me multiple messages daily and begged me to talk to him. When I finally agreed to let him come home to explain, he was at the door within minutes and spent hours apologizing, distraught at the prospect of losing me.

"I swear on my life I'll end the relationship." He groveled and pleaded for me to forgive him. "You've got to believe me, Casi—she seduced me. Please, listen to me. It was one time, not an affair. She means nothing to me." He begged me to try to understand how the excitement of momentary physical gratification caused a lapse in his judgment and he swore there was no emotion involved.

"If I kept my thinking above my belt, the event would have never happened." He reached out to pull me closer. "You and the boys are my life. God Casi, please believe me. I'll never hurt you or our boys again." He continued to grovel in desperation, and I wanted— needed to believe him.

Zack picked up the phone and dialed *her* number. He begged me to listen on the other extension while he called his mistress so I would hear him break up with her first hand.

"Hi," he paused and took a deep breath, "it's me."

"Zack, I'm so glad you called. I—"

"Stop. Please don't say a word. Just listen to what I have to say."

My hand shook as I held the phone tightly to my ear absorbing every word.

"I can't do this anymore. What we did was wrong and it's got to end. Now, today."

His words resonated in my head as he declared his undying love for me and told her that their one-night stand was a huge mistake.

"I'm sorry. I know I've hurt you, but I hurt my family more. I love my wife and boys, and I can't do this to them." The woman on the other end seemed stunned at her abrupt dismissal, but she said very little.

"Okay Zack, I get it. It's over." She abruptly hung up the phone.

It was over. I heard the affair end, and I wanted to forget the betrayal ever happened. I needed to put the whole thing in the past for the sake of my children as well as myself. Zack made a mistake, but we could start over. I desperately wanted to regain the integrity of our marriage and the intimacy she stole from us. If we could get that back, we could rebuild our lives.

Sleepless nights brought visions of Zack and his lover groping each other as I tossed and turned, tormented by my imagination. My world imploded—again, and I didn't have a clue how to restore the destruction. How do you repair a shattered diamond? For weeks I walked on eggshells trying to ignore the obvious elephant that planted itself firmly into our marriage. We needed passion to pull us through.

Zack said he loved me and wanted to recapture what we lost, but nothing I did made a difference. I finally decided I had lived with the status quo for far too long. If things were going to change between Zack and me, I needed to take the first step.

So, after a few weeks of ideas floating though my mind, I came up with a plan to remind Zack of the intimacy we once had together--intimacy we could build upon to flame passion within our marriage. I took the boys to my parents for the evening and cooked a fabulous dinner, preparing all of Zack's favorite dishes. When he opened the front door after his long workday, I greeted him dressed in a sexy, low-cut black dress.

The great room, bathed in candlelight and filled with tempting aromas of a gourmet meal, lured him toward the table where he saw our best china and silver arranged on a crisp white tablecloth accented by white linen napkins and a fresh floral centerpiece. Soft, romantic music drifted on the air and Zack's eyes glimmered with the reflection of sparkles reflected off the chandelier. I'll never forget that moment. For the first time in years, we sat down and enjoyed an intimate, romantic dinner for two.

Afterwards, I took his hand and led him upstairs to the bedroom. I dimmed the lights and unzipped my dress, letting the frock fall to the floor to reveal my sexy, black bra, black lace bikini panties, and a lacy black garter that held up my nylon stockings. I wanted so much for Zack to take me in his arms, carry me to our bed and spend the rest of the night making passionate love to me.

He looked up toward my reflection in the mirror and snapped around as if to confirm what he saw. His hands dropped to his side. My heart pounded so hard in my chest I was sure he could hear the rapid thump-thump-thump. His gaze traveled slowly, starting at my feet then inching upward before locking on mine.

His jaw dropped and my heart melted. Finally we would share the intimacy I longed for--but his stare turned icy cold. To this day, I still hear the echo of his biting words in the shadows of my mind, taunting me, berating my confidence, words that pierced into the core of my being:

"Casi, you look like a French whore. What are you trying to do?" He turned on his heel, strode out of the bedroom, down the stairs, and into the family room. A moment later, the television swallowed the sensual soft music while I stood there, frozen, alone, stunned. I felt cheapened, dirty, like I needed a shower to wash off the filth. Was I trying to pimp myself out to him, offering to sell my body in return for his affection or love? At that moment, something broke inside of me. The heart he swore to protect shattered.

We slept in separate rooms that night and for pretty much the rest of our marriage, but since the birth of my children I slept lightly, always listening for the occasional cough or cry in the night. So when Zack crept into my room late at night when he thought I was sleeping, my mommy alert flew into gear. Over and over he'd sneak to my bedside, hover over me, warm breath softly caressing my face. I felt his hard body lean against me, but I kept my eyes closed and my breathing slow and steady. Kneeling beside me, he'd brush a piece of hair from my eyes or kiss my cheek, then whisper in my ear—whispers that always held the same sentiment.

"Casi, I do love you. You are the only one I will ever love. I hate what has happened to us, but I just don't know what to do or how to stop it."

Then he would get up and slowly walk out of the room, back to his single bed, leaving me to struggle with my emptiness alone while I tried to drift into sleep. The intimacy we shared eclipsed when we tried to have a baby, and the resulting exhaustion from caring for two small children drove the wedge in deeper. But Zack's affair suffocated our relationship, shattered our trust, and shredded the very fabric our marriage needed to survive.

I forgave my husband and wanted to forget the past so we could restore our intimacy, but Zack drifted in limbo, trapped in the devastation of his choices. Our marriage disintegrated, dying a little more each day.

****

At some point the lack of intimacy became moot. Our relationship deteriorated and ebbed from conjugal to primarily platonic. A poison in Zack's soul filled his heart with anguish and caused him to grow increasingly impatient and irritated. Like acid, the toxicity ate away at him and pushed him closer and closer to the edge. An avalanche lurked inside of him, growing slowly, inching toward a cliff under pressure from a silent enemy and my naivety fell helpless to thwart the imminent disaster.

I stuffed my journal and pen back into my purse, left my half-empty second martini on the table and walked back toward my room. Josh would be wondering what was taking me so long. Deep in thought, I pressed the button and entered the elevator.

As a young adult, I struggled. For as long as I could remember, I searched for balance. As hard as I tried, I couldn't find the *happily ever after* I imagined as a small child. Now, as I looked back over my life, I saw everything from a different angle. My distorted reflection seared an unacceptable self-image into my mind and convinced me I was unworthy of love. I blamed myself for the actions and decisions of other people.

I realize now my husband may have been fighting demons of his own, and the choices he made reflected his own inner turmoil. It wasn't right, or smart, and his decisions created pain for everyone involved, but I have discovered people do what they do, based on their own frame of reference.

Whether they make decisions for self-preservation or simply to boost the quality their lives, their choices are usually crafted to benefit themselves and not to intentionally hurt other people. It takes a wise person to figure out the difference between the best thing to do and the right thing to do, but internal pain skews the competence of wisdom. The pain my children and I experienced did not evolve from intentional malice; they were collateral damage from Zack's poor decisions.

That's where real love should have come into play. Pure love is selfless. When you truly love, the needs and happiness of the person you love becomes paramount to your own. Marriage, in theory, unites two people who love each other in a partnership. They take solemn vows to protect and cherish their bond.

Zack and I didn't have that kind of love--not anymore. Our intimate love got lost somewhere along the way. And as much as I longed for my fairly tale, I couldn't cocoon myself to hide from pain or avoid being hurt. The balance I searched for throughout my life always existed, hidden behind my fears, faded in the shadows of my mind — until now.

I unlocked and opened the door to our hotel room. Josh, stretched out on the bed with his headphones on, listened to music while he flipped through a magazine. He glanced up as I entered the room and waved his hand in acknowledgement, then turned his attention back to his own world, oblivious that I just spent years of my life downstairs in that little hotel lounge, or that I uncovered precisely when and why his dad walked away from our lives and into the arms of his lover.

Chapter 9

The grave soul keeps it's own secrets, and takes it's own punishment in silence.
Dorothy Dix

The first crash set everything in motion. Another crash this time longer in duration, followed by the sound of broken glass and a screaming voice. I jumped up from my chair and raced toward the source of the explosion. Jace yelled obscenities and flung his fists wildly. A trail of dents in the walls added to the damage as he hit everything in his path.

"My God Jace, what's going on?"

My son curled his lip at me and continued his tantrum.

"What happened?" He punched the wall, then flung his hand back and forth quickly, obviously in pain.

"The damn printer isn't worth shit. That's what happened."

I looked in the direction of his pointed finger. What was left of the printer lay at the base of the stairs, having clipped several pictures on its way down and scarring the wall as well. The broken glass, frames and printer pieces scattered everywhere.

"Well, it certainly isn't worth much now." I spoke as calmly as I could manage to utter my words. "I suppose you have the money to go out and buy a new one?"

"Nope, and I guess I'll just have to get an 'F' on my paper too, Mom." He sneered and slammed the door behind him as he left the house.

I bent down to clean up yet another of Jace's messes. His outbursts were getting worse and I was at a loss. I couldn't seem to do anything to help him control his rage, but the explosions clearly spawned from his father's anger, a learned behavior I watched develop and felt helpless to stop. Zack displayed the same kind of temper so many times, and both of the boys mirrored anger issues.

Josh learned to control himself and funneled his anguish into more positive outlets, but Jace's rage consumed him. His low tolerance level for disappointment spiraled into an explosion at the least little problem. His early years displayed such a compassionate little boy, smart and talented, but now his temper, totally out of control, gripped his life in a death hold. For the next half hour I collected glass, broken printer pieces and scarred pictures, then I reached for my diary.

Journal entry, January 1999:
The children were still young when Zack and I began sleeping in separate rooms. We told them the change was because Daddy's snoring made sleeping difficult and he needed his own bed. The truth was, a slivered shard cut through us and, as hard as I tried, I couldn't understand how to melt the iceberg growing between us.

As time passed, Zack traveled more often, if that was possible. We went with him occasionally, which provided our family with mini vacations away from daily routines and Zack's temper. During those few days, my husband's jovial demeanor returned and I caught a glimpse of the man I once married, but vacations always ended and Zack's anger returned. His patience decreased and his weight proportionally increased...

> Secrets decay the soul, ruin lives and are almost always revealed ...

****

I begged Zack to talk to me so we could work things out and try to save our marriage. He finally agreed to go to counseling, but the therapist only fueled his anger. After a one-on-one session, my husband returned home enraged and refused to go back. His fury seethed in a violent outburst.

"Screw him." He screamed at me. "That damn shrink can't help. It's a waste of time—and money. He sits back in his ritzy office and interrogates me, but never has any answers. All these guys want is your money. They don't have a freakin' clue how to help anyone."

Zack's anger erupted more often now, and more intense. The smallest disturbance set him into a rage. I never knew when a simple gesture or passing comment would trigger his wrath. If Jace walked in front of the television, Zack fumed. He threw things and shouted. At one point he even kicked the dog across the room when the poor baby barked. His face contorted and his eyes—his eyes scared me. The boys and I cowered, often hiding in my bedroom to avoid the fury of Zack's explosive temper. I tried to protect them from their father's temper, but how do you thwart a tsunami?

Still, Zack loved his children and lived vicariously through their lives, especially their sports prowess. In spite of extensive travel, Zack found time to coach Josh's little league team and go to his baseball games. The children and their activities dictated the flow of our lives, but Jace always took a back seat to Josh.

I don't think Zack loved Jace less. Josh was merely older and as such, possessed more advanced skills with which his father could identify. Jace, talented in several sports, excelled, but no matter how hard he tried to impress his father, Zack focused on Josh. I could see the disappointment in my younger son's eyes when Josh innocently upstaged him.

Over time, even Josh questioned the inequality displayed by his father. Josh tried to compensate by supporting Jace, helping him whenever he could. I took Jace to all of his competitions attempting to build his confidence, but Jace needed his dad's approval and attention, not mine.

Despite my efforts to alert Zack to his son's feelings, the problem escalated, and Jace's low self-esteem manifested into frequent angry outbursts emulating his father. Not a surprise.

The negative behavior at least got Zack's attention, and the anger bubbling between them fueled more rage. Before long, Jace gave up on his father--and himself, putting little effort into anything he did. I watched him fall into the patterns I lived through. I couldn't bear the thought of the consequences he would surely face in his future but, the blueprint cast, he spiraled down a treacherous path.

I spoke with our pediatrician on numerous occasions, and we implemented various courses of action to reduce Jace's outbursts. When he was diagnosed with ADHD, attention deficit hyperactive disorder, we put him on medication, but the pills caused him to lose weight from his already thin frame, and he became lethargic and sad. It crushed me to hear him talk about how he felt on his meds.

"Mommy, I don't like my medicine." He whimpered and tugged on me. "When I take the pills I can't hear music in my head anymore."

I wasn't sure what my little boy meant by that comment but, nonetheless, hearing his pleas tore me apart and I finally chose to forego medication. Instead, I searched for alternative methods, diets and counseling, to ease my son's condition.

As for Zack, his irrational temper made no sense. I knew something troubled him, especially when the love he held for his boys didn't temper his rage. My heart broke when my innocent children asked me why I didn't divorce daddy. And the pictures they drew vividly displayed the torment in their hearts, drawings of daddy yelling, with crazed eyes and fire spewing from his ears.

Occasionally Zack's anger sparked physical abuse. His 6'4" athletic stature loomed over my 5'7" 110-pound body, so he easily overpowered me. Once, when his anger exploded, he picked me up like a rag doll, slammed me against the wall, and pinned my shoulders. My spine hit the attic light switch with a force so hard the entire plastic cover plate recessed into the drywall. I collapsed in pain. Days later my doctor confirmed that as a result of the injury, I sustained nerve damage between my shoulder blades.

But the emotional damage, a far more destructive and demoralizing pain than the physical, hurt worse. On many occasions Zack flew into a rage and stormed from the house threatening me.

"You better watch out, Casi." His voice drenched in fury, he yelled, throwing or kicking things out of his way. "One of these days I'm going to walk away and never come back, and I promise, you will not survive."

I thought about escaping. After all, our marriage held no intimacy and little respect, but his words rippled through my mind daily. With constant threats of my worst fear: abandonment, I guess I started to believe him—I couldn't survive without him. When someone says something like that to you enough times you just begin to accept the notion as fact. His words validated my broken confidence, mimicked the bully I saw in the mirror who taunted me my whole life. My self-perception told me I was insignificant, unable to function like everyone else. The more outside influences validated the notion, the more they set in stone. I easily fell into my old prototype, accepting I was inadequate and incapable of providing my children with a good life on my own.

Marital bliss seemed like a myth, at least for me. When I chose Zack, I dealt my own cards and divorce was not an option—not this time. I didn't want to be a two-time loser. I totally blew my chance at "forever love" when I pushed Brad from my life. In all my relationships, I was the common link. This marriage needed to last a lifetime.

Eventually, my happiness took a back seat to my children's. They deserved to know their father, a birthright that was stolen from me. They wouldn't grow up with that emptiness or doubt in their lives. I rationalized everything negative and focused on the positives while the cycle held me captive in a volatile marriage.

Like Scarlet O'Hara, I'd worry about it tomorrow. Motherhood kept me too busy to yearn for the comfort of familiar arms waiting at the end of a long day, or the passion that could make almost any crisis seem insignificant. It was only as I lay alone, late at night in my darkened room, that I brushed tears from my eyes and felt the sorrow at the loss of my dreams.

****

Night after night I drifted into sleep, tears escaping my swollen eyes to trickle down my cheeks, dampening my pillow. There had to be more to life. I loved my children and thanked God every day for them, but my marriage was violent and empty. There is a huge difference between loneliness and being alone. I wanted so much to feel the soft touch of a hand on my cheek—and my body. But unless we were on a family excursion, the only emotion Zack displayed was anger and though I loved my boys, I felt isolated and alone.

I tried for years to recapture the intimacy and love in my marriage but, the scapegoat for, and of, Zack's rage, I found it increasingly difficult to be affectionate. Nothing I did helped our situation and I had no idea why all of my efforts seemed useless. My only carnal exploits now evolved from romance novels, and I longed for physical, sensual contact. I couldn't continue to merely exist on autopilot. I needed more in my life.

Placing my journal on the seat next to me, I thought about my last entry. Too many people stay in loveless, broken, and abusive relationships. I just never thought I'd be one of them. Maybe it's human nature to resist change. For me, as bad as my circumstances morphed, admitting failure again was a harder pill to swallow ...and then there was the whole fear thing. I hated what happened between Zack and me, but the fight to hold on to our broken marriage drained my energy.

Our connection slipped away and I stood by and watched my life crumble. I felt numb and empty inside. For years, I rationalized my acceptance that happiness was unattainable for me, my plight in life.

Then one day I heard an interview with a man celebrating his 110th birthday. When he was asked to what he attributed his longevity, his reply was simple. "Every day when I wake up, I have a choice to be happy or sad. I choose to be happy." His beautifully clear explanation stunned me. Could life really be that simple?

The old man's philosophy stuck in my mind and I began to see how drama stole my happiness. There were valid reasons I wallowed, but the choices I made kept me stagnant in an unhappy situation. I knew life, by definition, was continual change. I mean, time moves forward, the spinning world doesn't stop and wait for anyone, so for better or worse, change happens. If I chose to let my marriage continue with the status quo, what would I accomplish? I wouldn't find happiness, love or any form of passion on my path any more than I could find my way to Florida by following a map to New York. Like the old man I needed to *choose* happiness, and that choice required some difficult decisions.

I was lost about how to reach Jace, but I knew rage would sabotage his happiness. I needed to find a way to save my son from the painful road ahead. More than anything I wanted my children to have a happy life.

I blamed myself for rationalizing Zack's anger. I should have done more to protect my boys, and from now on, I would. I wasted too much time wallowing in an impasse, praying we'd rekindle our marriage, but Zack was hiding something and I couldn't reach him. Some people use drugs or alcohol to anesthetize their pain. I didn't know then, but I was about to find out Zack's secret anguish and how he fell victim to a different kind of addiction.

Part III: Secrets and Lies

Chapter 10

We can throw stones, complain about them, stumble on them, climb over them, or build with them.
William Arthur Ward

I watched in horror as the toddler's head disappeared under the surface of the water. His arms flailed in a helpless, desperate struggle. I screamed to get his parents attention, but my words faded into the music and laughter of the crowd oblivious to the tragedy unfolding just a few feet away. There was no time to think. My reflex instincts fueled by adrenalin, took over.

Fully clothed, shoes and all, I dove into the water and swam to the frantic toddler as he thrashed about aimlessly. He struggled and kicked then desperately grabbed on to me with fear in his eyes. Safe above the surface, he coughed, spitting water until he finally managed to screech out a fearful cry for his mother. She spun around, recognizing her panic stricken little boy's voice. The color drained from her face as she saw him clinging to a complete stranger.

"Oh my God."

Her scream silenced the crowd. All eyes focused on the child and me as his mother fought her way through the water. She clutched him to her breast, ripping the child from my arms in an emotional, thankful embrace. Sopping wet, I slogged through the water and hoisted myself onto the side of the pool. My soaked t-shirt and shorts clung to my body leaving nothing underneath to imagination.

Josh's towel, tossed to the ground near the diving board, caught my eye. I snatched the terrycloth and wrapped it around me. Jace, still in the water at the far end of the pool, reached his hand out to Josh who pulled him out of the water and the two rushed toward me. I briefly described the incident as we gathered our belongings to head home. As we passed by the cluster still hovered over the small child, his mother's eyes met mine and she silently mouthed to me.

"Thank you so much."

Then she turned her attentions back to her still whimpering child.

"How did that happen, mom?" Jace asked.

I recounted the event from beginning to end while we walked home. Once inside, I ached to pull off my drenched clothing and take a shower. I trudged up the stairs to my bathroom, turned on the water, and pulled off my soggy clothing.

The spray of water pelted my face and my thoughts drifted back to the events of the day. Dear God, what if I hadn't seen him, or reacted quickly enough? The pain of losing a child was unimaginable.

A few days later, I received a thank-you note from the little boy's mother. I didn't know her, but she took the time to find out who saved her child's life. For one brief moment, we forged a connection. Her simple note touched me on more levels than she could possibly imagine.

Dear Casi,
I wanted to thank you again from the bottom of my heart for saving my son, Tommy today at the pool. I can't imagine what could have happened. I am so grateful you were there.

Angela Chastain

Eyes closed, I thanked God the boy survived. The impact of the incident changed Angela's future, but she would never know how much she and her son touched my life as well. I sucked in a deep breath and savored an amazing, unfamiliar feeling. For the first time in my life I felt significant and I relished in the moment.

Glancing back at Angela's note, my thoughts drifted back to my own mother, how she struggled to protect Brie and me and the legacy she left behind. I settled into my favorite chair, succumbing to the familiar comfort of my tattered journal while Mother's memory filled blank pages.

Journal entry, summer 2000:
By the summer of 1995 Mother began to show signs of senility, often forgetting simple events and discussions. Unfamiliar with aging, I assumed the incidents were a normal process of aging, but by October her behavior screamed something was very wrong...

The love between a mother and child transcends everything...

****

In the fall of 1991, Zack made a spontaneous decision to move back to Atlanta. Disillusioned with his job in Virginia, he felt the lure of the South, so the boys and I soon found ourselves back in familiar surroundings. My parents decided to join us a few years later, partly because of me, but mostly because my mother thought of Atlanta as her home. She was truly happy to be back where fond memories beckoned her.

Mom was never one to complain about how she felt and she hated to go to a physician for any reason, so when my dad called me and said he thought she was ill, his notion was reason for alarm. Dad pleaded with her to see a doctor, but she refused, insisting she was fine and, given a little time, was sure her health would improve. Neither Dad nor I agreed with her.

After weeks of concerned prodding, we managed to trick her into going to the hospital, hidden behind the guise of a family luncheon at her favorite restaurant. After lunch, we drove directly to the emergency room. Mom, furious at both of us, fought going inside, but we finally convinced her to at least check with a nurse.

Our plan worked but, despite our good intentions, mother's stage-four cancer had already metastasized. The doctor who evaluated Mom held little hope. She was dying, had little time, and no treatment options. She must have known she was ill for quite a while, as her liver cancer had spread throughout her body and into her brain. After Mother's diagnosis, I spent every day running to and from the hospital, while still struggling to maintain a normal life for the boys and support my Dad as he tried to accept his shattering world.

The doctor gave Mom a week to live at best. Zack, out of town as usual, withdrew from the drama. Overwhelmed by grief, I suppressed my emotions in front of the boys. The news alone would rip through their hearts without added pain of seeing their mother fall apart. I prayed for strength.

I'll never forget the day Mom slipped into a coma. As I left for the hospital that morning, I noticed a burned out bulb on the rear of my car. Replacing a taillight seemed trivial to spending time with Mom so I dismissed the notion, promising myself I'd attend to the issue as soon as practical.

Driving home that afternoon, half-dazed with emotion, I realized I was in the left lane but needed to make the approaching right turn. Remembering my broken light, I rolled down my window and made a hand signal as I edged my way into a right lane merge. Sufficiently spaced, I didn't cut off anyone, but I admittedly changed lanes a bit abruptly. The long, persistent horn that followed expressed the driver's temper in the car behind me. She obviously felt I squeezed in front of her and reacted with rage.

She honked and flipped me a recognizable hand gesture, screaming what I was sure were the choicest obscenities in her vocabulary. I mouthed "I'm sorry" then slowed down, signaling another right turn to go home, stunned the crazed woman followed close behind me, meeting my every turn. Ignoring her no longer an option, an uneasy shiver clenched my stomach shooting chills down my back and the hairs on my neck stood at attention. I didn't want her to know where I lived.

No telling what drove the woman's road rage, she could be dangerous. Taking the long way around the neighborhood with an eye on my rear view mirror, I finally pulled into my driveway. The distraught woman pulled over, blocking me in, and tore out of her car toward me. She ran forward spewing foul language and angry indignation. Aware I should have given her more warning before my turn, I attempted to apologize.

"I'm so sorry I pulled in front of you like that. I noticed my turn signal light was burned out this morning, but I spent all day at the hospital with my dying mother and my mind clearly wasn't on driving."

I literally groveled, fearful of her wrath, but her anger intense, she scarcely heard a word I said. I could see veins in her neck bulge as she shrieked her righteous fury.

"Right, like I'm really going to believe that one." Her eyes gleamed with a fiery gaze. "You should be ashamed of yourself trying to play on my compassion. It won't work. It's people like you who cause accidents and the innocent ones like me always end up the victims..."

My jaw dropped and a rush of unbridled fear washed over me, tightening my chest. Not only was she totally out of control, her fury strengthened by the second and she knew where I lived. What could I do to calm her? I turned away and walked up the hill to my front door, banged the knocker and rang the bell, as if the house were a friend's instead of my own.

Apparently concerned about who might appear, the woman scooted back in her car and peeled away. As she sped off, I glanced at her license plate and memorized the tag so I could call the police and report the irate woman's behavior. I needed to protect myself in case she truly was mentally disturbed.

Unlocking the door, I staggered inside, exhausted by the long day and raw emotion. I grabbed a scrap of paper, jotted down the license number then tossed the note and my keys onto the kitchen table. Outside I could see a storm looming in the distance. The deepening blue-gray clouds darkened the mid-November afternoon sky to an eerie midnight glow. Trees swayed with the wind as the breeze whipped through the yard tossing leaves to-and-fro randomly through the humid air. The scene was a fitting ambiance for the torment in my soul.

I stumbled to the sofa, clutched a pillow to my chest and collapsed into a curled fetal position. My mother was dying and I felt totally helpless and vulnerable. I didn't want to imagine a world without her. The wind whistled through the door casing like the forlorn purr of a distant train while deep feelings of total abandonment welled up inside of me.

I lay there sobbing for what seemed like hours, consumed by grief. Rain pelted the windows and a burst of thunder cracked a threatening warning, but the violent storm within felt far more treacherous. Wind whistled and lightening streaked through the darkness with moments of ghostly daylight. Shadows surrounded me and a surreal ambiance enveloped the room as my mind conjured visions of my mother. I couldn't shake the hollow emptiness drowning me. Dehydrated, I finally rolled off of the sofa and ambled toward the kitchen for a glass of water. The movement brought me back to reality and, realizing I now stood in total darkness, I switched on a light.

The scrap of paper on the table conjured visions of the distraught woman who followed me home. I wondered what could have happened in her day to warrant such hostility toward a complete stranger. My mother would never judge other people regardless of the situation. I could almost hear her words whisper to me.

"You have to walk a mile in someone else's shoes before you understand their actions."

Forgetting about my water, I reached for the paper with the woman's license plate number. I stared at the note for a long moment, then crumpled and tossed the scribbling into the garbage.

****

On December 2, 1995, my mother passed away, but I realized that day, curled up on my sofa, she would never be gone. So many memories lived on in my heart and her words of wisdom would forever guide my life and future.

Mom taught me a lot about compassion. She never judged other people. She knew first hand how inner pain could fog a person's objectivity and affect their behavior. She said that was why people took ordinary events and twisted them out of proportion.

When I was a child, Mom read to me constantly and quoted messages like, "Do unto others as you would have them do unto you." Through my young ears, I simply heard "be nice" but over the years I understood there was so much more to that simple phrase. Mom looked for the best in everyone and reminded me to choose my actions wisely because I touch other lives every day by what I say and do, and simple acts of kindness might just make a difference in their lives. Her words of wisdom live on within me.

The Starfish Story
Original story by Loren Eiseley

There was a young man walking down a deserted beach just before dawn. In the distance he saw a frail old man, picking up stranded starfish and throwing them back into the sea. The young man gazed in wonder as the old man again-and-again threw the small starfish from the sand to the water. He asked,
"Old man, why do you spend so much energy doing what seems to be a waste of time?"
The old man explained that the stranded starfish would die if left in the morning sun.
"But there must be thousands of beaches and millions of starfish," exclaimed the young man. "How can you make any difference?"
The old man looked down at the small starfish in his hand and as he threw it to the safety of the sea, he said, "I can make a difference to this one."

Remembering my mother's death triggered a stark wake-up call. I lived my entire life drying up on the beach of my own self-image, plagued by the unlovable and insignificant woman I saw in the mirror. Focused on pleasing everyone else, I never realized I was begging for someone to place me back in the ocean where I ached to be accepted.

As I put my journal down, I noticed my glass butterfly on the coffee table. Mother gave me the figurine years earlier when she explained the *Butterfly Effect*--an unforgettable story explaining how everyone's life ultimately has purpose. When a butterfly flaps its wings, air molecules move, which in turn move other air molecules and the perpetual motion continues on and on, like a wave reaching throughout the world for so long and so far that the fluttering eventually influences weather patterns on the other side of the earth.

The lesson seared in my mind. A seemingly insignificant event can cause dramatic consequences. Everything we do matters. Butterflies display such a strong presence in my life. Like a fragile butterfly I struggled within my cocoon, praying one day I would break free, take flight with new wings, and make my own mark on the world. I have heard people say one person can't really make a difference. I've even said the phrase myself on occasion, but saving a child made me realize each person makes a difference with every choice they make.

Someone once said:
"To the world, you might be just one person, but to one person, you just might be the world."

I saved the life of one small child on that mid-summer day, but I also realized my own significance and I knew I was destined to make a difference.

Chapter 11

Be careful what you wish for, it just might come true.
Anonymous

    The landing gear screeched, wheels lowered, and I felt the pull of the Boeing 747s engines as the captain prepared to land. I'd never visited Dallas before, or Texas for that matter. The final approach swirled around a cityscape like many others, which took me by surprise. On some level I expected to see plains with roving buffalo on the horizon and an airport filled with cowboy hats, boots and horse paraphernalia.

    On paper, Dallas based Millennium touted the perfect solution to Jace's problems and I prayed they would fulfill their promises. My youngest son was becoming more-and-more defiant and his anger erupted at the slightest annoyance. If only Jace could look beyond his current situation.

    Millennium offered hope. They said the program created a fundamental shift in the way my son would see the world, himself and the people around him. Of course there were no guarantees, but doing something was better than sitting back watching my child flush his life. I prayed they could at least provide Jace with tools to cope, or a safety net to catch him if he self-destructed.

    The baggage claim area stopped me cold. Apparently multiple flights of luggage hit the conveyer simultaneously and my plan of slipping in and out quickly faded. I stepped into a coffee shop and pulled out a notepad I bought in the Atlanta Airport. My journal pages filled now, I'd discovered the ease and convenience of our home computer as a far easier method for writing journal entries. Of course I couldn't lug the device with me so, for the time being, a notepad would suffice.

As headed for a small corner table, a newsstand rack with glaring headlines caught my eye. Visions of my mother, Jace, then the vacant face of my mysterious, black knight flashed through my mind. The vile word in bold print forced a knot to squeeze in my chest followed by a cold ripple of anxiety. It had been almost three years since Aunt Ginny unveiled the odious incident and the mere word still sent a chill to my core. I sat, picked up my pen, and scribbled the word, tracing the letters over and over, while the image of dark shadows spun through my mind.

Journal entry, July 2001:

My mother's sister, Virginia, was her best friend and my favorite aunt. She made plans to fly to Atlanta to be by Mom's side to comfort her, but Mom passed before Ginny arrived. Distraught she wasn't able to say goodbye, my aunt felt some consolation to know that in Mother's last moments a delirious stupor convinced her I was Ginny. As far as mom knew, Ginny was holding her hand as the life slipped from her body...

Sometimes knowing the truth hurts, but living with lies can do much more damage...

****

Ginny and I shared many long talks in the weeks and months following Mom's death and my aunt finally decided to come to Atlanta to spend some time with Dad and me. During her stay I pestered her relentlessly about my biological *father*. I needed to know the roots of my existence, who my *father* was and why he totally abandoned his two young daughters. I wanted to know the complete and total truth about what happened — and why.

Ginny hesitated to talk about Matthew or his relationship with Mom. Clearly my mother entrusted her sister with stories she wanted kept secret, but Mom was gone now, and I was very much alive. My aunt told me how my mother and *father* first met and how their relationship evolved. Immediately drawn to each other, they quickly fell in love. They wanted to marry, but his family wasn't in the same social class as Mother's, so gaining her parent's approval evolved into a big hurdle.

My mother, the baby of the family and as such overprotected, defied her strict, parents. The idea of being completely independent enticed her. Starry-eyed, she married Matthew and lived happily for the first few years, despite repeated efforts by her parents to separate them.

Ginny was curiously vague from that point on. Without going into detail, my aunt revealed that for some time before their divorce, my parents quarreled. Ginny described an incident where she jumped on my *father's* back to defend her little sister during a heated argument. She said Matthew abused my mother, verbally and physically, pushing her until she felt unsafe and, in order to protect herself as well as Brie and me, she decided to leave him.

Regardless of the underlying reason for their hostility, something didn't sound right to me. I wanted details and incessantly badgered my aunt for answers. Exhausted with evading me at every turn, Ginny sucked in a deep breath and glared at me with a chilling gaze before speaking.

"Are you one hundred percent sure you need to know the truth about your *father*?"

"Yes, of course I am. Don't you think I've waited long enough?"

"Perhaps, but be careful what you wish for, Casi." The cliché made my skin crawl like tiny ants parading down my arms. "I don't remember anything about the man who gave me life. What do I do with that?"

I fell back on the sofa like a defeated child. "I need to know who he is"—I hesitated, then gazed up to her with pleading eyes--"so I can figure out who I am. You know something. I know you do so please don't leave me in the dark."

"Who or what Matthew is has nothing to do with who *you* are, Casi." Her adamant comeback oozed with strong conviction. "Your mother is gone now, so I'll tell you—if you're absolutely sure you must know. I suppose hearing the truth from me is better than hearing sordid details from a stranger ...and knowing you, dear, I suspect you won't stop searching until you have all your answers." She drew in another long breath before continuing. "You know Laura, I mean your mother, loved you more than life itself."

"Of course, Mom loved me. I've never doubted that—why would I?"

"When Brie came along, your parents were thrilled at the birth of their new child, but over the next few years." She wavered. "Let's just say their relationship completely unraveled."

"What do you mean, Aunt Ginny?" I leaned in toward her and stared directly into her eyes. "What's with the drama? Just tell me. I'm not going to be shocked. I'm a big girl now and I don't need you to protect me or sugar coat the truth."

It was evident Ginny wasn't eager to share gory details of my parents' relationship, but at least I was learning something.

"Go on. Please, don't stop now."

"The discussions between them became more-and-more intense."

I raised an eyebrow. "You mean fights, right? So they fought. Believe me, I'm used to arguments. Been there."

"Yes, they fought, a lot, until the situation finally exploded." She paused again in an uncomfortably long moment of silence. "What do you mean the 'situation'? For God's sake, please tell me."

I pleaded, but her face told me I might be sorry to hear what she knew.

"Matthew got so angry one night he held Laura down and, uh—forced himself on her."

"Forced himself?" I paused in thought for a second before blurting out the connection my mind revealed. "Oh God. You mean he *raped* her?"

"Yes." My Aunt's face went pale. "You were born nine months later, almost to the day."

I felt the blood drain from my face and a tight clench encircle my throat. I expected to uncover some deep, dark secret, but nothing like that. Never in my wildest dreams, did I imagine I would discover such a violent core of my conception. The image smacked me right in the gut so hard I could barely breathe. The thought of my creation as the result of violence instead of love...the ultimate act of control—dear God, I was conceived in rape.

A shivering thought sent a chill down to my toes: if abortion was legal back then would I have been born? Suddenly, I possessed a completely new perspective of the whole abortion controversy.

Something horrible happened between my mother and *father* that poisoned the love they shared, infected them like a virus. What could have caused their relationship to deteriorate so profoundly that, in the heat of an argument, my *father* violently bedded my mother despite her desperate struggles to avert him? My conception occurred as the result of that violation. On some level I felt dirty.

Eventually the volatility between my parents propelled my mother underground. That's why she never talked about Matthew, why she packed up her life and fled, disappearing into the night. She feared for the safety of her children and herself. My parents' marriage, damaged beyond repair, ended in divorce, and in the 1950's divorce held a disgraceful stigma. My mother tried to protect Brie and me, but in the wake of that violence, two broken children were set adrift, condemned to float endlessly lost in a sea of toxic debris.

****

I began to understand the shadow that loomed over me for years. Even with Dad's monumental attempt to overcome my biological father's violence, and the vow of silence Dad and Mom forged, the contamination leached its way into my soul. I finally identified my birth father as the root of my internal struggles with trust and betrayal.

As an adult I recognized how my inner child warped and distorted those messages, and why emptiness in my heart fed deep-seated feelings of inadequacy. If I wanted to heal, I needed to rebuild my self-esteem.

I closed my notepad and grabbed my bag. The bold printed letters, R-A-P-E, on the newspaper headline faded into the distance as I walked away from the coffee shop toward the baggage claim. The crowd disbursed, leaving only my solitary suitcase endlessly circling around the carousel.

My focus now was Jace. I loved my son and would do anything to help him get through his emotional problems. He felt rejected by his father and he didn't think I could possibly understand his feelings. For the first time in my life I realized my mother and I weren't so different after all. Our maternal instincts compelled us to protect our children. I hoped Millennium taught me enough to weave a safety net for Jace.

The workshop, three days of intensive self-focus, cast a mirror into the corners of my mind I had tried to entomb. I flew halfway across the nation presumably to help Jace, but instead the program spiraled me into a jagged, dark pit locked inside my intimate soul.

Mid-afternoon on the second day the guide asked participants to lie down on mats and close our eyes. She turned out the lights, requesting everyone to imagine themselves as infants resting in their father's arms, while she attempted to paint a pleasant picture of a moment in our past where we felt safe and happy.

"What does he look like? Is he smiling? What do you smell? Is his face rough or smooth?"

The narrator went on with her imagery but instead of relaxation, my mind reeled with flashes of daddy intermingled with the faceless knight from my childhood dreams, each spinning together with the other in a crescendo of anxiety. I couldn't see faces. I didn't want to. I felt torn, afraid to envision details of the nefarious shadowy figure. I shot up and flew from the room, tears streaming, in an inconsolable dither. A counselor immediately pursued me; tried to calm me, but my emotions shattered into a wretched tirade.

"I came here to find help for my son." My rant flowed from deep within, so unlike me. Since my panic attacks, controlling my feelings played a huge role in my life. Why was I screaming at this man? "I have no interest in playing make-believe. I don't even know my real *father*. I couldn't imagine him even if I wanted too. He has no face—no emotion. He threw me away and never looked back."

I couldn't believe those words hid in my mind, let alone escaped from my lips. I broke down, trembling, plagued by a past I thought was put to rest. I never realized I cared about my *father*. He chose not to connect and I claimed not knowing me was his loss. I tried to convince myself of that premise for most of my life, but the truth surfaced from the depths of my soul, a truth always lurking, always tormenting me.

The workshop awakened a hidden fragment of my heart. I returned home with a whole new understanding of my inner turmoil and myself. The journey intended to acquire tools for my son, initiated a giant leap toward healing my own spirit.

Chapter 12

Every betrayal contains a perfect moment, a coin stamped heads or tails with salvation on the other side.
Barbara Kingsolver

A car swerved to avoid hitting him, slid, then hydroplaned over the flooded street, scarcely avoiding a ditch before the driver finally regained control. Jace, oblivious to his near catastrophe, straddled the double yellow line, his long stride focused straight ahead as if the freezing pelts of rain hypnotized him. Rain-soaked hair clung to my face, my arms and legs almost numb from icy, drenched clothing. I screamed for Jace to stop, but he ignored me, and the stormy night made his image increasingly difficult to see. The shadowy silhouette moved further and further away.

Klyce meant the world to Jace. She was his first real love and she made him feel special, treasured, a feeling he desperately needed. Perceived or reality, Jace's self-image faded each passing day proportionately to how he saw his father's attention focus on Josh. Klyce's affection dulled his emptiness but unfortunately he transferred the void, attaching his self-worth to her, which created a false feeling of content.

When she slept with Jace's best friend, he lost them both and betrayal was too much for him to bear. He broke into my locked wine cabinet, downed a $75.00 bottle of Cakebread chardonnay and was drunk and despondent by the time I got home. Grief and anxiety escalated into a frantic surge of emotion when he revealed his sordid story. His anger exploded into rage and he ran from the house into the rain-drenched night. I rushed after him, but at seventeen, even in his inebriated state, his athleticism shot him far ahead of me.

"I won't give up, Jace." I yelled toward his fading figure. "I'll keep following you. Please stop and talk to me."

After chasing him for almost an hour through chilling rain, I finally persuaded him to stop, get out of the middle of the street and tell me the story that prompted his erratic behavior.

"It's just not fair." He whimpered, sitting down on the curb. "You wouldn't understand, Mom. Nothing like this has ever happened to you."

I couldn't believe my mother's words poured from my mouth as I recalled a very similar discussion I had with her after Bryan betrayed me. "Jace, you'd be surprised at what I would understand."

Thirty minutes later and after an in-depth discussion, he reluctantly agreed to return home and at least warm up in the hot tub while we continued our conversation. I knew all too well what my son felt and my heart ached for him. We sat for hours in the spa that night and I shared some of the betrayals of my own life that later prompted a very significant journal entry, the ultimate infidelity from Zack.

Journal entry December 2001:
It wasn't long after my mother's death, mid-afternoon on a warm spring day when I received a phone call that would change my life. The woman on the other end of the line was obviously agitated, but her voice sounded determined, like she was on a mission and resolved to see it through...

May 23, 1997, I'll never forget that day. I discovered how lies obliterate trust and, once broken, trust can never truly be repaired...

****

"Hello, is this Casi?" The unfamiliar voice was laced with intent.

"Yes, who is this?"

"Hold on a second, I have to make sure Zack drove away." After a few moments of dead silence while my stomach rolled in knots, she returned to the phone, "He's gone. I warned him I'd call you."

I drew in a deep breath and, trying not to betray fear churning inside of me, managed to speak. "Who are you and how do you know my husband?"

"My name is Cheri. I'm"--She paused a beat as if working up the courage to continue--"Zack's fiancé."

The knot fisted in the pit of my stomach tightened as a tsunami of anxiety drowned me. I couldn't breathe. Nausea churned in my stomach and pushed into my throat. I swallowed hard to force the bile back down. Light headed, I reached for the arm of the sofa for stability and collapsed into the seat, while she recited a litany of her long, intimate relationship with my husband. My heart raced. My God, how could this be happening to me—AGAIN?

My head spinning, I gripped the phone tighter, holding the receiver rigidly against my ear.

"Zack and I have been together for years. He wants to marry me and it's time you knew the truth." Her voice drifted on-and-on, but I couldn't make sense of the surreal words. "He comes to see me whenever he can and we have a wonderful time, but when the weekend comes, or holiday, he creates some ridiculous reason to pick a fight, then leaves to go home to his boys.

I just couldn't take being pushed to the background anymore. I told him if he left this time, I would call you and tell you everything. He threw a glass of ice water on me and stormed out in a rage."

Zack would have done that. The scenario was definitely his *modus operandi*. Cheri went on for what felt like an eternity, babbling about how much she loved Zack and how she believed they had a future together.

"I love him so much, but after ten years, it's time you and I face the truth." She paused a beat before continuing. "I warned him. If he walked out this time I would end his secret life, tell you everything. I may be making a mistake by calling you, but you need to know Zack has another life — and that I'm his fiancé. Do you hear me, Casi? We are engaged."

I heard her words, but felt as if I were in a dream, no a nightmare, until she uttered the word "fiancé" again. That simple word pierced my heart. After all of his promises, all of my concessions, not to mention his affair, Zack did the same thing Bryan had done. Zack was engaged to another woman while he was married to me.

"We have fun together, and he's relaxed here. He's happy when we're together. But he's devoted to his boys and always leaves to go back to his children. Ten years. I just don't believe him anymore. He told me you were house bound and an invalid and I get that, but ..."

Still not speaking, I tried to listen more intently to what she was actually trying to tell me. The lies he fabricated were lame at best. How could she believe the bizarre stories he fed her — did she say ten years — what was she thinking? Any normal, sensible person, even someone with my insecurities, would have, at some point, figured out he was lying and wasn't going to suddenly abandon his wife and children to marry her.

My self-image was shot, but even I possessed enough self-respect not to waste ten years of my life waiting for random moments of affection from a married man. How could she not realize that if he would cheat on and lie to me, he was obviously capable of doing the same to her? The entire scenario blew me away. My mind flashed memories of my little boys, how much they missed their daddy while he claimed to be on the road working.

All the while, he led a separate life in a different state, in the arms of another woman. Zack's aloof behavior suddenly made complete sense. His affair with this woman was the root of his inner turmoil and subsequent angry outbursts.

Damn. I get that my husband skillfully hid his secret life from me--but for ten years? Was I totally oblivious? Beneath all of his anger and threats I still believed he loved me and would never consciously hurt me again. Although ...I never understood his escalating bouts of rage, or why we never recovered intimacy in our marriage. Wow, an affair, the betrayal stared at me like a crystal-clear reflection. Damn, Damn. How could I have been so naïve — so stupid?

My emotions ranged from devastation, to anger, and then in some warped, pathetic way, to compassion for Cheri. And there it was, my gullibility reared its misguided head yet again. I couldn't believe I was relating to her, just like I did with Becky, Bryan's mistress.

The phone beeped to signal an incoming call. I could see the caller was Zack. I didn't answer. What would I say to him? I needed to let the details sink in and process the devastation of this mammoth earthquake.

I spoke with my husband's fiancé for quite a while, setting her straight on many of Zack's preposterous stories about me. When we finally hung up, I had her phone number in hand. We had a lot more to discuss before this ordeal was put to bed. Okay, not the best metaphor, but appropriate. Racked with anger and betrayal, I was heartbroken, scared, and furious all at the same time. My head still spun and the feeling of nausea lingered long after the call ended.

The next time the phone rang I snatched the receiver. Zack, calm and cool, asked me how my day was, clearly testing the waters to see if Cheri was true to her threat. My expletive reply was clear and forceful before I slammed the receiver down.

The ten-hour return trip home from Maryland gave Zack plenty of time to prepare his defense. When he arrived, he was quiet, almost submissive as he pleaded his case. He told me that Cheri didn't take their original breakup well and didn't accept the end of their brief affair.

"She called me constantly." He wove a pitiful saga. "When I didn't return her messages, she showed up at work. She stalked me and threatened to call you, Casi. She swore to fill your head with lies unless I continued the relationship."

The bizarre chronicle took a moment to hit me. Oh my God. Cheri was his mistress. The same woman he supposedly broke up with years earlier. He was telling me he never stopped seeing her ...that she persuaded him to stay with her even after the phone call I heard him make proclaiming his love and devotion to me. She blackmailed him, promising to make sure he lost the boys as well as me unless he continued their relationship? Oh, come on. How naive did he think I was? Zack portrayed Cheri as a devious woman who held him emotionally captive, a story of fatal attraction at its best.

"I couldn't let her do that, Casi." He reminded me of Bryan with his award winning presentation. "She was blackmailing me and I couldn't take the chance of losing my family."

Ha, it was a little too late for that.

"Appeasing Cheri was the only way I could protect our life together."

Are you kidding me? I bit back a snide remark. "Did it ever cross your mind that the truth might work?"

"I hurt you so much the first time. I couldn't bear to cause you any more pain. I promise you, though, I hardly ever saw her, maybe once every few months. I honestly hoped she'd get tired of the whole ordeal and walk away, but she never did. She just pushed me to leave you and marry her."

"The lies, Zack. What about all the lies you told her about me? How could you do that?"

"Damn, Casi, I detested the entire situation. I was trapped, frantically trying to keep her satisfied to barter for her silence. When I wouldn't come to see her often enough, she threatened me. She even came to our house and parked across the street watching, waiting for me. I couldn't escape her. She was completely obsessed. If you don't believe me, just ask Wes."

"Wes? Wes knows about this? Damn. How many other people know how oblivious I have been for ten years?"

"Only Wes. He's my best friend and I needed to talk to someone. He knows the torment she put me through."

Zack flung his arm across the table sending its contents flying across the room. "I hate myself for what I did and I'm sure I'll rot in hell for hurting you and the boys." He portrayed his raging anger at Cheri as the root of his inexplicable violent temper and the fury toward her seethed for years.

"Damn it Zack, I'm your wife. If your situation was that bad, why couldn't you just talk to me? Anything would have been easier than what you say you were going through. And what about us—the boys and me? Your rage came out at us, Zack."

"I'm sorry. God Casi, I'm so sorry. I should have trusted you, trusted us, but I just couldn't hurt you again. I made the decision to move to Atlanta so I could put distance between Cheri and me. I didn't even tell her I was leaving. I just disappeared with no warning, but she found me anyway, through my mother, no less."

"Your mother knew?" I screamed at him.

"No, I mean yes, but that was an accident. Cheri called her and said she was a high school friend, trying to find me for a reunion. Mom gave her our new phone number and address."

According to Zack, he kept up the charade for as long as could. He ran out of excuses to pacify Cheri so he bought a cheap crystal ring she thought to be a diamond engagement ring to buy him some time, but time ran out.

Having had enough, my husband finally broke and stormed out of her house, daring her to call me. "Do what you want. I'd rather be forced to come clean and accept the collateral damage than put up with your vicious threats for one more minute." At least that's what he told me he said. He left her, slamming the door behind him.

"Thank God, it's finally over, Casi. I can't tell you how good that feels. You know everything. She can't blackmail me anymore."

"Over Zack?" I questioned. "Our whole marriage was a lie. Ten years? I can't do this anymore."

"Please Casi, don't let her destroy everything we have. I promise you we can finally be free and things will be different now. No more anger. We can get our lives back. Please, just give me the chance to prove it to you."

The entire weekend we cried and talked about the past and our options for the future. By Sunday evening exhaustion took over and Zack had me completely worn down. He swore ad-nauseam he hated hurting me, but felt a freedom and peace that was missing from his life for ten years. The guilt he endured triggered intense self-hatred followed by violent rage that poisoned our lives. Zack was nothing if not convincing and after two days of battle, I reluctantly agreed to give our marriage one more chance.

We went through the motions for two more years, playing our roles, but for me all trust disintegrated and I could no longer deny the piercing emptiness dwelling in my heart. I felt cold and hard inside and despite his desperate attempts to restore our marriage I could never trust him again.

****

That's what lies do--obliterate trust. I began to doubt everything: people, circumstances, and especially myself. Lies plagued my entire life starting with my father and I finally realized the devastating impact they spawned.

I couldn't erase the past or tell my thoughts to just go away. All I could do was try to create a better future. I was smart enough to know I needed to make some changes, but self-doubt loomed over my soul. The voice inside my head constantly reminded me I wasn't capable, but regardless of my instincts to turn tale and run, I was the only one who could transform my life. The challenge daunted me, but there was no turning back. I needed to walk away from Zack and stand on my own two feet, alone. The transition required a confidence that was completely foreign to me, courage to step off a cliff knowing I had no way to fly.

It was 2:00 a.m. before Jace hauled his waterlogged body out of the hot tub and drudged to the screen porch. He stripped down to his underwear, wrapped himself in a dry towel and finally went inside. I followed him, my mind reeling from the ordeal of the night.

After all I went through, like Jace, I could have really done a number on myself. I could have played a victim to the hilt and had every right to do so. He was right life wasn't fair. We did the *right* things, followed the rules, and did everything we should have done.

I shuddered, trying to accept I was nothing more than a starter wife. I made the sacrifices, put up with the affairs, lived a lonely and nearly celibate life, waiting for my husband to heal and praying he would return to our marriage. I watched my children cower at his rage and comforted them when they cried for him to come home, longing for his love and attention.

I scrimped and saved to buy used clothing and toys for my children and cut corners while my husband supported his clandestine addiction and mistress. Zack lived an alternate life where he could escape the pressures of family, finances and day-to-day problems that almost everyone experiences. He and his mistress enjoyed a carefree existence at his family's expense.

By all rights, I should be approaching a time in my life when I could finally sit back and relax, reap the benefits of the years of hard work and joint efforts Zack and I worked to attain. Instead, I was faced with starting my life completely over, alone.

I wanted to make changes in my life, to be happy, but fear of moving forward still battled with the emptiness of my broken marriage. I was torn between two paths, neither of which seemed viable. So, I chose to tread water for the time being, until I could figure out a game plan to move forward, and find the courage I needed to initiate the changes.

Despite my best efforts to the contrary, Zack placed himself in the long line of men who betrayed me with secrets and lies. I was knocked down so many times in the past, I felt counterproductive getting up again and yet, I knew the getting up would build my character and give me back my strength and self-worth. If I surrendered and recoiled into myself, I would spiral down and I wouldn't do that to my children — or myself.

Jace needed time to recover from his blow, but I would be there if he needed me. My children were my solace, my joy, and though I couldn't protect them from pain, I might be able to keep them from following patterns already set in motion. I would never give up on them, or myself. The only way I could help my children was to change my own life.

Chapter 13

It is not in the stars to hold our destiny but in ourselves.
William Shakespeare

"I don't know who I am anymore, Casi," Brie sobbed, plopping herself down onto my freshly made bed. "I know we've been looking for Matthew, but we've never really focused on the search. There's got to be a better way to track him down. Decatur is a small town and it's not like everyone who knew Mom and Matthew just disappeared. I wish I could just remember something, some little flash that would give us a lead?"

Brie was clearly frustrated. Her dreams of Matthew escalated as soon as we agreed to look for him. It was odd I had no childhood memories, but even more strange for Brie who was five years older than me. Finding Matthew would answer a lot of questions. We might uncover what really happened between our parents.

For years as a defense mechanism, I adamantly insisted the man meant nothing to me, but now I knew he hurt me deeply. To know my *father* felt nothing, no desire to learn anything about me. If only I could look him in the eyes, ask those nagging questions, and finally learn the truth.

I consoled my sister and promised to spend more time tracking down leads. By the time she left my house, I had already searched several Internet sites and generated numerous inquiries into the whereabouts of the ever so elusive Matthew Stafford.

I understood Brie's anguish. I searched for my own identity over the past few years and discovered a lot, but Aunt Ginny helped me realize my *father* had little to do with who I was. Brie made a good point though.

Finding Matthew might shed some light on our roots, lineage, and any future health concerns we may come across. Still, to truly understand myself I knew my search would be an internal one, independent of my bloodline.

There was a strange allure, some might say an obsession, connected to my own story. I found myself spending more-and-more time working on my laptop, researching my past and uncovering reluctant secrets. I compiled my findings first into my journal entries and then to a kind of manuscript, trying to pull everything together so I could see the whole picture. Wherever the path led me, I felt confident I would uncover the truth.

Journal entry, spring 2002:
For years my children were my lifelines and I was determined to be theirs, but the boys were in their late teens now, focused on their friends and activities and my busy-mom world slowed down to a trickle. Their mother was, as a rite of passage, no longer the most important woman in their lives. The evolution was difficult for me though. They were my life, filled the hole Zack left in his wake, and I wasn't sure how to have a life without them as my hub. I found increasingly more time to dream, but loneliness began to suffocate my spirit. Without small children or a viable marriage to give me purpose, I felt emptiness envelop me like a shroud...

The first step in changing your life is deciding you really want to change it...

****

As a stay-at-home mom during the boy's formative years, I took care of my children's every need. Now my own care moved into the foreground. I needed to determine what I wanted, change directions, and forge my new path. No longer willing to live a mundane existence, I knew big changes would be key to a fulfilling future. My decisions carved my destiny, but the thought of flying alone terrified me. There was no one left to hold my hand. I had been out of the work force for twelve years and wasn't even sure how or where to begin.

Serendipity or sheer luck, my high school friend, Nash, found his way back into my life just when I needed him. Out of the blue, he sent me an email:

Hi Casi,
I ran across your name in an alum update a few years ago and jotted down your email address, but I lost track of my scribbling before I had the chance to contact you. I discovered the note when I was reorganizing my office this week and took a chance it was still current.
Nash

When I received the unexpected note, a breath of fresh air instantly calmed me. We spent hours writing back and forth, chatting online and catching up on the paths our lives had taken. Somewhere between reminiscing and sharing life stories, we just connected.

Nash was never a scholar, but he was talented and articulate. I think school was too boring for his imaginative, artistic soul. He experimented with drugs in high school, barely making it into college and his subsequent four years were a blur of drug-induced lucidity. His addiction almost killed him, but he survived and now viewed life with clear perception of what was important. He cherished each day as if it were his last and lived every day to the fullest.

Nash accomplished what most people only dream of doing. He sailed for thirty days in a Transatlantic Race on a two-man trawler, acted in several movies and wrote and published novels. He searched the ocean floor for lost treasure, traveled the Northwest Passage, raced cars and followed his heart. His amazing zest for life inspired me. The only thing that held him back was society's confinements. He lived his dreams.

Nash's encouragement had me feeling I could accomplish anything my heart desired. I wasn't sure what that was, but I knew I'd discover my own dreams too. He became my long distance support system. We rarely talked by phone, but I couldn't wait to wake up in the morning to find his cheery IM message on my computer.

"Good morning, beautiful. Go out and have a wonderful day. You may not believe in yourself right now, Casi, but I sure as hell do."

Sometimes we would chat online for hours or I would see an inspirational message waiting for me upon returning home. He never went to sleep at night without leaving me a note. His missives evolved over months and I began to feel as important to Nash as he was to me. They kept me afloat.

I know we'll see each other soon. I think about you a tremendous amount of the time and when I'm away from my computer I miss you. Believe you can become everything you were always meant to be, and know I'm always here for you. I love you and promise I'll see you soon.

Love You, Me.

For years I wanted to start over, but my self-esteem ran on empty until Nash found me. He filled my tank, encouraging me to move forward with my life with enthusiasm and confidence. And I wanted that, I just wasn't sure how to begin.

One morning, my dad in his infinite wisdom, provided the nudge I needed to find my way again. He introduced me to a woman from his church who needed a designer for her small carpet company. I was certainly qualified, but old fears held me captive. The prospect of jumping back into the work force intimidated me. What if my goals were puffed up illusions of an unattainable distant dream? I was flat out scared, but despite my fear, I agreed to meet with her and astonishment besieged me when she offered me the job.

"You're perfect for my company, Casi. It's yours if you want it."

For as long as I could remember I hadn't felt "perfect" for anything, but the challenge intrigued me.

The thought of standing on my own two feet terrified me, but I knew from my battle with anxiety that I could do this if I just took one day—one step at a time. I wouldn't view the whole idea of starting over. That concept overwhelmed me. Instead, I'd take baby steps like an infant learning to walk. I resolved to change my life to set an example for my sons, and though insecurity loomed over my shoulder, I pushed through the fear. In doing so, I made a striking discovery. Living through panic attacks, infertility, abandonment and multiple betrayals gave me inner strength I never realized I possessed. My new position daunted me at the onset, but I quickly adjusted to proficiency.

The job agitated Zack, though. He appreciated the additional income, but went ballistic if an important client called me and took my concentration away from his needs or desires.

"Don't answer that call." He demanded my attention. "You can call them back later. I'm talking to you now."

"Zack, I have to get this. It's Derrick, and he's my biggest client. He wouldn't call me on the weekend unless his call was important." I turned away to grab the incoming call despite his badgering. "Hi Derrick..."

"Oh yeah, Oh sure." Zack yelled out so loudly, making sure he could be heard on the other end of the line. "It's so important you had to call her right away, on Sunday..."

Embarrassed, I rushed to get behind closed doors and covered the phone to shield my client from Zack's rant.

"Screw this crap, Casi. Tell him you'll call him later." He shouted, this time, to ensure at least I would hear his irritation so I'd returned my attention to him.

My phone calls weren't the only changes that annoyed Zack. My newfound independence intimidated him as if he felt threatened I no longer needed his support or income to survive. He teased me about my job, usually in front of Josh and Jace, and sarcastically belittled my position.

"Look boys, isn't Mommy cute? She has her little measuring tape and is going to work."

The odd thing was, his demeaning attitude only fueled my resolve. My job began to bring back a sense of self-assurance missing from my life for years, and Zack realized he lost some of his hold on me.

I don't remember the precise moment I decided to divorce him, but I do remember Joshua was a senior in high school and Jacob was a freshman. Zack and I were merely coexisting. I wanted more and one day I summoned the courage to tell him we needed to talk.

"My heart's on empty, Zack, and I can't walk through the motions anymore."

"What are you talking about, Casi?" He acted so surprised, like the revelation came from out of the blue and not from years of broken promises and betrayals. "Why are you doing this now? We've worked through everything and survived. You can't just give up now."

I knew a divorce wouldn't be easy. I'd have no means of support, and no back up plan. Together we lived paycheck-to-paycheck on two incomes and the children still had college ahead of them. Financial support from my husband would be little to nothing, but it was time to move forward and look at the world through fresh eyes.

After several lengthy discussions, my husband finally agreed our marriage was a train wreck. Zack moved to an apartment close by and I was left on my own for the first time since—perhaps the first time ever. I was always somebody's something: daughter, girlfriend, wife, mother--I had no idea who I really was and felt desperate to find out.

For twelve years, I was a devoted mom, but rejoining the work force changed me profoundly and quickly. Our divorce settlement provided for meager child support, for three years, barely enough to cover my mortgage. Then later reduced to half, which might cover utilities for another two years. My business needed to succeed. There would be no second chances. Our survival depended on me and I had basically three years to secure a steady income before my children and I would be in financial free-fall.

Nash continued to encourage me on a daily basis, but the responsibility fell to me alone. Even though the thought eluded me for most of my life, I had too much tenacity to cower and cry about how bad things were. I was angry with Zack and his mistress, but I didn't waste time dreaming up revenge. If there's one thing I learned, the lesson is that self-pity and schemes of vengeance do nothing but keep you wallowing in pain.

Life is too short to harbor anger. I would only end up hurting my children and myself in the long run, rather than the source of my contempt. I grieved the loss of what could have, and rightly should have been, but wallowing was not my style.

Every day would be a lost opportunity to create new dreams, and I wasted far too many days in my life waiting for, no expecting my *knight* to create a perfect life for me. I resolved not to squander one more day and refused to ever be a victim ever again.

****

My self-image imprisoned me, sucked me down into a whirlpool of fractured dreams that suffocated my aspirations. I needed to escape that spiral downward, to reach through murky waters of my past and thrust myself into freedom. I couldn't ignore what I went through. Instead, I'd learn from my experience, so I wouldn't repeat the mistakes. I tried to visualize goals and work toward a happier and more fulfilling future.

Once within my grasp, I held on to new visions and lifestyle as my lifeline. I immersed myself into positive reinforcement: self-improvement books, television and lectures. I placed myself in situations that bolstered my self-image and strengthened my confidence. This new phase of my life was exciting and looking backwards would only hold me in a broken past. Through sheer tenacity, I broke free.

I set my laptop down as my thoughts turned back to Brie. There wasn't any doubt I was curious about finding my *father* and uncovering my past, but I realized my miraculous breakthroughs didn't evolve from my search, but rather through my writing. The quest for my *father* began a journey to find myself. I had lived my life believing that life required submission to whatever was thrown my way. My passion slowly ebbed into a dull, numbing nothingness. That phase of my life ended.

Finding my *father* would be meaningful, but I knew now that finding myself and living to my potential would dramatically change my life forever.

Chapter 14

*You cannot always control circumstances,
but you can control your own thoughts.*
Charles Popplestone

I thrashed back and forth, desperately fighting to break free of the bonds trapping me. Beads of sweat cooled by the night air rolled down my face and a chill rippled through my body. Startled by the sensation, my eyes flew open and strained to see through pitch-blackness that engulfed the room. My hair was soaked, and the clammy moisture-drenched sheets held me captive like a silk encased cocoon. The soft, silk baby-doll lingerie I slipped into earlier, clung to my body. I fumbled for the bedside light, flipped the switch and trudged into the bathroom.

"Damn, night sweats suck."

The doctor used the term peri-menopause. The very idea of menopause made me feel so freaking old. I dreaded the thought of what else life had in store for me during this new stage. I pulled the nightgown off my shoulders, dropping the garment to the floor and turned the shower knob, then impulsively stripped the wet sheets from my bed and tossed them in the hamper before I stepped into the steamy enclosure. The hot streams of water cascaded down and warmth engulfed me.

It was 3:00 a.m., too early to get up. After a refreshing shower, I stepped out onto the plush throw rug and dried myself off, squinting to focus on the figure in the mirror. Shaking my head, I rolled my eyes but had to smile. God's creativity sure was genius when he made our eyes blur before our body began to wrinkle and sag. I snatched a nightshirt, absorbing cotton this time, put on clean bedding and slipped between fresh, cool sheets. My shower-warmed body instantly relaxed.

Maybe I could salvage what remained of the night after all. As I sunk deeper into serenity my thoughts wandered. I hated the loneliness that enveloped me at moments like that. The emptiness made me starkly aware of how unfulfilled my life was for such a long time.

Thank God for Nash. My mind drifted to my high school friend. If not for Nash, I might have wandered for many more years, never realizing why my life felt empty. I propped myself up in bed and reached for my trusty laptop.

Journal entry, winter 2002:
Nash supported me when I needed him. He reminded me of the young woman I once was. A woman filled with hopes, dreams, and creativity. For the first time in my life I began to believe I could do more than survive on my own. A glimmer of light pierced the walls of my self-perception. I wasn't sure what my future would hold but I knew I'd be okay. My high school friend helped me crawl out of an abyss I'd slipped into over the course of my life and propelled me on the journey to find myself...

Nash reminded me about someone important I'd completely forgotten about — me...

****

Early May brought rebirth as winter sputtered its last gasp. I grabbed a cup of coffee and drifted off to my office and a new day. A chat note from Nash was the first thing I saw as I woke up my computer.

Hi Casi,
I've got a surprise for you. I held off mentioning anything until I knew for sure, but my plans are firm now so I can tell you. I'm coming to Atlanta. I'm going to be racing my Formula One at Road Atlanta next week. I can't wait to see you, kiddo. We'll talk soon and make some plans.
Hugs, Nash

God, I hadn't seen him in so long. I wondered if I would even recognize him, or worse, would he recognize me. I beat back an impulse to pull out my mirror and study my face for wrinkles. Either way, I couldn't wait to look into his beautiful, blue eyes again.

His flight and hotel reservations were set and as the day approached, I felt nervous, overwhelmed with emotion. Nash was there for me when I was completely lost. He supported my new life, helped me rediscover a long-lost self-confidence. I owed him so much, was indebted to him, but I also felt deeply connected to him. I was sucked into a black vortex and he patiently dragged me out of that dark hole. I couldn't wait to run into his arms and press my lips against--

Press my lips? Where did that come from? At that moment I realized my high school friend not only stirred powerful emotion within me. The connection somehow morphed into a visceral attraction as well. Nash was coming to see me after countless years and our online relationship conjured more than a simple visit between high school friends.

The next few days dragged as I anxiously awaited his arrival. I trembled walking through the Atlanta International Airport concourse. When his flight arrived, my heart pounded so hard I thought my ribs would crack and my stomach flip-flopped. I scrutinized the passengers disembarking one by one until Nash finally came into view. I could scarcely breathe.

There was no mistaking him. He sauntered down the ramp toward me, dressed in blue jeans and a light blue dress shirt, with his sleeves rolled half way up, just as he had worn them in high school. He had a dark backpack slung over his shoulder. His hair was almost white now, but his blue eyes still sparkled with youthful energy. I ran to him and he dropped his bag, opened his arms, scooped me up off the floor and twirled me in circles.

"Hey kiddo," he whispered in my ear.

For a moment we were lost in time, holding on to each other in an almost desperate embrace. Finally separated, we stared into each other's eyes and grinned like children. Nash grabbed his backpack and, hand-in-hand, we moved toward the baggage claim area, talking, laughing like no one else existed.

I drove him to his hotel and for the next twenty-four hours, we were inseparable. We spent hours lying on his bed, wrapped in each other's arms talking and catching up on the events that became our lives. He filled me in on his recent move to the West coast, how the change made working on the screenplay of his newest book easier. When he made a casual remark about Teri reluctantly joining him a few months later, my heart froze. I swallowed hard but the lump in my throat didn't move.

"Teri? Who is Teri?"

I remembered Nash explaining his marriage in detail—and his divorce. We exchanged numerous instant messages as we chatted online, comparing our situations. He wrote about his son on many occasions, his boat, his books, his entire life, but he never mentioned anyone named Teri.

"Teri is my, uh—" He cleared his throat, stuttered. "My wife." He replied in a hesitant tone, his brow pinched. "I remarried a few years ago."

I listened, glued to every word as he described a less than ideal relationship, an almost dependent one on her part, and how he wanted to help her. He didn't intentionally deceive me. I guess the topic simply didn't come up. I mean we weren't in a romantic relationship. Perhaps he was just waiting for the right time, or maybe mentioning Teri never crossed his mind. Nash didn't really do anything wrong. Our emotions were of a deep and abiding friendship. I pulled my heart off my sleeve and placed the rather deflated lump firmly back into my chest.

****

For a brief moment, I ennobled my feelings for Nash, but in reality, my friend was there in my time of need and my displaced emotions managed to jumble things up for a while. The feelings evoked inside jarred an untapped emotion. I felt more than simple gratitude and friendship, but if I was honest with myself, I knew Nash filled a special place in my heart meant only for him, a wonderful friend.

For the next several days we shared everything. I watched his races, laughed and cried, as we reminisced about our youth. When he boarded the plane to return home, I knew he sparked a flame that changed my life...

I closed my laptop and set the computer aside. I was so tired of lugging around the sack of broken dreams I carried for a lifetime. The load was heavy and kept me trapped in the past. Reconnecting with Nash threw a new lifeline to me. He showed me how to live in the moment and let go of what I no longer needed. He awakened my dreams, renewed my self-confidence, and helped me realize I could follow those dreams if only if I released the hold on my wounded self-image.

My children were the center of my life for so many years. They distracted me from the emptiness of a broken marriage, but the boys were older now and would be out on their own in the blink of an eye. I wanted a career, a future, and love––especially love. Nash opened my eyes to see the woman filled with passion, hope and desire, a woman who'd merely lost her way.

I glanced at the bedside clock, 4:00 a.m. and I needed sleep. Slipping further between the cool sheets, I closed my eyes while visions of Shangri-La flashed through my mind. A distant mountain beckoned a sweet allure from the far side of a daunting fog.

The road ahead was long, jagged, and wouldn't be easy. I snuggled into my soft blanket thankful for what I had instead of what was lost. Drifting into sleep I remembered, "The butterfly only emerges after struggling with its cocoon." The beautiful metaphor would boost my resolve for tomorrows yet to come.

Chapter 15

When you have come to the edge of all light that you know, and are about to drop off into the darkness of the unknown, faith is knowing one of two things will happen: There will be something solid to stand on or you will be taught to fly.
                                    Patrick Overton

He stared directly into my eyes and the multitude of people in the auditorium simply evaporated. I sat there, alone, front and center absorbed in his every word and the significance penetrated the deepest corners of my soul as if he possessed a road map for my life. A magnetic speaker, he drew me into his aura like no one before. Andy Stanley preached sermons so relevant that the correlation to my life could be attributed to nothing short of divine inspiration. Oddly though, almost everyone I spoke to felt the same way.

"What is the WISE thing to do?" His question triggered deep reflection. "In light of your past experiences, your present situation and your future hopes and dreams, what is the wise thing to do?"

My mind reeled to the first time I saw this dynamic man and the profound affect he had on my life. I was lost; drowning in a sea of conflicting memories, betrayal and self-doubt, but his words forged a bridge across tumultuous waters.

Journal entry, summer 2003:
Nash was a thousand miles away now, back in his own life. Again I was faced with my own self-reliance and my own judgment without someone else guiding my way. Mom was gone and so was Zack, and I couldn't discuss my intimate struggles with my boys, especially in the wake of Zack. Regardless of our marital status, Zack was their father, the only father they would ever have, and I didn't want to tarnish whatever relationship they had with him...

Maybe I lost my way because I was headed in the wrong direction.

****

Zack and I had been separated for over a year and I still felt lonely, starved for a connection with a kindred soul, or someone who would help fill the deep emptiness inside of me. But meeting people, especially guys, required much more creativity than I expected. My memories of bar scenes with all the lecherous men and desperate women who frequented them totally depressed me. The chance of meeting my soul mate in one of those dives was about as likely as winning the lottery.

I considered placing a personal ad in the local newspaper. Maybe that would do the trick? I could just see it:

Wanted, a handsome, virile male. Candidates should be thoughtful, smart, loving, honest, have a great sense of humor, oh yes, and must be willing to fall in love with a total reject.

No, an ad wasn't the answer.

Internet dating was an option, but the thought of posting personal details about myself across cyberspace for the world to inspect intimidated me more than the work force.

In my mind, dating sites filled with desperate singles, probably set a virtual buffet of flesh for sexual predators, but I'd deleted or exhausted all my other options. Internet dating held some kind of attraction to singles and if I met a few people in public areas, I could at least form a better point of view of the idea.

I chose a popular company and filled out their questionnaire. Still a little skeptical, I scanned profiles of age appropriate men, and watched my inbox fill with messages, few of which remotely interested me. A week later, I actually pushed the send button on my first reply. Having made an effort, I began a process of exchanging emails, filtering out men who didn't fit my qualification list, and continued communication with those who piqued my interest.

The first few guys I met were a big disappointment. I shook my head in wonder why men would lie about themselves. Not that they displayed any difference from the laundry list of men who'd lied and betrayed me in the past, but did they really think I wouldn't notice the extra hundred pounds or the shining bare head when their pictures showed hair?

Did women lie about themselves too? I mean I could kind of see fudging on age. Who wants to admit how old they are, but how can you start a relationship with a lie. If I did that, I could expect no less from the men I dated. Over time, I became extremely selective with my responses and even more cautious.

One Sunday afternoon, I came across the profile of a man who described himself as tall and kind. The picture he posted attracted me and, according to his profile, our interests entwined so I agreed to meet him. Chris stood just short of seven feet and was one of the kindest men I ever met. We went out several times on super fun dates, but loneliness didn't prepare me to move into a physical relationship. After so many years with Zack, spending time with someone new felt awkward. My libido desired attention, but I needed time to catch up.

Chris and I forged a great friendship, though. One of the qualities that impressed me most about him was his intimate relationship with God. He raved about his church, an odd concept for me. I grew up a Christian, believed in God, and went to church religiously, but despite feeling deeply rooted in Christianity, something was missing from my spiritual life.

As a young woman, I visited multiple churches in various denominations searching for a church that felt right. The churches I attended as a child were didactic and judgmental. Their interpretation of God's word was simple enough: If you were good, which meant you followed their lists of do's and don'ts, you would go to Heaven when you died, and if not, you would be doomed to an eternity in hell.

As a child I envisioned the entrance to Heaven as a magnificent pearly gate glittering in the distance beyond a golden staircase that ascended through shimmering clouds. At the top, Saint Peter guarded the portal, and in his hand he held a lengthy list of my earthly performances, which would undoubtedly fall short of the expected perfection.

Over time, I grew up and my vision changed. I believed God was forgiving. He wouldn't really be at a Pearly Gate entrance with checklist in hand, waiting to tally up my score, but I was taught that performance was the key to Heaven, and what I did would determine my eternity. I tried to do the right things, but regardless of my intent, my life was far from pristine. I was divorced twice. Granted, both husbands hid secret lives and mistresses and, like my own *father*, they abandoned me. Memories of rejection haunted me as far back as I could remember and I wondered if God would reject me as well.

After Mom's death, going to church was difficult for me. I encouraged my children to attend and drove them to youth groups, but I chose to take a sabbatical. I still believed in God, I just wasn't sure about church, so for the past three or four years I struggled with my spirituality.

Chris found an incredible connection, but despite the numerous churches I visited, not one felt right or remotely close to what he experienced. So, one Sunday morning, I decided to try my friend's illustrious church to see what could possibly be the allure. The campus was nearly an hour from my house, so the convenience factor alone dissuaded me right from the start. Even if I loved the environment, I wasn't likely to attend a church that far away, but my innate curiosity enthralled me enough to take the jaunt at least once to check out Chris's illustrious pastor.

There was no mistaking North Point Community Church's location. The massive traffic jam headed toward a single destination stunned me. When I finally pulled into the enormous parking lot, I couldn't even see the church, and jockeying for a parking spot was like trying to find a space at the Super Bowl. No doubt something about this place attracted droves of people, but I couldn't calm the uneasy feeling that there was no way I could ever find an intimate relationship with God amongst this mass of people.

When I entered the church, the dual sanctuaries floored me. The right auditorium held a live pastor while the opposite theater showed a camera view of the man speaking on the opposite side of the building, which reflected on a ginormous screen. The total attendance had to be several thousand. Each stage sported a full band, massive electronics and extensive video equipment.

Completely overwhelmed by the organization, I shrunk into myself, but when the music began, the incredible, uplifting expression of worship filled me with an odd sense of courage and dignity. Energy filled the entire building and electrified the congregation. My anticipation of the pastor escalated with each verse. When the band finished, the crowds silenced and bowed their heads in prayer, while the minister took his place on stage.

I'm not sure what I expected, but Pastor Stanley's slight stature and simple appearance didn't fulfill my vision of Chris' spearhead. He wasn't dressed in robes or even a suit. In fact, he looked like an average man dressed in a simple blue and black plaid shirt with black slacks. My gaze zeroed in on him when he began expressing the uniqueness of Christianity.

"Jesus Christ made a profound difference in our lives. Most of us believe we are good people who occasionally do bad things, but the premise of Christianity is we were born in sin, so we are all sinners who occasionally do good things. If we were inherently good, then we could be consistently good. We could make a decision to do everything right and that would be the end of it. Instead, we all struggle with temptation."

Wow, his sermon resonated. Was he talking about me? My life unfolded in his every word. Why on this one day, did Andy Stanley choose the very topic that plagued my entire experience with church, and God for that matter? The relevance was uncanny. His delivery was animated and humorous, but his message was adamant.

"Something within us drives us to do bad things despite the knowledge we have of right and wrong. Sin is not only in us, but at times it even controls us." He referred to the Bible as he continued speaking of Adam and Eve, the original sin and the ultimate sacrifice Jesus made for humanity. "Christianity is not a code of conduct, and our salvation is not reliant upon our performance."

Psshuuu, this man blew me away. Totally different from the holier-than-thou preachers I heard growing up. He included himself as one of us, instead of standing behind a pulpit preaching down to his congregation. The sermon gripped me and held on through to the end. He enlightened me and, for the first time in my life, I began to realize that growing up believing something was factual didn't make the idea or event true. A new sense of freedom and contentment washed over me and I knew I'd found my home.

****

I looked forward to going to church every week. The sermons flew by and were always interesting and relevant. With over 5,000 participants in the singles ministry, I easily got involved in a small Bible study group and forged new friendships for the first time in what seemed like forever.

Like Nash, Chris played a key role in changing the course of my life. We didn't fall madly in love, but he became a great friend and helped me see there actually were amazing men in the world. Maybe my ideals weren't so far removed from reality after all.

Andy Stanley preached sermons so significant to my life struggles. One Sunday he said: "You should never evaluate a relationship based on where it is, instead base it on where it is headed. All relationships move. They get better or worse, stronger or weaker, more intimate or less intimate. You are wise to respond to the linear direction of a relationship from where it started to where it is. If you ignore that movement long enough, you will wake up one day with very poor options."

As I walked out of church, deep in thought, a large hand grasped my shoulder and pulled me backwards catching me off balance. I turned and fell into Chris' strong arms.

"Oops, sorry, Casi." He helped me regain my balance. "I'm glad to see you coming to church on a regular basis. How did you like Andy's sermon today?"

"Amazing, as always. It's like he talks directly to me, and his topics always hit home. I've never heard any pastor explain things like Andy."

Arm in arm, Chris and I walked back to my car comparing notes and laughing. We built a special bond, another friendship that would last over time and distance. As I headed toward home, I thought about the twisted and bumpy path my past took, but because of good friends and an amazing pastor I could finally see my life changing.

Chapter 16

A true friend knows your weaknesses but shows you your strengths, feels your fears but fortifies your faith, sees your anxieties but frees your spirit, recognizes your disabilities but emphasizes your possibilities.
William Arthur Ward

The fire roared as I stared, hypnotized by the flames. It was almost Christmas. My day was spent shopping with friends, and I was exhausted. Now 10:30 p.m. I sat in solitude, curled up into my favorite chair on the cold winter's night.

Old songs softly playing in the background comforted me, conjuring distant memories faded through the portals of time. I swirled the wine in my glass and watched the refracted firelight dance its reflection in the deep ruby pinot noir. The wind whistled around the chimney and pressed on the windows, humming its own lonely melody. Tucking my robe snugly around my stocking feet I took another sip of wine, while Paul Simon painted the canvas of my mind:

Old friends, old friends,
Sat on their park bench like bookends.
A newspaper blown through the grass falls on the round toes
Of the high shoes of the old friends
Can you imagine us years from today?
Sharing a park bench quietly
How terribly strange to be seventy
Time it was and what a time it was.
It was.
A time of innocence, a time of confidences
Long ago it must be, I have a photograph
Preserve your memories they're all that's left you.

Vivid visions of past memories flooded through the gateway.

Most of my life drifted through broken perceptions, wandering aimlessly, lonely, isolated, and rejected. Struggling to be noticed as something more than a pretty face or a trophy to achieve, longing to be valued, maybe even loved. Like a victim, I felt trapped, helpless to change my life. Too many nights, I cried myself to sleep, praying to God for my circumstances to change, hoping the next morning's light would chase away the darkness inside of me. Would I grow old, alone and empty? Would anyone show up at my funeral when I died? The emptiness I felt inside plagued me. I wanted to be able to look back on wonderful memories, of accomplishments, laughter, family, friends and love, but instead I wallowed, buried in a tomb of insignificance.

The last few years were different, though. For the first time, I approached a crossroads and turned away from the path of least resistance. I pushed forward with faith in God and believed in myself. Instead of letting life just happen to me, I made conscious choices, choosing to live well, despite my fear of failure. To walk the path less traveled felt foreign, daunting at times, but I stepped out on the ledge to follow my dreams and amazingly, I found there were people who held out their hands to support me. Andy Stanley inspired me and I met new friends through NPCC who helped me rebuild my confidence.

Swirling the rich, burgundy pinot around in my glass again, I noticed my laptop and reached for the comfort of my writing.

Journal entry, winter 2003:
When I made the decision to be a stay-at-home mom, my children became my entire world. Their lives took precedence and though acquaintances from their schools and sports activities provided me with occasional adult conversation, those connections were completely superficial. I remained in touch with a few high school and college classmates, but for the most part, I felt detached from the outside world.

For years my husband went to great lengths to conceal his affair so, in the process, Wes, Sharon and the few other friendships we managed to make during our early years together, virtually disappeared from our lives. We didn't even know our immediate neighbors except enough to smile and nod a pleasant gesture. I couldn't remember the last time we socialized or hung out with anyone besides my family. Zack never wanted to go to parties or get together with friends. Over time they turned in different directions and we no longer had friends. At least none close enough to be an integral part of our lives.

What fills the emptiness in life? Love is only the icing on the cake — and my ingredients weren't quite ready to bake.

****

NPCC's Christian ideology enriched my philosophy but, more importantly, my experiences with the congregation opened doors for a brighter, fulfilled future. Andy encouraged involvement in community groups and for the first time in countless years, I made strong female bonds. Befriended by Tracy, Lane, Lindsay and Allie, I finally found close female friends, the first since high school.

Tracy was quiet when I first met her, but when she finally opened her mouth and spoke, her wisdom amazed me. A wealth of knowledge, she knew more details about endless topics than anyone I had ever met yet she never bragged, and her incredible insight paled in comparison to her thoughtfulness and inspiration.

Lane rolled a spontaneous, fun-loving, free-spirited wild child. She always sported fashionable attire, perfect makeup and impeccable manners, except for one time in Vegas but as they say, what happens in Vegas ...Lane lived by the notion she deserved the best of everything. She expected success with whatever she attempted and her strength persevered.

Lindsay's bouncy, outgoing personality and edgy, dry sense of humor gave her a unique ability to make people laugh and she carried conversations with strangers as well as long-time friends. Her motherly attention nurtured all of us with a soothing conviction of a reliable friend.

It's curious comparing descriptions of high school and college classmates in my earlier journal entries to the women I now portrayed. My youthful emphasis hung on appearance, but now character and personality held complete significance. My perspective reflected how much I had grown, who I am.

But I digress. When I met Tracy, Lane and Lindsey, they intimidated me. Baring my soul to anyone, especially women had never been easy for me but, over time, bonds with my new girl friends evolved. They gradually chipped away at the walls of hurt, mistrust and anger I'd forged since childhood, a fortress that isolated my life.

The dynamics between friends brought us close enough to give and receive honest feedback and encourage accountability for our own poor choices. But we were equally quick to applaud each other's healthy decisions toward paths leading to positive futures––not an easy task when long established behavior patterns and toxic habits produce hidden roadblocks that sabotage our best intentions.

People tend to compare their inner selves to what they see on the exterior of their peers. I guess that's a natural tendency since we can't read minds. It's hard to know what lurks in the souls of the people around us--but it may be more difficult to recognize our own destructive behaviors. Our women's group decided to undertake a risky venture. We each agreed to exchange completely honest letters composed by the group describing how others perceived them. The premise: seeing ourselves through the eyes of others might help us see and understand ourselves and perhaps deal with the reality of our own weaknesses. But the project exposed my greatest insecurity.

As usual, Pollyanna smiled sweetly and agreed with the rest of the group. Inside, the idea of subjecting myself to the very disdain I avoided my whole life terrified me. Visions of blackballs hurled at me from every direction sent an army of ants marching up my arms until a fist clenched into a throbbing knot in my stomach.

It was one thing to open up to these women in discussions, but quite another to submit myself to a barrage of unsolicited opinions focused on my endless list of imperfections. How could I trust them to pierce my protective armor and expect to come out unscathed, let alone benefited?

Composing the letters for the other women went quickly. Writing came effortlessly to me so pulling together my thoughts and perceptions about the other members was an easy task. They each possessed so many wonderful qualities and few flaws, but me—what could they possibly see in me except an inept, mess who failed at almost everything she attempted? My Pollyanna act faked my way through casual situations in the past. I bent my life around everyone else's needs, but these women were going to dissect me from the inside out.

Who knows what they might find. Viewed through a microscope, all my deficiencies would be magnified. I'd worked too hard to succumb to a setback now, but if I backed out, the end result might be worse. I had to follow through and look at myself through their eyes.

By my outward appearance and nonchalant demeanor everyone thought I was totally together, but it took every discipline I could muster to walk into that meeting. My stomach churned with apprehension, but fighting anxiety attacks in the past prepared me to put on a calm appearance. I spent a lot of time practicing, chaos on the inside but cool as cream on the outside.

As my turn approached, I wanted to run from the room, but I took a deep breath, closed my eyes and listened as Tracy began to read:

Casi,

The thing we all wish for you the most in life is happiness and to find the one man who won't hurt you, but will truly love you and share with you, the life you deserve. At our age, we tend to wonder if it will ever happen for us, but we can see such a joyful and sincere heart in you. It is easy to picture you snuggled up in front of the TV with your perfect match.
The three of us get discouraged when we see you spending precious time with men you know are not the right choice for you. Our wish is that you experience a makeover in your frame of mind, beginning in your heart. Take time to spoil yourself with some new beautiful and feminine clothes and add a glow with the bare essentials of makeup so you truly show your wings and simply radiate a refined spirit.
Don't settle for less than you deserve. We know you are beyond ordinary, so shoot for the same in the men you date. God won't be able to open the right door for you if you are too busy with the wrong doors. You need to raise your level of amazement with yourself and let go of your insecurity.

You are a great catch for any man so wait for the right one and walk away from all others. WE have put you in a higher class. It's up to you to live it. We expect great things for you and you should too.

Since we are all parts of each other, it is also our wish you focus on yourself more. The endless drama with Jace has been draining you. You've been clear about your rules for him and you're doing well at holding to your decisions so concentrate less on Jace and more on your own spirit. Focus on being the strong Mom, not the good Mom. Jace's stuff will resolve itself; it's past the teaching stage.

Finally, we truly feel that wonderful surprises are around the corner for you. There is something special on the horizon for you, your passion for life is amazing. Only God knows your path, of course, but there is obviously preparation needed before he can move you forward or you would already be there. Be careful not to get side tracked by the weaknesses in your life. Thrive on the strengths. We all love you and support you. xoxo

Tracy, Lindsey & Lane

Stunned at hearing their letter, I was speechless. My friends saw a woman I had never seen. When I looked in the mirror I saw an insignificant, disposable outcast. But these women painted such a different picture. They saw my struggle with self-worth, how I accepted mediocrity, gave up and gave in to what fell in my path. For the first time in my life I saw how my self-perception trapped me in a broken, vicious cycle I believed was my destiny. Memories, fear, and resignation clutched me with an unrelenting death-grip.

Like the words of William Arthur Ward, my friends knew my weaknesses, but showed me my strengths. They felt my fears, but fortified my faith. They saw my anxieties, but freed my spirit and recognized my disabilities, but emphasized my possibilities. I didn't meet Allie until some time later, when we ended up in the same small group, but the timing was impeccable.

Allie was direct. If you didn't want to hear it like it was, you better not broach a subject. She possessed incredible insight, never hesitating to tell me the truth, even when I was pretty sure I didn't want to hear it, which is a gift everyone needs from time to time. Her blunt advice sometimes stung, but invariably she nailed the situation expressing exactly what I needed to hear, and usually what I already knew but managed to rationalize. Allie's frank attitude was purely altruistic, and her unique talent for stating the obvious forced me to peer into a virtual mirror.

William Ward described the essence of my friends as if they were his role models. Inspirational, motherly, wild and spirited, honestly direct or merely supportive and caring, my friends kept me grounded and profoundly influenced my life.

Nash awakened my aspirations and encouraged me to focus on the future. He helped me see my dreams and showed me I could realize them if I let go of my past. My old high school friend opened my eyes to see a woman I thought fragmented over the year and my new girlfriends continued my metamorphosis. Tracy, Lindsey, Lane and Allie were major players in my life, not just passersby. They showed me my significance, an image rarely seen through my own eyes, and only when I performed a noteworthy deed. I learned that who I am--who we all are--is not performance-based, but rather a state of being and that woman was good, strong, and able to reach for the stars.

Tracy guided me to realize my self-worth and inspired me to discover my passion. Lane helped me see I should never settle for anything less than what I truly want and to strive for the best. We are all worthy, but we have to believe to achieve. When the world pulled the rug out from beneath my feet, Lindsay caught me with a net of encouragement and always provided a kind word or a shoulder to cry on.

Allie wouldn't let me get away with feeling sorry for myself and in doing so, forced me to accept the reality of negative situations, so I could learn to get beyond them. Her mirror reflection showed me the truth when I wasted time and energy wallowing in self-pity and negative emotion. Moving forward requires completely letting go of the past. Allie broadened my horizons and I now look at both sides of whatever life casts my way.

Four women supported, motivated me to discover the woman inside. They taught me to believe in myself, showed me the inner strength and spirit I misplaced--not lost--somewhere in my childhood. True friends, they weren't always uplifting, but they encouraged and compassionately prodded me when I pulled back into my shell attempting to shut out the world.

****

We had fun. For a long time I forgot about fun. But now I hiked, went to festivals, barbecues, movies and parties, boating, horseback riding, biking, camping, and escaped the world for long weekends and vacations. In short, I found out there really was life after 40 and it wasn't centered on bending my life to fit everyone else's — or a revolving door of insincere of men.

The fire crackled, embers faded as the coolness of the wintry night air brought me back to the present. I placed my laptop back on the table next to my tattered journal and took a last sip of wine. My life no longer needed to be defined by a man, centered upon my young children, or jaded by my perception. I wondered how many people mindlessly meander through life accepting mediocrity and couldn't help but feel we were kindred spirits.

Friendships need nurturing, but each time I was hurt, I became more-and-more isolated and allowed fewer and fewer close enough to be part of my life. I was lucky though. I stumbled upon wonderful friends who refused to let me crash and burn. I've learned love is the essence of life, and good friends enrich and fortify the journey.

I recognized, albeit to my surprise and initial indignation, I lived the exact life I chose. It wasn't what I desired, but if I truly wanted to change the course of my life, I needed to take responsibility to change. No thing or person could magically make me happy. The choices were mine alone, and it was up to me to discover my own destiny. As long as I accepted mediocrity, that was precisely what I would get.

Wow, after what I lived through, I could write a book. I glanced at my old, worn journal and thought of how cathartic my writing was. "Hmm, I wonder..." I whispered softly. Silent embers lost their glow as I headed for bed.

Chapter 17

Whether you believe you can, or whether you believe you can't, you're absolutely right.
— Henry Ford

As the refrigerator door opened, a large bowl that was balancing on the edge of the shelf cascaded through my hands and fell to the floor. Baked beans splattered everywhere. The fridge, over-stuffed with preparations for the 4th of July festivities, demonstrated capacity with a vengeance. Rushed to prepare for my party, the last thing I needed was a major cleanup. I hated being late for anything, but hours vanished when my thoughts slid into the pages of my mind. Writing's secret solitude flew me to distant shores isolated from time.

Immersed in just that, the morning flew by. My journal evolved into a manuscript now, beckoning me with every heartbeat, even when I slept. Ideas or past events crept into my dreams and captivated me. For months I kept a notepad and pen on my nightstand, but finally realized a small tape recorder proved far more efficient to capture fleeting sleep-drenched thoughts or memories. Sometimes images danced in my mind so intensely the lure of my muse dragged me from the warmth of my bed tap on my keyboard, absorbed in writing, unaware night dissolved into daylight.

This morning my thoughts awakened me long before sunrise to capture mystic memories. Frustrated, I searched for the right words to encapsulate my brainchild. The ringing phone jolted me back to the present and the panicked realization my guests would arrive within the hour. In frenzy, I placed my dilemma on the back burner and rushed to the kitchen.

I cleaned up the bean disaster, still focused on the nagging question lingering in the back of my mind. Why do some people collapse in the face of adversity while others conquer problems and emerge with renewed resolve? As I pulled my ring off to wash my hands, it slipped from my fingers, and rolled across the floor under the fridge. Annoyed, I bent down on hands and knees to search for my treasured possession.

Neck strained with my cheek to the floor, I scanned the dusty darkness and noticed a piece of paper covered in filth, wedged between pipes and metal. I pulled the sheet from its hiding place and tossed it toward the trash, but the word "Attitude" caught my eye as the paper floated down to land atop broken glass and beans. I reached for the page again, brushed off a scrap of food and read further. A tsunami chill washed over me as I realized the relevance of the words on that worn scrap of paper:

Attitude

"The longer I live, the more I realize the impact of attitude on life. Attitude, to me, is more important than facts.

It is more important than the past, than education, than money, than circumstances, than failures, than success, than what other people think or say or do. It is more important than appearance, giftedness, or skill. It will make or break a company ...a church...a home.

The remarkable thing is we have a choice every day regarding the attitude we will embrace for that day. We cannot change our past...we cannot change the fact that people will act in a certain way. We cannot change the inevitable. The only thing we can do is play on the one string we have, and that is our attitude...

I am convinced that life is 10% what happens to me and 90% how I react to it. And so it is with you...we are in charge of our Attitudes.
                CHARLES SWINDOLL

The serendipity of a dusty piece of paper, yellowed with age, which years before slipped from worn tape and fallen to rest under my refrigerator, felt like more than coincidence. I can't confirm divine intervention. Perhaps dumb luck, but something conspired to break through my haze with the answer I needed. "Coincidences" influencing my manuscript continually amazed me. I couldn't help but wonder what I might have accomplished had I protected my own childhood hopes and dreams from jaded pessimism. I wanted to make a difference in the world, but how? Where would my passion lead me? I tucked the mysterious paper under my laptop and went back to my preparations.

It wasn't often I hosted a family gathering. I wanted today to be special so everyone, especially Daddy, would make wonderful memories. The party went off without a hitch, a fun get-together of family and friends culminating in a beautiful display of fireworks. Dad hugged me as he left, shaking his head,

"I always said, where there is a will, there's Casi." It wasn't the original quote, but invariably accurate.

By the time I cleaned up the dishes it was almost midnight. I walked into the family room to turn off the lights and thought about what Dad said. I did have a knack for finding ways to make things work. I might not have exact knowledge or ability to tackle a problem the best possible way, but I usually found an efficient method to get a job done. Still wide-awake and charged by the day's festivities, I felt the lure of my manuscript beckon again, so I sat down at my computer and drifted back in time.

Journal entry, summer 2004:
Dad was right, my Pollyanna outlook found ways to make things happen. It was part of who I was at my core. Zack's attitude gravitated toward the other end of the spectrum. When he confronted an obstacle or problem, his initial response broke in anger, followed shortly thereafter by resignation. When I asked him why he didn't at least try, he always responded the same way, "I wouldn't know what to do..."

I have found that attitude isn't anything--it's everything...

****

When I knew Zack and I were headed toward divorce, I sheltered my sons from the graphic details of our broken vows, but I never lied to them. If they asked direct questions, I told them an innocuous version of the truth, and tried to protect them from the barrage of unsolicited opinions that were bound to surface. Zack may have been an incompatible match for me and even a distant father at times, but he loved his children and despite his angry outbursts, they loved him as well. I didn't want them to hear any disparagement about him from me.

Resolved to find the direction my life lost, my focus shifted toward not repeating past mistakes. I continued to immerse myself in positive surroundings, read self-help books and articles, and looked toward the future, even when my warped gut instincts screamed at me to tuck my tail and run. Fear and failure weren't options, because mine wasn't the only life that hung in the balance. To break the cycle, empower my children with weapons to battle obstacles, I needed to be a role model to show them that despite pitfalls that grip your soul and twist your future, life can be better on the other side.

Angst plagued me for years influencing decisions I made, and changed the course of my life. I wanted my boys to be happy, healthy, determined men, independent and strong willed like their mother. They would chart their own direction, make their own mistakes, but I prayed they could learn from pain to move on and become confident adults who could handle the challenges life was sure to hurl their way. Their destiny depended upon their strength of heart.

Watching your children make toxic decisions that could dramatically affect their lives rips your soul. Josh and Jace, in their late teens now, insisted on testing waters and pushing boundaries like most teenagers. When they were small, I could pick them up, kiss the boo-boo and wipe their tears away, then watch them run off and play again, as if nothing happened. Broken hearts and dreams are not so easily repaired and, as much as I tried, my role was no longer to protect them, but rather to support and encourage them. They grew into intelligent, compassionate, creative and incredible young men, and I entrusted a greater power than mine to guide their way. Besides, my own life needed my focus now.

Work went well for me, so well my clients persuaded me to go into business for myself. The decision wasn't easy by any stretch of the imagination. I did well working for someone else and I had no idea how to start a new business of my own.

The thought of relying totally on my own knowledge and creativity to survive felt formidable and more than a little scary. My apprehension fortified by years of fear etched into my psyche made change difficult, especially at the thought of dismissing the security of a timely paycheck, but my work situation was becoming increasingly uncomfortable.

Change was not only inevitable it was imminent. With the support of clientele I developed on my own, I decided to take a chance at entrepreneurship, but I knew the task required spreading paralyzed wings—wings I wasn't sure I even had.

Not interested in competing with my mentor, I created my own niche in the industry by providing a unique spin on design services. The well-received idea generated enough initial income to pay my bills while instilling a sense of accomplishment foreign to me.

Zack, on the other hand, seemed to be spinning in the opposite direction. He gave up his managerial position to return to the company he worked for when we first moved to Atlanta, a sales representative again, this time working under a management team most of whom were once his peers. Tired of office politics and climbing the corporate ladder, he longed for a simpler way of life.

When Zack was a young boy, he was cute, charming, and smart. Academically, he made straight A's, but he was also popular, dynamic and a star athlete. It seemed like everything he touched turned to gold.

Throughout his youth he strove for a successful career in baseball, but his injury destroyed that dream. He missed the camaraderie and fun, but most of all, he missed the limelight he dominated, and as that light faded, the spark in his life fizzled too. He turned to sales to fulfill his need for competition and became an excellent salesman, but the job didn't satisfy the high he got from the spotlight. He learned to manipulate his circumstances to compensate. He charmed the skin off a snake and was at his best on stage at seminars or large-scale demonstrations, but he craved more.

I could see how much he missed playing baseball and tried to encourage him to at least look for a job in the sports industry. Maybe he couldn't be a famous baseball player in his forties, but he could find a way to stay involved in the industry, perhaps broadcasting games, or starting a baseball school to coach young athletes.

He purchased season tickets to the Braves games and watched baseball on TV for hours, calling the plays before the announcers uttered a sound. He knew the game inside out.

"You're a great salesperson," I said trying to encourage him. "Just knock on Ted Turner's door and sell yourself. The worst thing that could happen is Ted will say, no." I begged him to just take a chance.

"I wouldn't know where to start or what to do, Casi." It was always his pat answer. I think his repeated resignation and compliance to whatever fate threw at him slowly destroyed his passion for life. Zack gave up on himself years earlier, and nothing I said or suggested helped him find his passion again.

****

My husband never did follow his dreams. He didn't risk losing his safety net in sales. Instead, he searched to fill the emptiness in his heart in other ways--ways that led to the destruction of our marriage and negatively affected other areas of his life as well.

I've come to believe that emotions drive our thoughts and behavior. Happiness isn't a future event we have to wait for. It is a choice, a state of mind created by attitude. Zack couldn't see that, but I prayed my children would.

I closed my manuscript file and turned off the computer, but not my thoughts. To me, the only real failure is in not trying at all. I looked for options and at least found some kind of answers, while Zack simply gave up and said he didn't know what to do. I remembered so many times I said to my husband,

"If you took that attitude as an infant, you never would have walked. I mean think about it, Zack. Everyone begins life with incredible innate determination. Toddlers want to learn to walk and they keep trying no matter how many times they fall down in the process."

Children begin their lives with amazing conviction, confident that if they try, they will eventually succeed. What happens to that determination, as we grow older? Why do tragedies wear people down and define their destiny?

For me, following my dreams required faith. Sometimes I just clenched my teeth, closed my eyes and jumped in with both feet, pretty much what I did with my business. I wasn't sure what I was doing, but it didn't take long to learn, baptism by fire. I faked it at first and picked it up along the way.

The distant sound of fireworks lingered, illuminating the night sky. Independence Day filled me with a sense of pride. I slipped between soft, clean sheets, my mind still deep in thought. Necessity is the mother of invention. The early Americans did what they needed to do to survive. Maybe we are not so unlike our ancestors. Many people still do that today, create whatever they think is necessary to survive, but I truly believe life can be so much better than mere existence.

I spent so many years going through motions, settling for whatever came my way. Now, I wanted and needed more, like true love, passion, happiness, purpose and pride. I believed in myself, followed my heart and I knew the rest would take care of itself. The first step though was figuring out what I really wanted. I hadn't thought about that since my childhood fantasies. Fireworks rolled softly in the distance relaxing me as I drifted off in search of my dreams...

Chapter 18

*The first step in getting the things you want out of life is this:
Decide what you want.*
Ben Stein

Gardenias. The subtle scent floated through my slightly open windows. Eyes still closed, I stretched and breathed in deeply, filling my lungs, my body with the soothing, delicate aroma enveloping me. I loved to awaken to a crisp spring morning surrounded by fresh smells, brightness and colors, the ambiance of spring and new beginnings.

I threw the covers off and basked in the chill of the morning invigorated by the fresh, new day. Anticipation of a hot latte lured me into the kitchen. Saturday, today I would reinvent myself. "Today is the first day of the rest of my life," I said aloud as if talking to the hiss of the steaming milk. Okay, it sounds a little cliché, but fitting for Pollyanna, and it was time to put my talents to use. I wasted too much life bending my days around everyone else, fitting their mold of who they thought I should be. The decision to figure out my own dreams and the resolve to change my life was a new and promising milestone. I now believed I could find happiness, excitement and passion. The possibilities of that revelation invigorated me.

I poured fresh brewed latte into my cup, grabbed the newspaper and drifted toward the screened porch. Scanning the pages of the morning news, the word *dream* caught my eye and I read further:

U.S. Air Force Col. Rick Husband's childhood dream was to become an astronaut. He said the early human space flight program, Mercury, Gemini and Apollo, made an impression on him. "Watching the Moon landings and everything," he said.

"It was just so incredibly adventurous and exciting to me that I just thought, there is no doubt in my mind that's what I want to do when I grow up." The Amarillo, Texas, native was born in 1957. Growing up in West Texas he developed an interest in flying. *"I'd be out in my backyard playing,"* he said, *"and, any time I heard any kind of an airplane, you know, it's like, you stop what you're doing and take a look to see, 'Where's that airplane? What kind is it? Where is it going? How high is it? How fast is it going?'"*

While at Texas Tech, he sent a letter to NASA asking about requirements to become an astronaut. *"I got a package back, and it told about the pilots and the mission specialists and the requirements that were necessary,"* he said. *"And so, that kind of laid the pathway for what I needed to do if I wanted to be a pilot-astronaut."*

After applying four times and being interviewed twice, NASA selected Husband as an astronaut candidate and he reported to Johnson Space Center in Houston, Texas, in March 1995.

"And so, it was the achievement of a lifelong dream and a goal," he said. *"And, it's very humbling, I'd say, and exciting at the same time to be able to actually go and do the kind of thing that I'd wanted to do and the thing that I had looked forward to doing for such a long time."*

I looked up, distracted by the sound of two squirrels bantering in the back yard. Could life be that simple? Rick Husband, only four years old when he dreamed of becoming an astronaut. He followed his heart, his dreams, with a lifetime more fully lived than most people ever dare. Maybe figuring out what I wanted in life was as simple as remembering my youthful dreams. Writing already changed me. I thought about my childhood, moments that touched my passion and embraced my soul, times I felt so alive.

Tossing the paper aside I strolled back into the house toward my computer. Zack lost more than his dreams of playing professional baseball and I wasn't sure he would ever recover. I didn't want Josh or Jace to fall into that pit.

I wanted my boys to reach for the stars and their own dreams. Children learn what they live, by example—for my kids that example was me. I pulled up my manuscript and the next entry almost wrote itself.

Journal entry, spring 2005:
The turn of the century brought incredible change to my family. By spring of 2002, Zack resigned to my insistence that splitting up was not a mistake. He finally came to terms with my feelings and understood my future couldn't include him in any capacity beyond that of a friend and the father of our boys, despite his continual attempts to persuade me to the contrary.

I knew my destiny held far more promise than the struggles of my past. After several years of separation on August 8, 2003 our divorce finalized. Zack and I were far past romance by that time of course, but we shared two wonderful children and our love for them maintained the importance of an honest, close relationship.

The next month, Josh would head to college, Jace would enter his sophomore year in high school and Zack conceded to have hip replacement surgery to repair deterioration caused by the injuries from his athletic past.

The operation and recovery was difficult under any circumstances, but the rehab center displaced his new hip, forcing him to undergo a second operation within forty-eight hours of the first. The extensive recovery presented a tremendous struggle for him, and our family, but despite divorce, I stood right by Zack's side through his trauma and recovery...

Goals are rarely easy to attain, but it helps to focus on where you're heading, not the rearview mirror...

****

As autumn approached, Josh prepared for his first year in college. He earned a basketball scholarship and eagerly began a new chapter in his life. Jace returned to high school and I my new career, which required a lot of time.

But Zack's recuperative care demanded far more attention than we anticipated. He thought hiring a nurse to come in daily to help him for a few months would make life easier on everyone; the boys and I reluctantly agreed.

Kari's nursing skills apparently impressed Zack because he felt quite comfortable relying on her from day one so we all began to settle into our respective lives. My life embarked on a whole new era. Nash's computer chat messages dwindled to occasional emails inquiring about my achievements, and my church friends and various singles groups inspired a new sense of self that excited me. From the outside I presented a confident, self-assured façade, but inside I remained insecure and desperate for people to accept and see me as worthy, intelligent and competent. I had forty plus years of habitual programming and needed to erase the self-image etched in my soul.

It was hard to believe Josh started college, his first step toward manhood. It seemed like a blink ago I first brought him home from the hospital. I mentally scanned the pages of memories. When he first started playing basketball we were convinced the game was *not* his sport. Josh loved swimming, even as an infant he rolled and twisted with glee, smiling a huge underwater grin. At four he insisted on joining a swim team and by thirteen, he had earned countless ribbons, trophies and awards in the sport, some on a national level.

His coaches primed him for the Olympics, but the pressure of daybreak practices, dry-land workouts and daily evening swims stole the delight from his pastime. He wanted to have time to be a kid, try his hand at other sports. His new interest in drama surprised me, but when he added basketball he quit swimming all together.

Basketball captivated him, and his lung capacity from swimming provided endless energy on the court, but his first recreational game affirmed his prowess remained in a pool. As his doting mom, I watched between my fingers, hands shielding me from the view. He repeatedly tripped over his own feet. But Josh's tenacity endured.

His diligent swimming background instilled a persevering drive in him unmatched by most youths. Every day he ran for miles then returned home and spent hours shooting baskets. I felt sad for him on tryout day. Over nine hundred students entering his freshman class, including every member of the previously undefeated eighth grade basketball team, lined up for judgment. The fierce competition didn't dissuade my son, though. Josh's tenacity stood strong and when try-out results posted, my oldest son made the team. Josh's secure self-image gave him a strong sense of self, what he wanted and how to attain his goals. His drive and belief in himself inspired me.

Jace's experience as a youth yielded a quite different image, as if he lived merely in Josh's shadows. Both boys excelled in sports but regardless of what Jace did well Josh always performed a little better--not through talent, but rather age. Zack spent the vast majority of his time with his older son, rarely missing a swim meet, ball game or competition. In some sports, Jace possessed more God given ability, but Josh's three-year advantage captured his father's attention. True, at any given moment-in-time, Josh maintained a natural three-year lead over his younger brother. Jace's sensitivity perceived his father's lack of attention as self-inadequacy. Vanishing into Josh's shadows, my younger son felt rejected and his self-image dwindled.

I loved watching Josh's competitions and attended whenever I could, but my past made me acutely aware of Jace's mindset, and I attempted to fill in as his father's replacement. When Zack coached Josh's baseball team, I signed up for Jace's team coach and, in doing so, set a trend. I support Jace in everything he attempted, swimming, baseball, basketball, soccer and karate. I know he was happy I was there, but no matter how hard I tried, I couldn't replace his dad. Even Josh could see Zack's attentions focused on him and not his little brother.

As time went on, a distance wedged between Jace and his father; the larger the shard grew, the further Jace's self-image deteriorated. My younger son loved baseball and excelled with exceptional talent. He handled a bat beautifully, pitched curve balls, sliders, and fastballs beyond those in his age group, played a mean third-baseman and, as catcher, he popped out of a squat and threw to second tagging endless steals. But to him, regardless of his performance, he failed to catch his father's adoration.

A dwindling sense of importance, coupled with ADHD, created lack of confidence and Jace gave up on everything, including himself. One test away from a black belt in karate Jace quit. He stopped playing baseball and ultimately gave up sports altogether. Instead, he drifted toward guitar and music; something Josh didn't show interest in learning.

Jace began to hang out with a different group of people and, like a typical teen, his whole life wrapped around high school friends. At sixteen and independent, he grew increasingly disrespectful and belligerent, following in Kathleen's footsteps. Brie's youngest daughter, who was only a few years older than him, smoked, drank alcohol and experimented with drugs.

At seventeen Jace dropped out of high school. Terrified my son was heading down a dangerous path, I suggested counseling, but he would have no part of it. He lacked drive for anything except partying.

Jace lived recklessly on the edge and at times I feared for his life, but despite lack of self-worth he still maintained a close connection with me. As he matured, he realized dropping out of school remained the biggest mistake of his life, but the idea of going back to finish high school daunted him. He felt like a loser, and his reactive behavior only worsened his self-image. His life veered into an abyss and I felt helpless to change his path.

My friends lectured me for putting up with his destructive lifestyle.

"You coddle him, Casi." They honestly tried to help. "You just have to set down your rules. Stick to your guns and follow through."

Not an easy task when you are dealing with a 6'3" teenage boy who feels like his friends are his only family. Mom takes a back seat. And when I tried to be firm, Jace's rage took over.

My smart, quick-witted, and extremely articulate son knew my hot buttons. He nailed exactly the right words to sting then took off out the door and down the street.

"Just use tough-love Casi." My friends advised. "If he doesn't listen and follow your rules, kick him out of the house and force him to hit rock bottom. If you don't let him fail, his future--or lack of one--will be on your shoulders."

I know my friends meant well, but most of them didn't even have children and the ones who did, didn't have Jace. It's true his lifestyle wore me down and affected my health and social life as well, but I couldn't just sit back and watch him slip through the cracks, or throw him to the streets. He hurt inside and refused counseling. How can you save your child when he doesn't even realize he needs saving?

Millennium was the first step, but implementing the ideas I learned proved a formidable challenge. Jace was smart, smarter than me, but I couldn't turn my back on my child. Determined to come up with a way to help my son help himself, I explored every angle.

My dad worried about Jace too. We brainstormed to find a solution, until finally Dad hit on an ingenious idea.

"What if we use some of your mother's trust money to buy a house near by? Real estate is a good investment. We convince Jace you are managing the house for the uh—owner? It's not so far fetched, Casi. You're in that field already."

The simplicity and brilliance of Dad's idea didn't surprise me. Though I wasn't in the habit of lying to my children, Dad explained that Jace had to feel responsibility for something that was not rooted in family.

If my son knew we owned the property, he would see a safety net and would be lackadaisical about paying rent and keeping the property in good condition. The success of Jace's future depended upon his belief that he was truly on his own. At the same time, I felt secure about a roof over my son's head; he wouldn't be stung out on the streets. And I could help if he fell flat on his face.

Jace jumped at the chance to move into the house, excited to get out on his own, and found some roommates right away. With the sanity and silence restored to my home, my life improved immeasurably. I missed my son, but the drama subsided, thank God, and Jace's sense of independence and self-worth began to renew. The plan worked like a charm. After only a few short months on his own, Jace already realized the importance of a good night's sleep before work and apologized profusely for having kept me awake into the wee hours for the past several years.

****

The dark knight's taint didn't merely infect my mother; it seeped through her soul and implanted deep within my heart at conception, haunting me throughout my life. As hard as I struggled to protect my children, the venom leached through me into my boys. The wounds of the past have a way of passing down from generation to generation--could we ever break free? Daddy gave Jace an amazing gift. He helped him stand on his own and believe in himself. I realized I desperately needed to do that for myself.

Jace learned to balance his income and expenses. He found paying the heating bill usually held more importance than nightly beer parties, and that gas for his car and food in his stomach far outweighed a weekend trip to the beach. Acutely aware all roommates were not created equal, he chose friends more carefully.

In short, my exceedingly intelligent child began to see the real world, and over time realized living on a low income, dead-end job budget sucked. He wanted to make something of his life, to have a real future, but like his mom, decisions loomed regarding what that future looked like and how to get through his self-destructive patterns to find his destiny.

Life throws curve balls and, despite my children's hopes and dreams, grim reality often dictates our path. Josh's focused determination secured his self-image, which Zack reinforced with constant attention. Josh knew exactly what he wanted. He might get temporarily side tracked, but no doubt he would eventually reach his goals. He followed open doors wherever they led regardless of roadblocks along the way.

Jace was more like me, tough on the outside, but insecure on the inside. Our work cut out for us, finding self-assurance to look past hurtles dumped in our laps challenged us. Both Jace and I needed to continually stir our passion and rely on the insights we uncovered. With the right direction revealed, belief we could walk that path needed to come from within. Only with confidence could we dare to live our dreams.

I've always felt everyone was born to a divine calling. Each person held significance, with value and purpose, but it's easy to get lost along the way. Beginning my journal created a defining moment in my life. My dreams, the answers I yearned for, were always looming in front of me, within my reach if not my grasp. I just needed to discern what questions to ask.

Chapter 19

How much more grievous are the consequences of anger than the causes of it.
Marcus Aurelius

The subtle ebb and flow of the tepid waves caressed my body in surges as his strong hand lifted me closer into a passionate embrace. Consumed by lust and surf, my head tilted backwards in anticipation and desire. Soft lips pressed against my cheek then continued their journey down my neck and shoulders, stopping only briefly to nuzzle between strands of salt-water drenched hair. His naked body thrust against mine and our burning passion exploded in a frenzy of heated urgency enhanced further by the ocean's rhythm. I gasped for breath, desperate to hold on to fleeting ecstasy.

My mind in a haze, I struggled to a seated position and threw the covers off my sweating body. These dreams tormented me, but at the same time released pent up lust locked inside of me for far too long and I longed for their return. Craving the touch of a man, the pressure of his body next to mine, the scent and taste of masculinity seethed through my entire body. I yearned for arms around me, holding me at night as I drifted off to sleep and ached for love—for sex and passion. God, I lived so much of my life without the intimacy of a man, reading melodramatic romance novels instead. I hungered for the lust and tenderness tempting me within the pages.

"Pathetic," I whispered.

It wasn't like I didn't have opportunities to establish relationships, or have sex for that matter, but I self-destructed, sabotaged every personal connection I entered. A plethora of reasons flashed before me, but the common denominator was me.

Sometimes my choices were just plain toxic, but even when I managed to stumble upon a great guy, I found a way to derail the train. By forty, my baggage could fill an airport terminal.

I realized honest communication held the key, but sometimes pasts just collide, like Jack's with mine. I sucked in a deep breath and clenched my eyes tightly as I envisioned him. I could almost smell the musky sweat dripping from his bulging muscles after a workout. Strong yet gentle, Jack's touch sent desire writhing through my limbs, but like me his past gripped his soul. As I reached for my laptop, his aura flooded my memories.

Journal entry summer 2005:
Jack's sincerity impressed me the moment we met. His personality combined little-boy innocence, compassion, and honesty with articulate integrity only seen in a person whose education included hard life-lessons as well as book learning. I couldn't help but be drawn in by his noble virtue. His handsome, muscular stature only enhanced his charming first impression. After so many years, I forgot how amazing romance felt but Jack's attention roused my appetite. I felt desirable again. He sparked a physical reaction in me I thought withered and died years before, and I basked in the fervor. I knew he wanted me too...

My relationship with Jack spawned a remarkable transformation in me. But after seven years of banter, I finally understood the dynamics of love and anger could never coexist together...

****

"You are my fantasy, Casi." He grabbed my hands and looked straight into my eyes with innocent honesty. "You're the image of a soul mate I've dreamed of since I was twelve years old."

Jack was falling in love with me and for the first time I could remember, I felt valuable, he showed me a kind of love I never experienced. The chemistry between us exhilarated me--especially having come from a marriage completely devoid of touch for far too many years--but I knew chemistry played only one card. A good relationship required a full deck.

At first, Jack displayed compassion, with an ear to listen, or advice to offer support when I faltered. Ten years younger than me, our age difference didn't faze him. We hiked, biked, went dancing, and he even got me to join a gym where I actually worked out under his supervision. Talking flowed easily too, but true to my past patterns, I felt the need to protect my heart.

In a sense, I was starting over, beginning a new life. I loved my newfound independence and needed to stretch my wings. At times I acted like a teenager and, in a way, I guess I was, like a young girl waking up to a world she never knew existed. I wanted to socialize, meet people, make new friends and, for the first time ever, live my life without relying on anyone else. I hesitated settling down, but one trip to Asheville, North Carolina, dissolved my shaky determination and Jack became a part of my life.

Over one weekend, we talked about our pasts and he opened his soul sharing a sad story of his childhood. Like me, Jack's childhood damaged him. His parents loved him deeply, so deeply he became an obsession to his mother and paired with a series of devastating events, Jack's life cocooned into isolation.

"When I was little, tons of friends surrounded me and I was always happy." He continued as he sat down on an old wooden swing in the backyard of our bed-and-breakfast. "But when my parents sent me to a private school, my life fell apart. My eyesight weakened, but I hated glasses. I was the "new kid" in school and wanted to fit in, but my thick-rimmed glasses made me look like a nerd."

He pushed the swing back with his feet and set it in motion. "It was difficult to make new friends. They nodded or smiled but not seeing their friendly gestures, I walked right by. Everyone thought I was unfriendly, a loner, and that's exactly what I became. The solitude consumed me and at one point, I even quit speaking for months. Isolation filled me with resentment and rage."

The compassion I felt when I heard his story drew me closer to him and our injured, kindred souls connected, but after a few months of dating, the depth of his damage surfaced and cut me at my deepest level.

Once Jack felt comfortable in a relationship, he relaxed his guard. On the surface that sounds like a good thing, but whenever he felt overwhelmed or frustrated, an inner rage seething just below the surface exploded. His rage took over and the resulting dynamics between our broken pasts collided.

Jack hated the overbearing control he felt from his mom and the devastating affect her obsession released on his parents' relationship. His mother completely overshadowed his submissive father and Jack feared he'd somehow evolve into his dad.

As a defense, he subconsciously sabotaged every relationship he entered, by projecting his mother on the women he loved. His defensiveness caused fights, an excuse to keep women at a distance, hiding the real issue: fear of commitment, to truly love, no holds barred. Of course, overshadowing Jack never entered my mind. I had no desire to control anyone, least of all him. In fact, I still expected my white knight to rescue and take care of me.

But to be fair, my baggage created just as many problems. I learned at an early age to never get attached to anyone because eventually, they all walked out of my life. Disguised as Pollyanna, I bent my life around the needs of people I cared about, hoping I could compensate, but at the same time terrified they'd abandon me.

When my biological father deserted us, abandonment issues stifled me as if he ripped away my fragile wings. Like a *wingless butterfly*, I staggered through life, unable to fly.

Jack mourned the loss of his youth, the time he could never regain, and grieved for what should have been; completely blind to the man he was. He reminded me of Eyore, the lonely, depressed little donkey from Winnie-the-Pooh who always saw the negative side of life. Jack wanted me, as his mom, to "fix things" and the broken child within me felt compelled to try—but failed. I needed my knight, to put me first and take care of me. A knight slays dragons, protects and defends, he puts his princess on a pedestal.

Virtually everyone has an inherent need to be accepted, valued and loved. When someone's tank registers empty, ideally a partner fills it up, but regardless of how I tried to help Jack, my efforts always backfired. We both needed the same thing from each other but, ironically, neither of us could fulfill the other's requisite.

As long as life streamed easily, Jack and I felt blissful. Our relationship flowed with passion and fun, but inevitable daily pressures preyed on Jack's low frustration threshold, sparking rage. When that happened, he no longer saw me. Instead he cast me in the role of his mom, the focus of indignation and resentment. His anger exploded and pierced the core of my own pain.

Jack's rage seethed for most of his life. In high school he strove for perfection. Salutatorian of his class, he saw second place as a failure which triggered disappointment, anger and self-hate. His fury, though rooted in childhood, still tormented and controlled him twenty-five years later, even in business.

"I hate my damn job." He slammed his hand on the car horn and leaned on it, taking his anger out on an innocent driver whom he felt cut him off. "Davidson is a moron incapable of listening to suggestions. I have to sit back and take orders from people who don't have a clue what they're doing, and my hands are tied." Baffled at how to help Jack I still felt compelled to try.

"Find a better job situation, Jack." I tried to comfort him. "Just be patient and keep looking. Please, don't let your boss get to you. Don't give him that power."

"I thought you'd understand and support me, but all you do is patronize me. You should be mad now, right along with me. Instead you tell me I shouldn't get upset. You're just like my mother."

I got that Jack wanted me to get angry with him, not try to calm him down, but my past caused me to cringe at anger. My broken child wanted to help. Jack was smart and talented, but in his eyes he wasn't successful and that fueled his fury. I tried desperately to come up with suggestions.

"You could go into business for yourself." I laughed and tried to lighten his tension. "Hey, if I can do it, anyone can. You're great at what you do. Maybe you could be a consultant?"

"I hate what I'm doing. I never liked accounting. It's what my mother wanted me to do, not what I wanted. I wish I had become a builder ...or taught school. I'm great with kids and now I'll probably never even have any of my own."

Making decisions based on other people felt all too familiar to me, but a distinct jab from his comment about never having kids ripped through my heart. My children were young adults now, well, almost, and that phase of my life was over. I was just beginning to focus on who I was and I had no desire to start another family. If Jack stayed in a relationship with me, he would have no children.

"Besides, I can't just start over, Casi. I'm too old to do that." We pulled into my driveway and walked inside the house. "Why do you always think things can be so easy? That's not the way life is."

"You have so many contacts in your field and if you don't like working under people, then a consultant could be the answer. You would at least be your own boss."

Jack did become a consultant, loved his business and eventually quit his job, but he wanted more. One day he was at my house complaining about where he thought he should be in life. Again I tried to come up with answers, anything to help.

"You're great with money and finance, and you have tons of other skills. Think about something you'd love to do and then, just go after it." I scrambled for something to get him off his pitiful-me roller coaster ride. Glancing down at the mail on the table, I noticed a flier. "Hey, there's an investing seminar here this weekend. Do you want to go? Maybe you'll get some ideas." The idea sounded great when I said the words, but that little flier evolved into the nemesis of our entire relationship.

We went to the seminar and the speaker hooked Jack. While I took a bathroom break, he purchased the entire program. It was easy for Jack to absorb new material and he studied the method in depth. Inspired to flip foreclosed homes, he urged me to go into business with him. My business contacts provided the perfect source for cosmetic improvements on houses so the premise seemed like a good fit.

Jack wanted to change his life, but his broken perspective prevented him from changing anything more than his clothes. Instead, he kept me in the "Mom" role, demanding I manage contracts, negotiations and secretarial minutiae, while he basked in the sun at the pool. It's not that I didn't want to do whatever I could to help. Pollyanna would have done anything to make him happy, but I knew nothing about contract negations, and math intimidated me. Besides, my own business soared, requiring my full attention, which left me little time to learn a completely new business.

If that wasn't enough to drive a wedge between us, no problem, there was more. My dad hooked me into attending stock classes with him, so when the foreclosure venture that Jack and I attempted failed miserably, Jack expressed interest in the stock market as well.

He decided to learn with me. Both students, novices, just beginning to trade using our own savings, the timing of our venture couldn't have been worse. Our first "real money" trade hit right about the time the economy crashed, and we both lost money—a lot of money. Jack wagered more than me, ultimately losing more, but proportionally, we sank in the same boat. People say misery loves company, but Jack didn't. His rage seethed directly at me.

"It's your fault." His dead serious, bellowing scream shook the walls. "Why did I ever let you talk me into investing, Casi? Because of you I flushed my entire savings. I'll never recover from this."

"I talked you into stock investing? Dear God, I could never talk you into anything, Jack."

"You introduced me to all of it." He snapped back, a sneer of fury plastered to his face. "If it wasn't for you, I never would have thought about real estate or investing. I would have never gotten involved in any of it. You destroyed my entire future."

"Jack, you are the one who bought the real estate program without even telling me, and I didn't ask you to learn about the stock market or make any of your trades. The market crash caught everyone off guard, even seasoned investors. I lost money too, but I would never think of blaming you."

"You didn't lose as much as I did, and your crazy idea to go listen to the real estate seminar got me sucked into that."

"So how does my idea to go to a seminar make it my fault you purchased the program?" I defended, myself as best I could. "I wasn't even there when you bought the thing and getting involved with stock investing was entirely your decision. You wanted to learn with me. Damn, you know so much more about money than I do. Your career is in finance. I know nothing, but you—"

"I'll never forgive you Casi, for making me lose my savings." ...and he never did. In his mind, everything he lost was all on me. His resentment festered, slowly decaying our relationship. He continued to look at the negative side of life instead of embracing the positive. I had to escape that mentality and attitude. No matter how much I tried to open his eyes, Eyore couldn't see the Tigger side of life.

I prayed he would open his eyes and cherish the **now** he had. Attitude is everything. But Jack was lost, adrift in a smothering fog of memories that blocked his view of the future. When he felt rage, warranted or not, I got the brunt of his fury. And each time he exploded, my battered self-image tattered again until I felt the pull of old habits and feelings I couldn't bear.

Jack and I experienced a natural allure toward each other, like magnets drawn together by an inner pull. But despite chemistry and deep affection, our pasts continued to collide. Jack's greatest fear reflected his fear of ending up like his dad, and I knew from my life with Zack, anger and resentment couldn't be a part of my life again. Jack and I existed torn between a past and a future that splintered our ever elusive now.

Time is fickle and disguises truth. Our relationship morphed into a distorted, addictive dependency. Jack was solidly in my life and my childhood traumas kept him there. We broke up, and dated other people, but the thought of losing our connection fueled our innermost fears, his isolation and my abandonment.

For years, we held on to each other with the notion we would, over time evolve healed and whole, and come full circle to renew what we once had. He didn't move forward with other relationships because he knew he would lose me—and he was right. Tracy once told me people come into our lives for a reason, a season or a lifetime. There were several reasons for Jack and I to have shared a connection.

I learned a lot from him and he from me. Most significantly, I helped him start a business he loved, and encouraged him through years of self-growth. I inspired Jack to change eating habits and focus on his health. As a result, he enjoyed far better health for the weightlifting he loved.

Jack taught me patience and sharpened my ability to see things through the eyes of others. He helped me discover the importance of physical fitness, which I incorporated into my life. I set goals, even ran a few 5K races. I came in seventh in my age category in one of them--and yes, there were a lot more than seven women entered. The point wasn't that I win or even place, but rather that I ran the race and finished, and Jack supported me.

Oddly enough though, I learned even more in trying to help Jack than I learned from him. I discovered everyone is affected by his or her own unique past. And no one should live with displaced rage no matter what the source. I couldn't help Jack heal his damage, healing comes from within. And when his anger deteriorated my self-image, we couldn't avoid the collision course our pasts created.

Still, knowing him shed a beautiful light on my future. Now, acutely aware that jobs, experiences, or people around me don't define me, I shifted the mirror away from the men in my life. Aunt Ginny nailed the premise years earlier when she told me who I was had little to do with my past or my relationships. Instead of dwelling in memories, I now looked at each day as a new chance, a new beginning.

****

For years, souls entwined, Jack and I moved forward enmeshed. We supported each other, became more than friends, but stayed less than lovers. We put each other before others in our lives and slowly healed while we waited from a slight distance for the moment we could try again, a moment we knew would never come...

Closing my laptop I thought of my past relationships. My inner strength gave me courage to escape my destructive situation with Zack. I made choices to change the course of my life, despite my fears. I believe making a choice is like treating a headache. If my head hurts, I take an aspirin. It may taste bad or be difficult to swallow, but it provides relief and I function more productively. It's a simple idea to grasp, but hadn't been an easy one to implement.

Divorcing Zack was an aspirin for my life. Walking away from Jack would be another one. Jack and I both needed a lifeline to help us heal. We grew through each other. He helped me see the world through different eyes and discover things aren't always black or white. Compassion and tolerance for others would be key ingredients to my own happiness. Jack was not my soul mate, but the aura between us was as addictive as a drug.

In the book A New Earth, Eckhart Tolle wrote: "There is a way out of suffering and into peace ...Someone who in childhood was abused, neglected or abandoned by one or both parents will likely develop a pain-body that becomes triggered in any situation that resonates even remotely with their primordial pain of abandonment ...her pain body becomes easily activated in any close relationship with a man ...(and she) may feel a magnetic pull to someone who it senses will give her more of the same pain. That pain is sometimes misinterpreted as falling in love."

Tolle's words hit the core of my soul and I wondered if his description was the root of the connection between Jack and me. Like magnets drawn together, our like-poles repelled and our inner torment pushed us apart. But we couldn't walk away from each other; the magnetic pull was too strong. Over the course of seven years we danced around the issues, fooled ourselves on several occasions and dated other people in between, but in the end, we needed to heal ourselves, choose a direction of our own individual and separate destinies.

I laid my laptop on the bedside table and wiped at the back of my neck, still damp from my lustful dream. The night sky dissolved into a soft glow of daybreak. Breathing deeply as if to capture the new day, I slipped from my bed and headed toward the sink to splash water on my face. For too many years I created a vacuum where closeness couldn't be sustained. Jack opened my heart and now I craved warmth, and the passion of love and intimacy. My repeating dreams supplied ample evidence of my strong desire to feel love, and to love someone. I would find passion with the right man. It was time to take another aspirin—let go, and move on.

Chapter 20

Never allow someone to be your priority, while you are merely his or her option.
Unknown

I struggled to open my eyes but a drug-induced fog paralyzed me. Whispers drifted around me in slow motion as my mind slipped in and out of a half-dazed coma, my body tingling with surreal numbness. It wasn't until I heard Josh's voice call me that I struggled to find consciousness.

Finally aware of my surroundings, I grabbed my chest, yanking an IV attached to my wrist along with the apparatus at the end of the tubes. The nurse grappled with my arm and held it still before the equipment crashed to the floor. Wrapped in bandages cinching my torso, I wriggled to loosen confinement, but a sharp stabbing pain took my breath away.

Surgery terrified me. Add in a doctor splitting and rearranging my chest, my emotionally charged consciousness writhed. I opened my eyes a slit to see Josh, Jace, and Daddy gazing down at me.

"See Mom, surgery wasn't that bad. It didn't hurt me a bit." Jace joked and I forced a smile, but pain made finding humor in my son's wit difficult.

Typical to form, Josh handed me a note pad. "Here, you're better at writing anyway, Mom." He chuckled. Josh was right from day one about my writing. My craft became my salvation.

The boys left with their grandfather to eat lunch, leaving me with my thoughts and aching body. It would be a few hours before the doctor would release me to go home. Recuperation of about a week lay ahead, but I could already tell the surgery lightened my load.

Despite excruciating back problems, the accessibility of clothing that fit, and the apparent inability for anyone to meet me with their eyes focused on my face, the decision to undergo breast reduction surgery didn't come easily. But, at 5'7" and 123 pounds, my small frame struggled to support my size 34-G breasts. I'd considered reduction for years, but when my doctor discussed problems I'd face without the surgery, and my insurance company agreed to pay for the procedure, my choice seemed a no-brainer.

The hardest obstacles I faced in life evolved from fear. Apprehension strapped me to toxic relationships and anxiety nailed the coffin, preventing me from accomplishing anything outside my comfort zone. If I wanted to find happiness, I needed to rip the seal from my self-imposed fate.

Life by definition is continual change. For better or worse, there was no way of avoiding natural progression. But regardless of what life brought, I still could make choices. I didn't have to be a victim.

It may sound simple, but realizing I had options, that my choices--or lack thereof--created my life, changed everything. I guess I missed that memo sometime in my youth. Now, my relationships evolved and my friendships thrived. Enter, Mark, a man who helped me understand how my own patterns drove my relationships.

Journal entry, January 2006:

Mark hated drama. He didn't sweep me off my feet like the white knight of my dreams, but his endearing qualities sparked a flame for me nonetheless. Intelligent, successful and a great father, he turned my head with how he abhorred conflict. Still, yin and yang occur to balance life and when Mark completely sidestepped confrontation, he detached communication as well.

After a marriage with Zack and a mess with Jack, meeting someone who took great pains to avoid heated situations enticed me. Mark evoked a sense of calm in my storm.

He liked cooking and stuck to a fairly nutritious diet. Preparing dinners with him, exploring ethnic foods, and creating different taste sensations added spice to my humdrum routine and I found I loved a variety of international cuisine. Mark appreciated antiques, and loved to spend hours driving aimlessly over obscure countryside roads looking for quaint shops and off the track auctions. He opened my eyes to a plethora of new horizons. Mark presented down time for me, an eye in an ever-twisting cyclone of my life that paused the tempest long enough for me discover changes I craved...

Like Dorothy in the Wizard of Oz, I spun to another world before I discovered there's no place like home...

****

Mark swept into my life in February of 2005. His unfaithful wife bruised his ego. I never considered women betraying men before, but Mark's marriage revealed a stark reality and I felt a kindred spirit.

From day one, I sensed Mark's attraction to me. Roving hands and attempts to embrace me reflected his desire and intent, but I found myself unintentionally pushing him away. I wanted to date, but possessed little desire for a committed relationship, let alone marriage. For me, those lurked only in distant dreams. As much as I treasured the idea of love, I refused to dive in quickly, fearing only regrets would reside in my happily ever after.

Mark, on the other hand, loved being married and despite his divorce, saw matrimony as his goal. In truth, I think the idea of marriage held stability for him, but ready for marriage--not so much. I didn't sense his desire to create a new life with me. Mark loved his life. He simply wanted someone to fit into the empty spaces.

A vivid red flag waved feverishly in my face when he blew off events of major importance to me, to work on his car, run errands, or tend to the whims of his children—not important issues, but whims like taking his daughter shopping for make-up or watching a high school baseball practice with his son. Mark's own agenda continually took precedence over important happenings in my life. I never felt like a priority to him. I merely fit into his present need for an emotional and physical companion, the image of what he wanted his next wife to look like.

I admit a relationship with anyone at that point didn't tempt me. Mark was a sweet, good man, but I yearned for a spark, passion, and fulfillment. To move forward with Mark would mean giving up on ever finding that missing something. For a while I simply needed to be me, independent of anyone else, to figure out who I was and why I made such colossal mistakes in the past. I didn't trust myself and I didn't want to commit to a relationship, let alone a future with anyone, at least until I worked through my own issues. Mark didn't like that. He controlled his objectives and I wasn't cooperating.

When he told me he loved me, he wanted to move forward. His goals firmly in his sites, his persistence didn't wane—until he did.

Mark didn't deal well with his own drama, but mine he saw as complete chaos. He tried to persuade me to walk away from what he deemed theatrics.

"You're always wound up in some kind of melodrama." His cavalier attitude frustrated me and I rolled my eyes like a teenager annoyed by my dad's lecture. "The easiest way out is to just walk away, Casi."

"You don't understand." I blurted out keeping in character. "It's not like I create the issues. Brie and I need to find answers about our biological *father* and the boys are still teenagers. And I'm their mom."

The truth is there was other turmoil in my life as well. Divorce hit Jace like a bat to his head. He never felt close to Zack in the first place and now the distance made a relationship with Zack more difficult than ever, so unlike Mark's straight-A, all-star children, Jace experienced trouble in school and life in general. He needed focus and parental attention, attention Mark wanted and didn't want to share.

My new business became a hurdle too, with financial commitments and client obligations, which also took my focus and time away from whomever I dated. Mark considered my response aloof and his premise caused him to walk out of my life more times than I can count. When the spotlight turned elsewhere, he simply stopped talking to me, sometimes for several months at a time. Mark consistently made decisions affecting both of us and acted upon them without ever discussing the situation with me. The problem festered until his pot bubbled over...damn, he never even let me know there *was* a problem.

One Friday evening, he asked me to come to his house for dinner. After a long drive returning from a business trip, he kissed me and ran upstairs for a quick shower, and asked me to start dinner. Before I set the table, I cleared some papers, picked up his phone and wallet and placed everything on the kitchen counter. But moving his phone sparked a thought, I sent him a sweet text earlier that day, but he never replied. Mark complained about his phone turning off without his knowledge, so on innocent impulse, I checked to make sure he received my text. He did...the missive I sent survived cyberspace, but a barrage of other messages overshadowed my note. As I flipped the phone closed, the images processed and I hesitantly reopened the phone to verify the cause of the knot in my stomach: at least ten texts to and from his ex-girlfriend, Victoria.

I glared at the conversation trying to tame the not-again river stinging my skin as it tumbled over jagged shards of I-should-have-known.

Despite my past, the thought of snooping never occurred to me. With Mark's constant advances and talk of marriage, I never dreamed he would carry on with someone else while trying to convince me to move forward. Of course my Pollyanna innocence never expected any man to cheat. I guess that's why they caught me off guard. Still, regardless of past betrayals, I firmly believe trust is the foundation for love and one can't exist without the other. I wished I could un-see the damning evidence, but the messages etched into my mind.

"It was wonderful seeing you this week, Vicky. You excited me the first day, just sitting across the table from me..."
"...I'm lying here in bed and I can't stop thinking of you next to me. I can still smell you beside me..."
"...Victoria, you are the sexiest woman in the world."

My heart hurt. Damn, why did I continually get involved with insincere men? Mark said he loved me, wanted to marry me...but he kept his options open. Could I blame him? Our relationship didn't move as fast as he wanted, but why didn't he talk to me about the issues instead of making a decision that affected me without my input?

Like the laundry list of men before him, Mark's stoic reaction when confronted spoke volumes.

"I don't know what you want me to say, Casi."

No apology, no fumbling for fabricated excuses, not even resentful indignation. He simply turned and disappeared into the next room. I walked out to my car and Mark made no attempt to come after me.

It was almost six months before I heard from him again. When he called me he never mentioned Victoria. His modus operandi regarding confrontation held firm. He acted matter-of-fact.

"Our relationship wasn't going anywhere, so I made a choice. But that's in the past. Can we keep it there? How about dinner tonight?"

Mark's aversion to anger repelled the polar opposite of Jack's compulsion. He never talked about emotion, especially the past. Instead, he bailed. As far as he was concerned when something was over, dredging up unpleasant memories would dredge up the worst in a relationship. I guess he figured six months gave me enough time to get past his indiscretion.

His sabbaticals triggered my old fears. When Mark made up his mind to walk out he offered no explanation or warning. He just suddenly stopped calls or communication for weeks or months at a time. He invariably struck up a rapport with some woman on the sidelines to fit into his life, leaving me feeling completely disposable—my deepest fear. But oddly, after the dust settled, I regained a slight sense of relief. I can only assume my reaction provided a momentary solace, a reason to crawl back into a familiar shell for a while, to lick my wounds.

Lesson learned, when a relationship hits a speed bump, as they all inevitably do, I don't see cutting losses and running as a viable option. In my humble opinion, love should be treasured like the finest diamond, never compromised for sexual pleasure or momentary boost to one's esteem. Mark fell into the arms of another woman whom he hoped would move faster into his plan, but he only slipped further away. Finally a realization: when I made decisions based in fear, I put my life on hold and allowed others to control my future.

That discovery held merit. Unfortunately, I started avoiding decisions altogether. In hindsight, I'm convinced Mark's avoidance of confrontation sabotaged his previous relationships too. Unable or at least unwilling to communicate his emotions or listen to his partner's put the brakes on what he wanted to escalate. He said talking about emotions made him feel *squirrelly* so he walked away from uncomfortable situations. A few months later when he returned, he expected to pick up where he left off, no harm, no foul, but dodging a bullet didn't solve the problem. Instead a wedge shot into the foundation.

I believe love requires patience and trust, neither of which, were my strong suites, but the bond also takes honesty, communication, and self-restraint. Temptations lurk everywhere, but if you're lucky enough to find someone who fits your dreams, you need to have enough strength of character to walk away from enticement. Mark said he loved me, but when things didn't go according to his blueprint, he replaced the defective puzzle piece. Love or need, you be the judge.

His patterns didn't change and though his many wonderful attributes enticed me, I decided to break the on again/off again pattern. A coward's way out, typical of Pollyanna, I picked a fight and let him walk away, convinced this time I wouldn't go back. I let go of another safety net and dove into free-fall, praying I would be strong enough to catch myself.

****

The ability to handle difficult situations is an essential survival tool. I believe working through inevitable bumps helps couples thrive. When you love someone you share your lives, the good, bad and ugly, and his or her happiness is essential to your own. Mark was a good man, and he taught me a valuable lesson: never allow someone to be a priority in your life when you are only an option in his.

The pen slipped from my hand and rolled off the hospital bed. I closed the notepad, but my thoughts lingered. I spent most of my life bending over backwards, trying to change *myself* to make things *work* in my relationships, the same pattern I repeated with family and friends. My twisted childhood belief that it was my responsibility to make everyone else happy morphed into distorted relationships.

I finally realized I am responsible only for my own happiness. As my friends so accurately pointed out to me, I lived the exact life I wanted—not what I desired on a conscious level, but my choices and patterns put me in impossible situations. I let life happen to me; let people choose me, instead of choosing a relationship or direction myself. As the good Wizard of Oz reminded Dorothy, the power was always within me.

Jack opened my heart and Mark helped me realize I never wanted to settle for less than exactly the perfect relationship for me. Not a perfect man, that obviously doesn't exist, but someone who fits perfectly with me, who loves and respects me and shares the same philosophy in life as I do. Maybe if I merged the best qualities of Jack and Mark into one man, I might see the elusive *right* man for me. At the time, I needed to pull away from both of them. They provided safety nets. It terrified me to think of letting go and flying on my own, but that was the only way to find what my heart truly desired.

The damage Matthew Stafford inflicted made it difficult to see clearly the distinction between truly loving someone, and my need to be loved, but Jack and Mark helped me learn the difference between those two concepts, giving me clarity regarding my future and the relationships I chose to enter. Two people have to fit together, beyond lust and physical attraction, although that was definitely an important qualification too. I realized the uncertainty and confusion about my *birth father* catapulted me into the arms of whoever offered words of love, usually insincere men.

Like the pieces in a puzzle, thoughts, goals, ideals and interests interlink with attraction, communication, trust and honesty. I'd prayed I find that connection with one special man someday, but in the meantime I planned to laugh, learn and find my own way. For the first time, my future truly wasn't dependent upon someone else and I knew the revolving door of insincere men would eventually disappear from my life forever.

Chapter 21

Secrets are made to be found out in time.
Charles Sanford

    I dropped the phone and stood for a moment in a daze of disbelief, regained my composure and dialed the number again. Surely I was mistaken. No way. The recorded message played again and I listened intently, praying I was wrong, but there was no mistake.

    I threw the door open, marched into the back yard and collapsed onto the thick grass carpet. The sky, a deep azure blue accented with puffs of white cotton-candy clouds drifted above. I stared at the vast beauty that somehow put my dismay in perspective. Secrets and lies continued to plague my life. I was so tired of drama I could scream, and couldn't understand why a theatrical production reeled endlessly in my life. Stop the merry-go-round--I want off.

    A beautiful, blue butterfly flitted around me before landing on my bent knee. I watched its wings move ever so slightly, deep blue intricately edged in white. A sense of calmness washed over me. The analogy between my own life and that of a butterfly radiated with significance. Though fragile, a butterfly has unparalleled inner strength. The insect never knows its parents and is a stranger to affection, thus representing loneliness and a constant struggle to survive. Yet despite their solitary existence, butterflies transform within their cocoon and emerge again, reborn as strong, free, beautiful creatures.

Like a butterfly I went through a metamorphosis of mind, body and soul. There was no turning back, and I wouldn't want to even if I could. I liked who and where I was in my life and yearned for the mystery my future held. Determined not to relive the dregs of my dysfunctional past, I drew in a deep, cleansing breath.

Zack kept secrets from me throughout our marriage and, even now, he continued to lie when the truth was easier. I dragged myself inside drawn to the lure of my dusty manuscript.

Journal entry, July 2007:
I had no control over the decisions other people made, or the secrets and lies they chose to impose on me, but I could control my own thoughts and reactions. The secrets that were kept from me were set in place to protect me, but instead they created a domino affect that snowballed against me in a downward spiral, redefining my life...

Painful truths eventually surface, but sometimes they can take more than 50 years...

****

"Oh my gosh, Casi, you look amazing." Brie plopped on the bed and watched as I put on a touch of makeup. "It's not fair. It's like you are growing younger instead of older, and it's not just your appearance. You act more like you used to in high school. I lost my little sister for decades, but you're back, the passionate girl I remember growing up with me is here again, and I'm so glad."

Ecstatic at seeing her baby sister recapture youthful passion, Brie shared some of her own past. Like me, her relationships caused heartbreak throughout her life. Her first husband's abuse and infidelity resulted in a difficult divorce, but numerous other turbulent relationships haunted her as well. We compared our insecurities and toxic romances. Traumas wore her down, but she survived by walking away from her dreams and throwing herself into projects and hobbies.

Her husband Steve was a good man, faithful and kind with the patience of Job. He and Brie were best friends, but I always perceived a good marriage would have to include passion and romance. I never saw that between Brie and her husband. Still, I had to admit their marriage worked for them and I guess that's the important thing.

Over time, Zack and I lost all intimacy. We didn't even share the same bed toward the end, but we managed to stay friends. Maybe Brie had the right idea, but I felt such a strong yearning inside to find the love of my life and though friendship played a part of that connection my desire for passion and intimacy remained too strong to dismiss.

It was easy to see Brie missed something in her life. She went through motions, spinning from hobby to hobby in search of satisfaction to nourish her sense of self, but never settled on anything for very long. We both felt emptiness deep inside that sucked passion from our lives, a missing puzzle piece that needed to fit snugly into our souls to fill a hollow hole.

Brie's silent stare halted my train of thought.

"There's a reason for the blank spaces in our childhood memories." She grabbed the bottle of nail polish sitting on my bedside table and began to polish her toenails while she spoke. "When we find Matthew, he'll help us figure everything out. I wouldn't have pushed this issue when Mother was alive, but she's gone now, Casi. It won't hurt her, and Daddy doesn't even have to know. I hope we discover something soon. I can't continue living in this fog wondering what really happened. Don't you want to know the truth too?"

Since mother's death, Brie's memory shot her hazy images, bits and pieces about our *father,* and she dug in her heels about finding him. I promised Mom years earlier I'd drop the search and, despite her death, I still felt obligated to keep my word.

But Brie's relentless insistence made sense, if for no other reasons than our medical history, finding our father played a part in our future. Still, I wasn't sure how I felt about this elusive man.

"Brie, Mom kept us in the dark for a reason." I stopped my primping and sat down on the bed next to her. "What if there's something really BIG tied to our past? Clearly she felt the need to protect us. Aunt Ginny said Matthew raped Mom when I was conceived. What if we find him and learn he's dangerous? And why hasn't he tried to find us? We just might open up old wounds that could threaten our family?"

My feeble attempt to play devil's advocate wasn't working. Brie continued pleading.

"I told you, Casi, we don't even need to contact him. We can just investigate his life." She put the cap back on the polish and admired her bright, pink toenails. "My breakthrough memories are not of a violent man. He's smiling and happy in all of them. That sentiment conflicts with everything we've learned so far. I've got to know the truth."

The truth enticed me too. For months Brie and I investigated leads hoping to discover more about Matthew. Searching the Internet, reading microfiche and putting together a paternal family tree was time consuming and we consistently ran into dead ends. Knowing our *father's* name and that our maternal grandparents lived in Decatur, Illinois was key, but our birth records didn't reflect what we knew to be true.

There wasn't any question that Daddy adopted my sister and me, but when I applied for a passport, they required copies of my birth certificate to process and the father listed on the document listed Daddy, not Matthew Stafford. Brie experienced the same results. Our birth records were altered.

We turned our focus to newspapers and after an extensive search of Mother's maiden name, we pulled up the obits of our maternal and paternal grandparents, but there was another obituary we found that blew us away. There in black and white was the obituary of one Michael Andrew Stafford. Born on December 18, 1950, to Matthew and Laura Stafford and died December 28, 1950. Michael Andrew Stafford was—our brother. My mother gave birth to three children with her first husband, not two. A brother I never knew existed died a year before my birth. The drama of my life continued to unfold.

****

I've heard that everyone lies. Some are little white lies told to protect people from unnecessary, hurtful comments or opinions. But bolder, premeditated lies are created to hide actions and cover selfish desires. We rationalize them away; justify lies that hide secrets under the guise of self-preservation, but secrets have a way of coming out over time. Some just take longer than others.

As the story of my life unfolded, secrets unraveled too. Drama held me tightly in its grasp with a stranglehold and I was desperate to free myself. My mother kept her past secrets to protect Brie and me from pain. Zack lied to protect his family too, but I have found that secrets don't protect...they erode and destroy.

My cell phone rang drawing me back to the present. One more lie slapped me right in the face and I didn't know how to deal with the collateral damage. Reaching for the cell, I couldn't help but wonder if anyone really benefits from lies, especially lies told to protect them.

Chapter 22

A leopard doesn't change it spots.
Unknown

"You have to lie. I'll call you back on speaker and you have to say you made up everything you said." I sensed desperation in Zack's voice and suddenly realized how he led his life over the last 20 plus years. Only now, the shoe slipped on the other foot. I morphed into the other woman—except I wasn't. His new wife lived in darkness in the shadows of Zack's lies. How ironic. Did she know? I wondered if the irony even occurred to her and I couldn't help but savor the moment—I'm only human. She overheard us talking on the phone and Zack frantically scrambled to cover our conversation. The scenario warmed my heart just a bit, but at the same time, I felt sad for both of them.

Zack believed his wife went shopping and wouldn't be home for hours. Why he put the phone on speaker remains a mystery, but when she unexpectedly walked in his office and confronted him, he promptly hung up on me. I knew immediately she heard at least a portion of our conversation.

Though Zack and I divorced years earlier, he insisted he still loved me. He continually baited me by professing he wanted me back. I knew his declaration held little if any truth, he still felt guilty and didn't want me to feel hurt over the way our lives played out, and I let him continue the bravado. Unfortunately, that was the topic of conversation his wife inadvertently heard me laughing about when she walked into his office.

Journal entry, January 2008:
Zack and the truth were an oxymoron and if by chance the truth ever came out, he would have probably broken out in a rash. I will never forget the day I made a grim discovery...

July 17, 2007, was one of the most significant dates in my transformation. It was the day I discovered Zack's ultimate betrayal...

****

It had been seven years since Zack and I ventured into our separate lives and despite the fact he developed a relationship with his nurse, Kari, he was diligent in his pursuit to win me back. Even after she moved in with him he swore his devotion to me and said he would "burn in hell" for what he did to me and the boys. Zack adamantly promised he would come back in a heartbeat if I would have him, which I knew was his warped way of protecting my feelings, the way he had always *protected* me in the past--with lies.

The truth is my life blossomed since our divorce and I felt satisfied with the way our lives evolved. Our relationship was better than ever. The refreshing honesty meant we could finally talk with each other about almost anything. We were good friends and on top of that we shared two incredible children together.

Zack thought I would be the first of the two of us to marry, but the appreciation he felt toward his nurse apparently developed into something more significant. For months he coaxed and teased me, "Are you sure you won't change your mind? Marry me again, Casi.

"Ha, I'm positive, Zack," I assured him. "I'm happy the way things are. We get along so well, better than we have since we were dating, and I like what we have together. I'm not going to change my mind. Why do you keep probing me?"

"I don't know, I guess I just want to make sure, you're okay."

I didn't understand his concern at the time, but not long after our conversation, the situation became vividly clear. On March 4, 2006, on an impulse according to Zack, he and nurse Kari stole away and got married. According to Zack, the bond was an unceremonious union performed at the local courthouse. The boys weren't invited to the wedding and I wasn't even informed until a few weeks later. Zack said he married Kari because she was having health problems and needed insurance coverage, but my X was never forthright about any relationship and I doubted the validity of his explanation. In truth, he didn't need one, but I couldn't help but feel he was hiding something, perhaps he just didn't want me to feel replaced.

It was strange to think of Zack married to someone else. We were connected for over twenty years and though our romantic interest faded completely, his presence soothed me like a comfortable old chair you don't want to throw out.

After his marriage we stayed close, but he kept Kari at a distance, oddly claiming I intimidated her. She seemed pleasant enough and I acted cordial on the few occasions we crossed paths, but Zack's life turned down a new path and I had no interest in making waves between Kari and him. I truly wanted him to forgive himself and be happy, at least I did until I stumbled upon the biggest lie he ever told me.

Five years after his initial hip surgery, Zack contracted a Staphylococcus/Streptococcus infection that progressed throughout his body, ultimately settling into his prosthetic hip. The doctors appeared bewildered about the initial trigger of the illness and couldn't diagnose the infection for weeks.

By the time they discovered the contamination, his prosthetic hip needed replacement and his condition was listed as gravely ill. His life seemed touch and go for some time. The boys were terrified their dad was dying, so I naturally became quite involved with his trauma.

He required two hip revision surgeries over a three-month period with constant antibiotics during the interim to kill the resistant bacteria. It was July 17, 2007, during the second surgery that I made an unexpected discovery. I stayed in the family waiting room at the hospital with Kari throughout Zack's seven-hour surgery. When they moved him into recovery, I decided to run home to update the boys on the details of the surgery. Kari gave me her cell number in case of an emergency.

A few hours later, I called to ask her if she needed me to bring anything when I returned with Josh and Jace. There was no answer, but her voice mail picked up and I heard a simple message:

"Hi, this is *Cheri*. You've reached my voice mail. Leave me a message and I'll call you back."

I dropped the phone, frozen in a confused daze. Surely I had heard the message incorrectly. A few moments later I regained my composure and slowly pressed the numbers again, expecting to validate my mistake. The message couldn't have said Cheri. Her voice repeated and there was no mistake. Stunned, I repeated the premise aloud.

"Zack's wife was *Cheri* not Kari. He married the woman with whom he had an ongoing affair throughout our entire marriage."

Zack lied to me—again--the grand Tsunami of lies. I shook my head in disbelief then slammed out to the back yard in a tizzy. Was there some innate instinct in this man that caused him to lie when the truth was much easier? Maybe some people are just incapable of honesty. His lies made no sense, especially now. We developed such a great friendship with our children as a foundation.

The boys and I returned to the hospital and I kept my emotions under wraps, never saying a word about my unintentional discovery. I stopped myself from glaring at Cheri, but my mind raced with memories of our past encounters. I never understood how anyone could sustain a fifteen-year relationship with a married man. What could possibly drive them to continue when the outcome appeared so obvious? Zack would never leave his family. But I guess the joke was on me after all. Her persistence paid off. *Cheri* ended up with *my* husband.

The next time I called, her voice mail played a re-recorded message leaving out her name entirely. Zack caught her mistake and knew his elaborate secret would be out unless she changed the message immediately.

I waited until Zack recovered before I confronted him with my discovery.

"Why Zack, why did you lie about Cheri? The truth was easier."

"What are you talking about, Casi? Where did you get the idea that Kari was Cheri? Why would I do that?"

"Good question. I've asked myself the same question repeatedly. Don't try to weasel out of this, Zack. I know the truth. I heard her voice message, more than once. You're busted. Just admit it, please, for once in your life, just be honest."

Zack paused and, realizing he was cornered, tentatively spoke.

"It wasn't *really* a lie. Cheri's real name is Kari Cherise, so technically I didn't lie."

"Please Zack, don't pull that crap. Manipulating the truth is a lie. Just like all the other lies. You manipulated the truth and our lives for the past twenty years. Isn't that enough?"

"I just couldn't bring myself to tell you. I couldn't hurt you or the boys again."

"God, don't you think the idea of hurting us could have come before you made the initial lie? It's a little late to think about hurting us now. I mean the damage was done a long time ago. I thought we were so far past that. I truly believed we found an honest ground where we could coexist. We were friends, but now..."

"I lied to *protect* you, Casi. I never wanted to hurt you again. I hate myself for what I did to you and the boys. I will never forgive myself and I deserve whatever happens to me, but I didn't try to hurt you."

"So you created this extravagant lie. Did you really think we would never find out? I mean how can you even think you could pull off something of that magnitude? I can't believe Cheri would agree to something so absurd." I paused for a second and then admitted, "On second thought, maybe I do. She certainly participated in a fifteen-year long affair behind my back. God, I feel like such an idiot."

"I'm sorry, Casi, please believe that, and don't blame Cheri for any of this. She begged me to tell you and I wouldn't listen to her."

"You just don't get it Zack. Maybe you never did. I feel betrayed all over again, and disposable. You threw away our relationship, again."

I should have realized it would be hard for Zack to admit what he did, even to himself. Over time I saw so many pictures of them together throughout the course of the past twenty-one years. They'd been together since shortly after Jace's birth. Pictures of them wrapped in each other's arms, happy and laughing at parties and on vacations, all of which were taken while he was married to me and supposedly off on business trips.

God, when I think of how much I missed him, how the children wanted and needed their daddy while he chose to wine, dine, and bed his mistress, I felt ill. The money he spent on her left little to the imagination why we struggled financially and even fell into bankruptcy at one point.

Even worse, Zack's pictures showed Wes, the best man in *our* wedding, and Sharon, his wife, in the background. Wes, who coerced me into meeting his best friend Zack, who he insisted was "the most honest man he ever knew." Wes and Sharon knew about Zack and Cheri from the beginning, another stab in the back from my so-called friends. I guess they were just *better* friends of Zack's, but the truth is if they were truly his friends, they would have made sure I found out years ago. When would all the lies and deception in my life end?

I trusted Wes and called to cry on his shoulder so many times over the years to ask his advice and lean on him for support. One time I was in a panic because I thought I was pregnant again and with Zack's erratic behavior, I wasn't sure whether to be happy or terrified. Damn, Wes comforted me and promised Zack's actions were merely pressures of his job, and he would be elated to have another child.

I leaned on Wes so many times while he covered for my husband. Now, I felt like a clueless fool when I thought of the times Wes told me Zack loved me with all of his heart, insisting Zack simply needed to "work through some issues." Perhaps Wes felt that to be true.

The most difficult admission to myself came from seeing how happy Zack looked in those pictures, while my children and I lived in silent torment. The final lie ripped through me. According to Zack, Cheri wanted him to tell me the truth about her identity from the beginning. Damn, I'll bet she did. What better way to shove it to me after all those years? He and his mistress destroyed our marriage, and the poison leached into our friendship as well. Explaining might have been painful, but the novelty of truth would have gone a long way toward healing my raw wounds.

****

Zack protected the people he loved with lies. He was a master manipulator. It was the only way he could handle his choices, but I truly believe he felt he kept us from pain. He wasn't a malicious man. I just couldn't figure out what drove him to be a pathological liar.

I grieved a moment, for what was lost — for my children and for myself, but my future, not my past held my destiny. I wouldn't hold on to or wallow in old pain.

They say time heals all wounds, but I'm convinced time doesn't heal; it just helps us to forget so we can move on. Time opened a new door for me. I wanted to walk through, let go of the past and move on.

Zack panicked to protect his new marriage to Cheri and I had no intentions of disrupting his life, but I have to admit I found a soothing sense of satisfaction knowing that when Cheri overheard us talking on the phone, she experienced a minuscule touch of the pain she caused in my life for 25 years. Karma is hell.

Still, Zack was the father of my children and that bond would always tie us together. Cheri became a part of my children's lives, so it made no sense to hold on to animosity. True to form, I felt compassion for her. She was a victim of Zack's fabricated world as well. A world he created for his own self-preservation. Truth be told, I really liked her. Under any other circumstances, we might have been good friends. Who knows, maybe someday we still could be.

I walked away from Zack that day and vowed to take out of his hands the opportunity to ever hurt me again, but a part of me felt a strange sadness for him. His patterns remained firmly intact.

He continued to manipulate the truth, even though there was no longer a need to do so. Letting go of my past brought me an increasing sense of peace, fulfillment and happiness. I couldn't help but wish that Zack could find that too. Cheri, though never a nurse, truly loved him. If only he could let go of his obsessive need, he just might discover what his life needed for so many years. Maybe Cheri could help him do that someday.

Chapter 23

Awful events can sometimes lead to a wonderful future.
Casi McLean

The desolate, black terrain stretched as far as I could see. In the distance, the outline of grayish-brown trees connected land to sky, but there weren't any leaves, no green, red or gold colors of the familiar panorama of north Georgia. The eerie absence of pigment induced a surreal aura that engulfed me, evoking a feeling of isolation from the world. The endless flat asphalt road disappeared into the horizon, luring me forward with hypnotic beckoning.

Thank God the rental car included a satellite radio. Familiar seventies music tamed the silence and soothed me within a more reassuring environment cocooned between the locked car doors. The hotel clerk insisted the trip from Chicago to Decatur would take only forty-five minutes to an hour, but my GPS didn't lie. One p.m. central time and I still wasn't there. Two hours into the drive, alone on a deserted highway in the middle of nowhere, I began to question my rationale for embarking on this trip.

Betsy and Alicia's excitement prompted my decision. My mind drifted back to my first conversation with the two women, and the events that lead to that initial chat. I turned down the radio, grabbed my I-Phone and touched the record button. I couldn't write in my journal or computer while I was driving, but I could record my thoughts and type them later. Setting the phone on my lap, I searched my memories.

Journal entry, March 2008:
I couldn't stop wondering what transpired between my mother and Matthew. Perhaps the death of their son caused too much grief for their marriage to survive. I was more intrigued than ever to discover the truth.

Obituaries of my paternal grandparents supplied the first break in our search. Brie and I found microfiche copies from a local Decatur newspaper and discovered our father, Matthew Stafford, grew up with one brother and three sisters.

According to the article, his brother John, several years older than he, died of a massive heart attack years earlier. As of the death of our paternal grandmother, Matthew's sister, Leann, lived in Arizona, and two other sisters, Elizabeth and Alicia still lived in Decatur, Illinois. My father lived in Dallas, Texas...

Knowledge can open up new worlds. The question is, will the aliens be friendly...

****

I reached for the phone book to pull up the area code for Decatur, Illinois, picked up the receiver and dialed information. My heart pounding in my throat made swallowing difficult as I anticipated what might transpire.

I wanted to know more about my *father*, but at the same time a part of me dreaded what *more* might be. Aunt Ginny's warning, "Be careful what you wish for" rang in my ears in unison with the phone. A cordial operator searched for a few seconds then gave me a number. Brie scrambled for a pen as I reached for my notepad.

Moments later I stared down at the number written on the scrap of paper I held tightly in my hand. The scribbles on the page had the potential to change my life. It wasn't the phone number of my *father* of course, but if he were still alive, his sister would know where he was.

Brie grabbed the phone and stretched her arm toward me. "You call, Casi," she insisted pushing the receiver in my direction. I reached hesitantly to take her offering.

"Are you sure you want to do this?" I questioned not really expecting Brie to answer. I glanced at her one more time with a scrunched face and raised eyebrows before I began to enter the number, then took a deep breath and continued, faltering briefly before entering the last digit. The phone rang repeatedly with no answer and no voice mail picked up for messages either. I couldn't decide if I felt relieved or disappointed.

"It was probably a bogus number anyway." I muttered to my sister. "Life just isn't that easy." We held little stock in the possibility that Matthew's sister never married or that she still lived in Decatur after all these years, and Stafford was a fairly common name. I placed the number in our files and we turned our attention to other more viable sources. Our first thought turned to Dallas. We called to see if our *father* still lived in the area, but we hit a dead end there too.

It took months before we were able to track down another significant lead. Finally, I discovered a website created by a group of volunteers in Texas who aided adopted children in their search for biological parents. The law prevented them from providing birth or death certificates, but they were able to search the social security index.

I'll never forget the day I got an email from Patricia, a volunteer sympathetic to our cause. She searched everything at her disposal to help us. Her message read:

According to the index, your father was born September 13, 1927, in Illinois, and died in Nacogdoches, Texas on February 16, 1990.

My eyes froze on the word — *died* — we waited too long. Matthew Stafford, our biological *father*, was dead.

Patricia faxed a copy of his obituary to me. Mixed emotions washed over me as I read the chronicle. He didn't sound like a horrible man, but of course whoever wrote his obit would have likely documented positive qualities. My feelings jumbled. I felt contentment to finally learn what happened to him, but at the same time, angry with him for dying, for never even trying to find me. I detested him for taking his secrets to his grave and for the damage he caused to my self-image. Even if his actions weren't intentional, he triggered a lifetime of toxic relationships for me. Yet part of me felt a twinge of relief in not having to know the truth, at least for now.

I continued reading the account of his death, astonished to discover that his obituary mentioned Brie and I, the first two names of the *six* daughters who survived him.

"Oh my God Brie." I grabbed my sister's shoulder with excitement. "Do you know what this means? We have *four sisters*." Stunned and elated, I processed the idea. Regardless of who our *father* was, our sisters played no part in his shenanigans. Wow, sisters connected by blood. I continued to read the names, *Marisa, Emily, Sarah and Katherine.*

"We have to find them." Brie contended with exuberance that fueled mine. As we anticipated the next steps in our search, a whole new saga began to evolve.

****

Matthew died, but our questions mounted. We turned our attention to the other names listed in our grandparent's obits, those of our aunts. Then I remembered the scrap of paper we filed earlier and retrieved the number that might belong to Aunt Elizabeth. I picked up the phone and dialed...

The sign, Decatur, Illinois lay just ahead and I glanced at my watch as I approached the exit ramp. It was three p.m., central time. The drive took almost four hours. I sucked in a deep breath trying to calm my racing thoughts and nerves.

I waited a lifetime for this moment and I knew once I opened the door, what lay ahead could never be closed off again.

Chapter 24

Learning is accompanied by pain.
Aristotle

The stench drifting on the air made breathing difficult. A distinctive, familiar odor flooded my head with soothing, yet strangely unsettling feelings. Staley's was an icon in Decatur since A.E. Staley created the production of food starch in 1912 and the pungent aroma was as significant to the town as red brick streets. I crossed the bridge and entered the city limits, while a rush of anxiety tingled through my body. My heart raced. Betsy's home was less than five minutes away. My aunts were both there, anticipating my arrival. It was only a few months earlier I first learned they existed and now, in the next few minutes I would meet them face-to-face. I pulled into the driveway of Betsy's quaint little home, took a breath and blew out anxiety with a forceful whoosh before opening the door. I stepped out of the car into a new phase of my life.

Four hours later, I drove toward my Chicago hotel, my mind filled with emotion and new memories. I couldn't wait to call Brie to give her details. We lived through so much together, but when Brie couldn't make the trip to Decatur to meet our aunts, I vowed to provide a complete play-by-play. My thoughts drifted back to the day Brie and I first spoke to Elizabeth Stafford. I touched *record* on my I-Phone and recorded my memories.

Journal entry March 2008:

I stared at the phone in my hand. It was a link to my past, and I knew if I opened the door, I would have to walk through. Regardless of what I found on the other side, my life would change forever. I slowly dialed the number; my stomach churned. I wasn't sure what to say, but had little time to think before the voice on the other end answered, "Hello..."

Once you open the door of knowledge, you can never close it again...

****

"Hi, um—is this Elizabeth Stafford?" I stuttered. "The sister of Matthew Stafford?"

"Yes," the voice replied. "Who is this?"

I began to speak, faltering at first, then fluid in my discourse. "This is Casi, Matthew's—uh—daughter. I—"

The woman interrupted me with excitement in her voice. "Oh my Lord, Cassandra, Matthew's daughter?"

I could hear intense emotion blossom.

"We prayed every night for you girls. How are you? And Brianna? I thought we would never hear from you girls again. What happened to you?"

This woman, our aunt, was genuinely excited to hear from us.

Brie and I chitchatted to Aunt Betsy non-stop, probing her with questions and details about whatever popped into our minds. Her younger sister, Alicia, lived only a few blocks away. Leann, her older sister, died a few years back and Matthew, our *father*, died some years ago. She was sad we didn't find him before his death.

"He never stopped looking for you girls." Her voice trembled. "We couldn't understand why your mother took you and left. They were crazy in love, your mother and *father*, and Matthew never recovered from losing his girls."

Aunt Betsy chatted with us for close to an hour. Matthew was a carpenter and she described the house he built with his own hands for Mother. She talked about how he handmade dollhouses and furniture for his beloved girls. I remembered Mom gave me a carved wooden doll cradle when I was two or three and she told me my grandfather made the bed for my dollies.

But grandpa was a doctor. It wasn't likely he had the interest or ability to execute such intricate carpentry work. In fact there were a couple of small tables mother gave Brie and me that grandpa supposedly made as well. I wondered if those gifts were her way of passing to us some part of our *father*.

Betsy told us of our Indian heritage. Matthew's mother was a full-blooded Cherokee. That meant Brie and I were both one-quarter Cherokee. Mom told me English and Italian ancestry dominated our culture, but never Indian. As Aunt Betsy continued, my mind drifted to what I learned about Indians in history classes, the *Trail of Tears* and oppression the Cherokees endured. Cherokee, North Carolina was only a few hours drive from Atlanta and I planned a mental road-trip to learn more of my heritage.

Mother left Brie and me several pieces of Indian jewelry, silver and turquoise bracelets and rings. Perhaps those gifts came from Matthew as well. Regardless of what transpired between my mother and father, she still apparently wanted to give us a *piece* of him, albeit without our knowledge.

Betsy talked of how close she was to Laura, and that she never once heard Matthew so much as raise his voice to his cherished wife. She described how his face lit up every time Mother walked in the room and how distraught he was at her disappearance. My aunt painted such a different picture than mother did, and I was more confused than ever.

"Our sisters." I blurted out. "Tell us about our sisters." We doted on every word as our aunt retraced lost moments of our lives.

"After your mother took you and left, Matthew was desperate to find you, but his finances ran out and eventually his desperation turned to despair. He grew more-and-more bitter as years passed. I'm afraid he became a bit stern over time." Betsy sighed. "I don't think your sisters had a very happy childhood. Matthew was so strict with them, and the harsh childhood made them hesitant and quiet..."

The end of the conversation left us vowing to call back soon and promising to contact Alicia as well. Aunt Betsy promised to rummage through her desk for the addresses of our sisters and old photos of our family. Finally, we saw light at the end of our dark tunnel, and a chance to see my faceless dark knight in pictures of our elusive *father*.

I knew about my biological *father* for many years now, but when I thought of him I saw only an obscure vision of a faceless man, or sometimes a monster lurking in shadows. How odd the image Elizabeth portrayed painted a loving and devoted husband and father devastated by the loss of his family.

It seemed like an eternity before the pictures arrived, more likely proof of how spoiled we've become by instant messaging and email. The envelope in hand, I stared at the parcel as if the package held a magic potion. To see my *father's* face for the first time in my life, at least the first time I could remember, shot a chill rippling through me from head to toe. Pulling the photos from their packet, I took a deep breath and gazed at each one before placing them neatly on the table. One by one I examined each treasured snapshot and ran my finger across the face of this man who was in part responsible for my existence.

He was a handsome man with curly dark brown hair and an infectious smile. I certainly saw what initially attracted my Mom. Matthew stood at least 6 feet in height. Tall for a man of that era, he towered over his siblings. Aunt Betsy painstakingly identified each person in every photo.

She stood between Aunt Alicia and Aunt Leann, with Uncle John and Matthew to the rear. Grandmother Lucille and Grandfather Thomas Stafford sat in front of their children. The words "your daddy" were scratched next to Matthew with an arrow pointing to his face.

There were other pictures too. I recognized my mother's parents; grandma and grandpa looked so young though, younger than I'd ever seen them. There were snapshots of Matthew holding Brie, and several of our aunts, uncles and cousins, but the shots that struck me the most were of mother. Standing next to Matthew, there was no doubt she was in love. She absolutely beamed with an adoring smile, happier than I had ever seen her. Whatever happened between my *parents* devastated her and the damage left scars she carried throughout her entire life.

The months that followed revealed so many facets of our roots. My first conversation with Emily came unexpectedly. Aunt Betsy was ill, bedridden, and couldn't come up with our sisters' phone numbers right away, but our curiosity was in overdrive. We knew their names and where they lived, so it seemed like an easy task to at least try to reach them through directory assistance. The first two attempts proved unsuccessful. Katherine and Marisa didn't leave a trail, but we found a listing in New York City for one Emily Williamson. I reached for the phone, pressed the numbers, and waited excitedly as the extension rang.

"Hi, you have reached the voice mail of Emily Williamson. Please leave a message, and I will get back to you as soon as possible." I stuttered as I spoke, not knowing what to say.

"Hi, uh—Emily." I stumbled over the words that fell from my lips. "My name is Casi McLean. I'm not sure if I even have the right Emily Williamson, but if you are the daughter of Matthew Stafford, I—uh--"

"WE." Brie corrected me.

"WE are your sisters, Brie and Casi. If you are the Emily Williamson we are searching for, we would love to talk to you. Please call me back at 404-555-4738."

I hung up the phone, fully aware the woman who would pick up my message probably wasn't our *Emily* and I shouldn't be surprised if I never heard from her. Brie went home and I went out for dinner with some friends. When I returned home, I checked my voice mail.

"This is Emily Williamson, the daughter of Matthew Stafford. Casi, please return my phone call when you get this message." I immediately hung up on my voice mail and called her number. Emily answered the phone.

"Hi Emily, this is your sister, Casi." I trembled with awkward anticipation. "I guess you were pretty surprised to hear from us after all these years." I could hear Emily breathe in deeply before she spoke.

"I guess you could say that." He voice was laced with sarcasm. "I had to pick myself up from the floor, um—you see, I had no idea you even existed, so it was quite a surprise to get your message."

Emily had no knowledge of us? But, we were mentioned in Matthew's obituary.

"Daddy divorced my Mom and remarried several years before he died." She went on to explain. "I never even saw his obituary. Wow, two sisters, I can't believe it."

We talked for a while comparing notes, amazed at our similarities. Emily told me about the sisters she grew up with, her youth, and what being the daughter of Matthew Stafford actually meant. She told me about health issues, and that our *father* died February 16, 1990, at age 62 of cardiopulmonary arrest due to coronary atherosclerosis. I had to write that one down so I could look up the illness later, but from what she explained, my *father* died of a heart attack due to cholesterol build up.

Emily shed light on what may have been the reasons behind my mother's abrupt departure from Matthew's life. Like Brie and I, she had little memory of her childhood and, after some discussion, confessed a shocking family secret.

"I really hate to be the one to tell you this." She hesitated. "But your biological *father* was—uh—" her voice dropped off and she paused again for a moment before taking a deep breath and continuing. "*A pedophile.*"

I felt a tightening in my chest. I remembered mother's warning: *He is the kind of man who pulls wings off of butterflies.* My mind reeled at the thought of a perfect metaphor, an encrypted description of a pedophile who would shatter innocence of a child, warping her self-image and emotionally disabling her. Finally, mother's message made sense.

Like ours, Emily's childhood memories were sketchy at best and for several years she questioned the source behind her lack of recollection. She suspected a trauma might have caused her lapse in memory and Katherine, the eldest of our four sisters, confirmed her suspicions. Katherine confessed she inadvertently walked in on Matthew one day, while he was molesting Emily. Kat suffered repeated rapes herself, but hid her shame and torture because she believed she was his only victim. When she discovered Matthew with Emily, she threatened him, vowed to: "Kill him in the dark of night if he ever touched any of them again."

Emily made clear she did not want Brie or me to discuss the dark side of Matthew with Marisa or Sarah. There was too much at stake. Both of our younger sisters appeared to be well adjusted, and if they were abused, they surely retained no memory of the abuse. Matthew was gone and no longer a threat, so to uncover the truth would, in Emily's mind, do nothing but harm. I reluctantly agreed. But secrets and the lies created to cover them tormented my life and I wasn't sure that keeping more secrets would be an advantage to anyone.

When I hung up the phone I felt mentally spent. I collapsed on my bed and try to sort out and process everything Emily told me. Brie would have to wait until the next day to hear what I learned from our younger sister.

My conversation with Marisa, the youngest of my newly discovered sisters, painted a completely different picture than the one I shared with Emily. Marisa's memories of Matthew clearly painted a lighter picture. Strangely, she knew about us since she was twenty...some thirty-two years earlier. Marisa didn't mention abuse by her father, but she did say he was sorry he hurt Brie and me.

Matthew called Marisa to his side when he was quite ill and fearful he might die. He asked her to bring him his will, told her about us and begged her to find his two oldest daughters to let us know how sorry he was that he was such a horrible father. No more explanation was given.

Marisa vowed to look for us and always intended to do so. She often thought of contacting *Unsolved Mysteries* to see if they could help her with the search. Matthew recovered from that near-death affliction after he received bypass surgery, and I guess finding Brie and me slipped to the back of Marisa's mind. Perhaps his illness softened him somehow or caused him to change his deviant behavior. The more I found out about our *father*, the more questions needed answering.

My thoughts wandered when I thought of how different my own life might have been if my mother stayed with Matthew. I was thankful for so many things, especially Daddy and my boys. Still, I couldn't help but wonder.

There was no denying that Emily's story about Matthew held truth. Katherine remembered everything and she saw him molest Emily. Matthew Stafford *was* a pedophile. The story fit my mother's reaction too.

If my mother discovered him touching either Brie or me, leaving him to protect us would have been her logical response. And her warning, the warning that haunted me: "He's the kind of man who pulls wings off of butterflies." I didn't know what to do with the information I now held.

Over time, we spoke to three of our four sisters and discovered in them, treasures missing throughout our lives. Our forth sister, Sarah, chose not to speak with us.

She viewed communication as a kind of betrayal to her mother. I have to respect that, but I hope she reconsiders sometime in the future.

***

My questions continued to mount, even more now. If Marisa found us years ago, perhaps we might have met our father, but I believe everything happens for a reason. Life is as it was meant to be. Knowing Matthew might have altered who I became. Perhaps I would never discover who I was inside, never put pen to paper to write this manuscript and you might never have read these words.

Brie and I kept close contact with Marisa through email. She is such a delightful woman and I look forward to meeting her. Katherine and Emily are involved in their own lives and the distance between us prevents us from meeting face-to-face. Sarah refuses to accept Brie and me. Being close to her mother, perhaps she knows more than the rest of us.

I pulled up in front of the hotel, parked my car and entered the lobby. The day's events spiraled through my head while I tried to absorb an entire lifetime. Knowledge was a fickle friend. It could enlighten or destroy in the same breath. The *Matthew* my aunts described was the complete opposite of the one Emily described to me. Who was right, and how would I ever be able to find out? I guess the most important question was did I really need to know the truth?

Exhausted, I checked into the hotel then dragged my luggage as I staggered toward the elevator and my room. The king-sized bed enticed me. I stripped off my clothes, slid between the sheets and lay there, in a comfortable, almost comatose state, my mind drifting between fact, fiction and fantasy. For a moment, the ringing seemed like part of a dream. Realizing the phone blasted next to me, I reached through darkness and grabbed at the nightstand. It was Brie.

Chapter 25

Life is like riding a bicycle. To keep your balance you must keep moving.
Albert Einstein

Approaching the door I drew in a long breath, pressed the bell and waited. It was a defining moment, the only way to obliterate emotional bondage that held us captive for so many years. Cheri slipped outside and walked silently next to me toward my car. The awkward first few moments dissipated. We agreed to meet, but breaking through lies that built walls between us was no easy task. Sometimes the only way to escape the past is to look straight in the demon's eyes. Facing the truth relinquishes its hold on you.

It's strange, but in another world, Cheri and I might have been friends. She was likable, sweet and sincere. On the outside, exactly the type of person I gravitated toward, but tough questions I needed to ask her loomed between us and I doubted she could justify her answers.

We pulled up and parked in front of a Caribbean restaurant close by and, still making light conversation, wandered inside. I hoped the atmosphere would make purging our souls a bit easier, but my stomach churned at the thought of secrets unraveling right in my face. Cheri excused herself and went to the bathroom the moment we sat. I squirmed in my chair, my mind flooding with recent memories.

I reached in my purse for a small pad of paper and began scribbling to offset my angst. The last time I visited this restaurant Dad revealed some major secrets from my past. Another page of my story beckoned.

Journal entry, September 2008:
Dad, a constant source of strength for me, began showing signs of his years in 2008--or so I thought. For so many years his overall health remained indestructible, but by-pass surgery, osteoarthritis and prostate cancer wore him down. At 82, his short-term memory blurred. No longer the vision of strength and fortitude, my dad's sharp, unfaltering aptitude faltered, but I still trusted his decision...

It's miraculous how one event or a seemingly insignificant decision can change the course of so many lives. The tiniest shift could alter a future forever. In only one moment, dreams could unfold beyond the wildest imagination or plunge lives into the depths of hell...

****

Eleven years passed since mother's death and though he denied it, Daddy was lonely. He missed Mom and longed for the companionship and support they shared. He met some women through church and various social activities, but no one could fill the emptiness in his life where Mother dwelled.

On a whim, I encouraged him to fill out a profile for an Internet dating site. The responses floored me. Once we eliminated young women searching for *sugar daddies*, quite a few women remained who seemed to be in a position similar to Daddy's.

Over the course of the next two years he dated, enjoying the company of several lovely women, until he found one in particular. Thrilled he met someone special, I was taken aback when he announced his intension of marriage after knowing her for only fourteen days. My concern had nothing to do with replacing mom. I just never imagined that at eighty-two, he'd want to get married again--especially after dating the woman only two weeks. I questioned her intent.

Knowing what I know now, I would have advised him to steer clear. Not that he would have listened, but his decision created devastating consequences for our entire family. Dad's choice to remarry taught us all that decisions based in loneliness, like those made in fear, empower others to manipulate our futures.

For the next few months, he spent time planning for imminent changes. He revised his will and included a prenuptial agreement to protect his assets. He needed paperwork kept in a safety deposit box at his bank. As a precaution, Dad gave me a key to the box years before, but I never used it. He called me and asked if I would meet him at the bank, which was about five minutes from my home, so I grabbed my key and headed out the door.

Arriving well before Daddy, I went into the back room, unlocked the box and pulled out a stack of papers. I took his treasured documents into one of the small private rooms, sat down and began sifting through them, finding sales receipts for jewelry Dad purchased over the years for us, a few old IOUs, newspaper clippings, birth certificates, my parents' marriage license, and a number of legal documents.

Curious, I opened a document and froze. The paper read:

At a session of the Circuit Court held in and for the county of Macon, State of Illinois, in the county building in the city of Decatur on the 23rd day of December A. D. 1954. Laura M. Stafford, Plaintiff, VS Matthew E. Stafford, Defendant...

I read further, a chill slithering over my arms toward my stomach. The paper, the first of several documents, opened doors to my past in black and white. My biological parents married on May 8, 1946. That made sense, Brie was born February 7, 1947. They lived together until 25 October 1953.

Okay, I was born January 16, 1952, so they were together when mom gave birth to me, but Aunt Ginny said they had a major falling out nine months before I was born, which resulted in my mother's rape and my conception. That meant from April 1951 to October 1953 they lived in a turbulent marriage as best. Unanswered questions mounted higher.

Mom divorced on 23 December 1954. The documents stated: on 25 October 1953, Matthew:

Wholly regardless of his obligations as a husband, willfully and unlawfully deserted and absented himself from Laura without reasonable cause and without fault on her part, and has persisted in such desertion and yet continued to absent himself from Laura for more than one year immediately prior to filing of the complaint.

What? These divorce papers said my *father* abandoned and left Brie and me with my mother. I glanced at the bottom of the page and saw signatures of *both* of my parents. Additional separation papers showed they split up when I was two, *on February 6, 1954.*

Newspaper clippings posted the divorce on *December 23, 1954*, and a subsequent marriage license issued to Matthew on *December 29, 1954* further proved a discrepancy to what I understood as facts. A birth announcement came next, for baby girl Stafford (Sarah, one of my new sisters) born on *September 19, 1952*. Damn, that was 8 months *after* my birth and well before Matthew and Laura divorced.

My life's mystery continued to unfold; Brianna Marie Stafford and Cassandra Kathleen Stafford...adopted by Mr. Robert Gordon McLean, (Daddy). Granted in the state of Georgia on the premise that Matthew's whereabouts were unknown, which meant Matthew never gave his consent because no one could find him. I found letters sent to and from lawyers requesting Brie and I be issued new legal birth certificates showing Daddy as our *birth father*, and legal documents to verify the legality of the procedure.

The documents certainly answered a lot of questions, but even though I saw dates and paperwork, I wasn't convinced Matthew deserted his wife and children for some woman. Did he start a new family with the mother of his illegitimate child? And what about the scenario described by Aunt Betsy?

The puzzle pieces didn't fit together, but I finally began to realize why I harbored such deep feelings of inadequacy and abandonment. My childhood dreams of a tarnished knight evolved from fractured memories, seeds planted by a confused toddler. A volatile relationship between Matthew and Laura intermingled with a loving marriage of my Dad and Mom. The reflection I saw in the mirror burst into existence from shattered shards of memories, affecting every relationship, male and female, forged throughout my life. And all of my decisions reflected off of that damage and confusion.

A firm hand clenched my shoulder, and I felt Daddy standing behind me.

"Ahhh." He gazed over my shoulder at the papers spread across the table. "I was wondering when you'd decide to give in to your curiosity."

"Curiosity?"

"You've had that key for years, but the thought never occurred to you to look into Pandora's box?"

"Why didn't you say something, Daddy? You knew all this"--I threw my hand outward across the expanse of the table--"yet you never said a word. Why?"

"I promised your mother I wouldn't tell you. She spent a lifetime hiding a truth to protect you, but maybe you needed to know." He paused then added. "I left that in God's hands."

"You'd never break a promise." I felt the blood drain from my face.

I confessed to searching for Matthew to find medical background, and told Dad he died.

"But we discovered four sisters we never knew existed."

Dad knew about at least three sisters. "Did you try to find them?"

"Yes, we spoke to Emily and Marisa, but we haven't met them yet. I hope to someday." Then, dropping the subject, I asked him how he wanted to change his will to include his wife-to-be.

****

Dad didn't appear hurt at all and I felt relieved I didn't break my promise to Mom either. Over the next few weeks I probed him from time to time, asking what he knew of the relationship between Matthew and Mom and the events of my early childhood. He really knew very little, or at least that's what he said. Mother never spoke much about Matthew, and Daddy said he didn't push her to tell him anything.

I might not ever discover the whole story, but one fact remained undeniable: the decisions Matthew and Mother created caused secrets and lies that plagued my life and changed its course. And they affected Brie's life as well. Decisions often have a domino affect, and little decisions we make every day could have profound consequences.

Brie and I still have no recollection of our childhood or our *father*, which may be a blessing. However we can't deny the role he played in charting the course of our lives. I'm not angry with him anymore. I don't resent him either. The decisions he made were his alone and, like everyone, he lived and died with the fallout. My life needed to move forward instead of clinging to the past. Finding out the truth about Zack and Cheri from her point of view provided a huge step.

The dinner with Cheri went well and I was glad we decided to have that tough conversation. We broke through barriers, shared our individual views of the past and I found out Cheri lived through a childhood trauma as well. One that left her as vulnerable as I was. We uncovered a lot of lies Zack told, but our talk healed wounds that festered for too many years. And Cheri answered the one question that haunted me:

"Why did you stay with Zack for fifteen years when you knew he was married with two children who needed and loved him?"

"Because I loved him." Her simple reply was laced with innocence. She paused for a moment before continuing. "He lied about you, and he continually promised that if I was patient, we would be together some day. I wanted—needed to believe him."

"Oddly, that was the only promise he kept. Maybe you were right to believe him." We walked out the door toward my car. " It took almost two decades, but you're together now."

Cheri didn't make up excuses for the part she played, what she did--what they did, but she explained how the affair started and why their relationship lasted for so many years. People do strange things for love, especially when they're lonely or needy. Married or not, love triangles trap and destroy.

Many years ago, Allie fell for a married man. Though she regretted the affair, the experience gave her a first hand viewpoint as the other woman and we discussed the topic on many occasions. My take from my own love triangle: our perspective guides us in everything we do.

Though I didn't condone her comportment, I believed Cheri. We concluded Zack loved us both in different ways. We fed his addiction and, terrified to lose either one of us, he created his own hell. In some perverted way, he did manage to protect our hearts for a long time. His actions weren't right or fair, but they crafted our reality and forever connected us.

Zack never understood that everyone involved would have been better off had he simply left me when he met Cheri. His rage toward himself damaged our children. If he'd walked away to be with Cheri, maybe rage wouldn't have controlled his life or fractured ours. The boys might have seen a very different father, and I wouldn't have slept through twenty years of my life in an empty marriage. As for Cheri, I often wonder how her life might have changed as well.

Zack watched, first hand, the destruction of his life and he blamed no one but himself. His elaborate lies enabled an obsession. Like a snowball rolling down a mountain the abscess swallowed everything in its path. The sad part: I still believe he loved me. He tried to end things with Cheri, over and over, but he didn't know how to stop the snowball he set in motion and over time he began to love her too.

He was as damaged as me. Like Jack, the dynamics of our pasts collided. It took a long time before I understood Zack but, like love, pain can seduce a person to do many things they never thought capable of doing.

It may sound naive when I say I believe Zack never intended to hurt anyone. He focused on his own demons and I get that. I made plenty of mistakes and poor decisions because of my own. Zack and Cheri made poor choices, but their intent, though self-centered and indulgent, wasn't malicious.

Our pasts set us on a collision course that destroyed more than a marriage. I pray Zack forgives himself someday and I hope Cheri helps him find happiness. As for me, I'm looking forward, not backward, holding on to only the good, like Josh and Jace. I thank God for helping me to let go of anger and pray He will give me guidance, direction and strength to make decisions with positive impacts on my future. Every decision we make matters.

Chapter 26

Love is a condition in which the happiness of another person is essential to your own.
Robert Heinlein

Totally in free-fall, I couldn't breathe. Adrenalin gushed through my veins, pulsing in tandem with the fist clenched in the pit of my stomach. Words blurred through tears and my hands trembled as I tried to focus on his email. Words that made no sense...

My *birth father* began a cycle when he walked away from his children and never looked back. A broken child, I spent the next fifty years protecting myself from ever having to endure that pain again. Every intimate relationship I experienced reflected a destructive pattern. I spent years trying to unravel, understand, and break down walls.

I made poor choices, accepted insincerity as a Band-Aid for a gapping hole in my heart and tried to prove my worth by bending my life around others. But I still loved, and hurt when what I perceived as love abandoned me.

Enter Jim. I fell in love with a man who I believed loved me and, despite my fears, opened the door of the fortress forged around my heart. Jim and I dated for a year and a half. I trusted him, shared my history with him, and he knew how hard I struggled to overcome my past. But when he grew weary of our connection, he cavalierly dumped me like a piece of trash. Does that sound like the whining of a poor-me syndrome? Perhaps. The twisted endings of my love life continued regardless of what I learned.

My mother told me God never gives you more than you can handle. I wanted to believe that, but my faith wavered when a few days later, my dad was diagnosed with lung cancer, followed by my business succumbing to the pressures of a failing economy. Three traumatic events entwined to shatter my world, all within a matter of a few days. For a solid week I couldn't eat or sleep and felt completely defeated, a difficult position for a Pollyanna. I sat in silent solitude for hours each day until I dragged myself to bed and collapsed. My eyes were swollen and my head throbbed. There were no more tears left to shed.

For weeks, I halfheartedly walked through the motions of my daily routine. Responsibilities and commitments held no interest to me. Dad needed support through his illness. Jace lived on the edge always at a crucial point in his life that required mom to guide and encourage him, and Josh was getting married. I needed to pull myself together—for my family if not myself.

Five thirty a.m. sitting in my hot tub, I watched hovering steam swell from the water, drift upward then dissipate into to the dim morning sky. Birds chirped, welcoming a new day. The world awakened to a new beginning. I yearned to do the same.

I tried to understand what happened and why. Dad's cancer and the economy were beyond my control, but Jim? Was I still that naïve, completely oblivious, or was Jim an expert, skilled at creating a romantic aura to get what he wanted? In my mind, I ruminated over our entire relationship. Everything seemed perfect when we were together, what could have gone so wrong when we were apart?

I stepped out of the spa, wrapped a towel around my body and scuffed inside to the kitchen to make coffee. If he at least talked to me, let me know what was in his head… Damn, how could he say I was the love of his life—and then just walk away?

I poured steaming coffee into my cup and headed toward the bathroom. Letters were always easier than saying something unpleasant to someone face to face, but didn't a year and a half of sharing our thoughts, problems, and dreams merit more than a *Dear John* email? A phone call, would that be too much to ask?

As I reached for my robe, my towel dropped to the floor and I glanced at my naked reflection in the mirror. The image of my emaciated body brought me back to reality with a jolt.

Weeks of sleepless nights and lack of appetite took a toll. A sudden rage bubbled to the surface. I came too far to fall back into emotionally ravaging myself again.

"No!" I screamed at the mirror. "Not this time." I couldn't and wouldn't let drama in my life defeat me, or let Jim take away the self-respect I worked years to achieve. I changed my life through grit and determination and pursued my dream. A lot of drama dumped into my life at once. Anyone would be overwhelmed.

I gazed at my reflection. I survived the very fears I spent a lifetime desperately running from—a revelation, and at that moment I knew I would never lose myself again.

There would be no self-pity or helplessness. A new sense of freedom and strength washed over me and I knew I found the woman I was meant to be. I saw a future, a purpose and belief in myself I never knew I possessed. Finally, the face staring back at me in the mirror radiated with confidence. I pulled my robe back over my shoulders, smiled and grabbed my coffee. Life can turn around in the blink of an eye, and I might have missed it if my gaze still focused on the past.

My manuscript beckoned. The cold silence of daybreak engulfed me as I sifted through emotions that previously consumed me. According to Elizabeth Kübler-Ross, grief progresses through five stages: denial, anger, bargaining, depression and acceptance.

When we lose someone we love, regardless of the reason, grief creeps into our heart, but loss isn't limited to death. Sometimes we have to grieve what *life* brings our way. I drifted through the first four stages and now embraced the fifth, accept and move on. I could finally write my last chapter.

Journal entry, October 2009

Physical attraction is an indefinable, natural phenomenon. Chemistry and lust between a man and woman are as primal as it gets. The creator's genius was at its best when he made attraction feel so incredible. Designed to carry on the species, the chemistry of lust initiates with powerful force. But sustained mutual monogamous love, that's another story. Over the years I found out love was never easy, but I believed if chemistry drew me toward someone, the connection was worth investigating. I have no doubt love is the greatest gift life offers, and I thought I found that gift with Jim...

April 23, 2009...

****

From the first moment our eyes met, his tall, slender stature, clean-cut appearance and deep blue eyes pierced my heart. Our interests complemented each other and after spending only one evening over dinner and conversation, heat sweltered between us. Despite what he termed a "messy divorce" Jim wanted to find love again. I knew if I ever fell in love again, I needed a man who wanted marriage, not a serial dater.

Our first kiss sparked a whirlwind romance, awakening lyrics and soft melodies of old music etched in my mind. Jim's s touch sent a sensual tingle to places I forgot I possessed. When he held me close, his hot, hard body and warm lips--I melted into him.

"You make me feel young again, Casi." He laced his fingers through my hair and pulled me closer, softly nibbling my neck. "I can't stop thinking about you. You must see how crazy I am about you."

His touch awakened every primal instinct sleeping beneath the surface of my prim and proper shell. Jim's desire fueled my passion and he treated me like a princess with unyielding attention and undeniable lust. He cooked for me, took me to extravagant restaurants and wonderful weekend excursions, snuggled with me and stole kisses, playing and toying with me, luring me into his web. He knew exactly what I needed as if he owned a blueprint to my soul.

Jim was a gourmet cook, intelligent and romantic beyond any man I had ever met. He created a fantasy world every moment we spent together, with soft music, amazing food, wine and rooms bathed in candlelight. The intoxication was addictive and my primed heart melted. Finally, someone saw me for who I was inside. He wanted me and I fell hard and fast. The man of my dreams romanced me like the knight I imagined as a child. In hindsight, I'm pretty sure his well-perfected performance targeted vulnerable women, and I fit his prospectus like a glove.

The first time he whisked me off to a romantic getaway, I thought I'd hit the lottery: a man who loved me in a remote cabin secluded in the North Georgia Mountains complete with fireplace and hot tub. What could be better? A light dusting of snow made the ambiance flawless. We sat in the spa, drank wine in front of the fire, talked, kissed and wrapped ourselves in each other, exchanging details about jagged paths our lives had taken. He told me his story, his incredible relationship with his 20-year-old daughter, Starr, and mistakes he made with his first marriage.

Everything about us clicked as if we were two parts of one whole. When the fantasy weekend ended, the ambiance lingered. I felt the walls around my heart crumble. When Jim asked to read my manuscript, I reluctantly let him see me from the inside out. His astonishment brought us closer. He vowed he would never betray me and would always be honest. He told me he wanted to be my final chapter, the happy ending where I find him, my soul mate.

"You're the love of my life, Casi."

My coy reply, "We'll see," but I knew his words read my heart.

Jim was the first man since Brad to break through my defenses and touch a piece of my soul. For a while, everything was perfect. We never disagreed about anything. When we were together, Jim created a romantic ambiance down to every detail to make me feel special and loved--why couldn't I see the aura was too perfect to be real?

Several months into our relationship, during an intimate romantic dinner, Jim acted distracted, so I asked him what was wrong.

"I need to talk to you, sweetheart." He touched my cheek and whispered. "I should have come forward earlier, but every time we're together, everything is so perfect, I keep putting off discussing this with you."

He was right. Things were always perfect when we were together. I gazed deep into his troubled eyes, and took a deep breath to prepare myself for what I feared could devastate our lives. My stomach churned. *God please don't let him say he was dying.*

Tears rolled down his cheek as he shared his story. "I've mentioned my disastrous divorce before, but I've never told you what happened." He took my hand, led me to the sofa and snuggled close, his eyes never leaving mine. Jim explained details of his relationship with Tara, his ex-wife, dissecting an entire timeline through their divorce.

Tara, increasingly enraged by judicial decisions favoring Jim, accused him of criminal offenses starting with spousal abuse, progressing to child abuse, and ultimately accusing him of child molestation. According to Jim, her vengeance set a nightmare in motion.

"Once a person is suspected of molesting a child, Amber's law protects the victim. Right or falsely accused, the suspect is prohibited from contact with the child. My divorce has been a living hell. The break up disputed more than just property division and child support. Tara's allegations spiraled me into a prolonged battle with the criminal justice system, a fight for my life."

I watched Jim relive each detail he endured. I felt an ache in the pit of my stomach with each silent tear as he described emptiness and frustration.

"Casi, child molestation is a felony, and because of Tara's accusation, I haven't been allowed to see Madison since she was two—she'll be six soon. She probably doesn't even remember me. Not only that, my company let me go after a financial investor ran a personnel background check on all employees and my name came up as an alleged felon. I am only a consultant now, not an employee. Tara destroyed my reputation, my career and my relationship with my daughter. I even spent a brief period under house arrest, forced to wear an ankle bracelet to ensure the justice system could track my whereabouts every moment."

Jim poured out his heart for several hours before he fell silent. Then he grabbed my hand, his voice quivering.

"I would understand if you wanted to walk out and never look back." He hitched his chin toward the door.

I found it incredible such a gentle man could have done anything to warrant such serious accusations. I wiped a tear from his cheek.

"I'm not going to walk out of your life. I'm not going anywhere."

Over the next few months, I met Jim's mother, older daughter, and her mother (Jim's first wife), all of whom validated Jim's story. My belief in him strengthened. The thought of Jim dealing with such a devastating situation falsely imposed on him by a vindictive woman broke my heart. The ensuing months brought so much anguish and fear into his life, I scarcely knew how to support him, so I just let him know that no matter what the future held for him, I would be by his side.

I trusted Jim, and my judgment regarding him as well. Tension surrounded Jim's defense though. He missed Madison terribly. And the pending court case, added to his workload, created a constant stream of stress. Consulting as the head of operations for his company was taxing under any circumstance, but his new project was the first of it's kind.

Jim's responsibility: to build out an operation using a state-of-the-art processing facility that took bio-solids and, instead of creating fertilizer, transformed the waste into e-fuel. His success could provide a potential replacement for fossil fuel, a method that could expand globally, especially with the world's recent focus on "going green." The entire future of the company depended upon his success. Jim, terrified of losing his consultant position because of the felony charge, worked twice as hard to compensate and prove himself invaluable. The pressure, internal and external would devastate most people.

His job site, located on the West coast, had Jim spending weeks at a time on the other side of the country. When he couldn't come home to Atlanta over the weekend he flew me out to California. Whether in San Diego, Laguna Beach or Santa Monica, we stayed in the most romantic settings, but the time apart strained our relationship.

Plenty of things occupied my time when Jim was in L.A. The economy took a huge hit, the hardest of which focused on residential building, and builders suffered. Four of my clients went bankrupt including one who owed me over $33,000. When his properties went to the courthouse steps for auction, they took my company with them.

The stock market plummeted and my savings disappeared. I felt lost with no control over anything in my life, while everything I worked for, everything I became, disintegrated. But when Dad was diagnosed with lung cancer, he took precedence over everything and the cumulative stress knocked me off my feet.

As much as I needed Jim's strength to lean on, his plate was full, so I tried to sugar coat my situation. True to form, Pollyanna put *him* first. The last thing he needed was to worry about me. So, I dealt with my own problems in silence.

As the plant got closer to completion, Jim's work required a lot more of his time and we seemed to have trouble finding a weekend to spend time together. The trial date finally set, he put on a strong façade, but the fear in his eyes betrayed him. His ex-wife's case was weak at best, there was simply no evidence, and his character witnesses, who included Starr, his now 21-year-old daughter, her friends, and Jim's first wife, gave overwhelmingly positive testimonies. Still, on the outside chance the jury returned a guilty verdict, Jim could spend the next 20 years in prison. On the outside, his strength never faltered, but I knew the prospects of his future terrified him.

When we were together, the world took a backseat, but I sensed a distance growing between us as the trial date approached. The day-to-day participation in each other's lives disappeared. I felt as if I was a distraction from his life instead of a part of it.

On Tuesday, January 20, 2009, late in the afternoon, I got a simple text from him: "The DA dropped the case, I'll call you in a bit."

I texted back: "Oh my God, that's amazing. I don't have any more appointments today. I'll come see you. What time can you break away from work?" Ecstatic, I drew in a deep breath and exhaled slowly, then continued my note. "Jim, you'll see Madison again."

"If Tara hasn't poisoned her mind." He replied. "I can only imagine what she's been told about me."

"You're an incredible father. Starr is proof of that. It may take time, but Madison will see the truth."

"We'll see. Got to run. I'll call you soon."

Hours later, he phoned.

"Hi Sweetie. Listen, it's been an emotionally exhausting day. Everyone wants to celebrate, but I can't. I just need to be alone to absorb everything. Do you mind if we get together in the next day or two?"

The next day or two--I was stunned. I wanted to hold him, feel the relief drain from us both, but instead, I gave him space. Jim made plans to be with Starr the next evening and I didn't see him until Friday night. I tried to imagine the emotions he was experiencing, so I backed off, just thankful the ordeal was over. It would take time to get Madison back.

The custody battle would be ugly, and Lord only knew what Tara filled her head with over the past three years. Madison would need counseling, as would Jim, but the important thing was he could see his little girl again. Finally, he could take a breath and look toward a future free of prison bars, and we could get our lives back.

That didn't happen. The nightmare was over, and Jim's consulting job turned back into a prominent position, but his work schedule demanded more time than ever. The start up met with difficulties, which took him to the West coast more often, sometimes for two to three week stints.

Still, when we managed to find time together, our connection was magical, but issues at the plant endlessly pulled him away and when he corrected one problem, another popped up.

Jim texted me every day and called once or twice during the week. He told me how exhausted he was working constantly, that he missed and loved me, but something in his voice felt different, distant. I knew the project demanded time of an already stressed-out man, but I couldn't shake the feeling something bothered him beyond work.

His nightmare was over and he survived, but *my* stress still loomed endlessly. With no support system, I felt my world crashing in on me. I needed Jim, and the lonely nights away from him with minimal communication nagged at me.

One morning my friend Sara emailed me an Internet link she wanted me to see. I pulled up the site on my computer—and felt the blood drain from my face. I stared at the pictures while my entire body went numb. Jim—on an Internet dating sight, profile listed in black and white, with full color pictures. The post said he lived in California, not Atlanta, which I guess wasn't that much of a stretch. He was looking for "that special someone" searching for—all the things we already had.

Jim looked into my eyes so many times and swore he would never cheat...and I believed him. It wasn't as if he randomly met someone and felt an attraction. With all the time we spent apart, that might have made some kind of perverted sense. Instead, he purposefully posted an advertisement, solicited to meet someone, a search to find the love of his life. I can't explain the pain, the emptiness I felt when I read his profile. I shook my head as if to shake away a bad dream.

All of my past betrayals exploded into a flood of unbridled emotion. Then numbness...I felt no anger, but I trembled with complete deflation. How could Jim do that to me? I wanted to make everything go away, my past, the profile, the ache piercing my chest, Dad's illness, the troubled economy—but I couldn't. This was my reality.

When Jim came back in town for three days I pretended I knew nothing. It wasn't easy, especially when he held me in his arms and slept beside me. By Sunday morning I found the confidence to confront him. My heart raced and hands quivered as I reached for the printed profile tucked in my over night bag. I stared into his eyes, holding the paper out to him and shuddered.

"Jim, what do I do with this?"

He silently perched his glasses on the end of his nose and looked over the words as if he was reading, but eyes never moved. He knew exactly what the paper said and gathered his thoughts to determine what he would say. A few moments later his gaze shifted to me and the paper fell to the floor.

"I'm so sorry." He tried to pull me close, but my rigid body refused. "I never meant for you to see this. And I promise, I never acted on it. It's just that I was so far from you and missed you. Posting the profile was just Internet entertainment. It meant nothing. I'll get off of the site immediately. Believe me, Casi, I love you with all that I am."

"I thought I knew you, Jim, knew us, but maybe we are looking for different things. You said you wanted a future with me."

"I did—I do, Casi. We are on the same page, I promise you. It's just that there's one thing I can't seem to get past."

"I'm listening. But I'm not sure anything explains why you'd post a profile on a dating site."

"When the whole Tara and Madison ordeal started, everything snowballed so fast." He took his glasses off, turned my face toward his and stared into my eyes. "I went from having a family to becoming an accused felon over night and I couldn't deal with it. Between work, losing Madison, and defending myself from a continual barrage of Tara's accusations, I couldn't function.

When they put me under house arrest I fell apart, ended up in a therapist's chair just trying to find a way to get through each day. The thought of spending my life in prison for something I didn't do terrified me. The only way I was able to survive was to stop thinking about it. I know you know what I'm talking about, Casi. You've been in a place like that before, when you have to force yourself to stop thinking."

"I guess you're referring to my anxiety attacks. Yes, I learned to change my thoughts, to stop adrenalin reactions."

"Right, and I had to learn how to live each day thinking of only that day—just to survive. So for the last four years I focused on the present. I completely block out what the future might hold."

"I get that—and I'm sorry, but how does that have anything to do with me, or you posting a profile to find your special someone?"

"The problem is, I can't seem to stop doing that. I can't see a future anymore, as hard as I try. Can you understand that at all?"

I sat and glared at him, trying to read his mind over his words.

"I want a life with you, Casi, and I promise I'll try to work through this. Please give me that chance. I'll go back to my therapist. I truly love you and I want us."

I still felt numb, but his eyes convinced me he couldn't be lying. Maybe I was naive to believe him, but sometimes your heart just takes control. I could see he was hurting too, and his ordeal was agonizing. I wanted--needed to believe him.

Wow, did I really just say the same words Cheri said about Zack? That should have been a huge red flag, but the thought never crossed my mind.

I left Jim's home that afternoon. He said he had a company business event he needed to attend. The next morning he flew back to California for another three weeks, but called and texted me as if nothing happened. He got back in town on a Monday and said he couldn't wait to see me.

I'll never forget that evening—it was the last time I ever saw him. Too exhausted to go out to dinner, he picked up some hot wings and wine (totally unlike Jim) and we sat and watched the basketball championship on TV. Afterwards, we went to bed and spent hours entwined in passion. He whispered he loved me over and over as we drifted off to sleep in each other's arms.

Jim woke up early the next morning, showered and slipped out for an early breakfast meeting, but not before kissing me passionately.

"Enjoy your day, sweetheart. I'll see you tonight. I love you so much."

I didn't see Jim that night or any night afterwards. Problems erupted at the project site and he was called away to the West coast again. He spent the next two weeks in California. The day before he was scheduled to come home, I got an email from him amazingly entitled "Hi Sweetheart"— Jim walked out of my life.

Hi Sweetheart,
I've talked to you about my fears and protective feelings related to you and all "my stuff." The protective feelings I spoke of had mostly to do with my love and respect for you and the intimate details I know about your past relationships. I guess that's the downside to writing such a transparent book. Anyway, I seem to be consumed with NOT being one of "the same".
I guess the bottom line Casi is that I just flat don't believe I'm capable of a "real" relationship right now. Regardless of how hard I have tried, at the end of the day I'm just not being honest with myself and I'm not being honest with you, and therein lies the major burden I bear (well one of them).

At the very beginning of "us" and after hearing (and reading) your story I promised you that I wouldn't lie to you or cheat on you as others have done. Well, I've held up that end of the promise, but I also promised you that if I didn't feel we were going to grow like a relationship needs to do that I would tell you that as well. That is the part of the promise that I don't feel like I've kept with you and it bothers me.

I had hoped that once my legal burden was behind me that my attitude about relationships would change. I now realize Casi that I may never let my guard down enough for that to happen. I truly believe the hurt and pain has affected me beyond repair and hurting and disappointing someone as wonderful as you just makes matters worse.

On days when I'm honest with myself I know what I am truly doing is giving you false expectations of our future together and basically putting your life on hold. My love, respect and admiration for you is beyond description. So I need for you to go and live the full life that you deserve. I want you to write and paint and spread your infectious smile to everyone you meet.

Hopefully one day when emotions are a little less overwhelming we can sit down and talk through love, life, friendships, and hope, while also talking about disappointments, hurt and mind-boggling pain. There is a book in your mind about my story. I truly want to help you tell that story one day, but right now it's still too real for me.

I love you with all my heart, Casi and can't stand the thought of my unhappiness rubbing off on you for one more minute. Please be happy...

I'll Love You Always,

Jim.

That was the last time I heard from Jim, a year and a half together and he dumped me in an email that pierced my heart with a near fatal wound.

****

Like Kübler-Ross said, there are five stages of grief: denial, anger, bargaining, depression and acceptance. I spent weeks grieving the loss of Jim, the lifetime of losses I endured as a child, teen and adult. It was time for acceptance. It wasn't the black knight of death that took Jim from me, it was life. Like a thief that lurked in the shadows life stole an essence from my soul time-and-time again, but I finally recognized the tarnished knight who haunted me — the embodiment of my biological father who stood guard over my heart and stifled my relationships since my childhood nightmares created him.

The culminating grief of a lifetime of loss ended in overwhelming gut-wrenching emotion with pain so intense I couldn't breathe. I couldn't run, or hide, and for a moment, the hurt held onto my core, consumed my life and took away my drive, but eventually we all have to face our own demons...

I spent my life longing for love and, at the same time, running from it, until I met Jim. I loved him — and I treasured finally feeling love so much I shut my eyes, dismissing red flags as my own baggage, determined not to let anything destroy our relationship. Jim and I had incredible chemistry, and we built a connection, a foundation of compassion held us together, but sometimes that's just not enough.

It may sound odd, but after I got Jim's email, I read the words over and over, until somehow the words changed with the passage of time. At first I saw them contorted through tears and hurt. I could only react in pain. "How could he do this to me?"

But I really didn't want to know the answer to that question. If there was one thing I learned in life, it's that knowing details behind your pain doesn't make the hurt any less severe. Sometimes knowing the particulars intensifies agony even more. Maybe Jim was the perfect player expertly skilled at obtaining his prey, or maybe he truly was broken inside—the truth is, it really makes no difference.

Over time I could see Jim's life was in constant chaos. Every day he battled to survive. The fight for his life and his daughter was his priority. That wasn't a reflection on me, but rather the reality of his circumstances. He dealt with his own pain and loss the only way he knew how. I realize now that's what we all do. We struggle to survive the inevitable pain and grief that life bestows upon us the best way we can. We endure.

As much as Jim wanted love, wanted to love me, he was too hurt and broken to sustain our relationship. Maybe his Internet entertainment manifested as a search to escape the pressures in his life. I never meant to be one of those pressures, but our relationship was just one more thing he fought to hold on to.

Throughout my life, I gravitated toward broken men. Not because those men were jerks, but because I was so needy and vulnerable, I entered the wrong relationships, at the wrong time—at least wrong for me. The choices I made were mine alone and fit a perpetual pattern created by me that only I could break. Looking back, my pain was very real, but I wasn't the only one hurting. The men in my life fought demons of their own and the dynamics between us proved lethal.

The most important lesson I learned to date is this: If I can find a way to shatter the broken reflection in the mirror of my past, I can heal—then I can find true happiness.

Final journal entry, October 25, 2009

I chose to stay with Jim through his pain and I got burned. Maybe his agenda totally played me—maybe not, but it doesn't matter. He kept his word when he wrote that email to me and I know now the words came from love, not rejection. Love is a condition in which the happiness of another person is essential to your own. Sometimes the greatest act of selfless love is letting someone go.

I learned the hard way that growth is usually accompanied by pain, but I still believe the power of love is stronger than any other force on earth. If you defy it, fear it, or turn away and ignore it, you imprison your own heart. Trusting makes me vulnerable—makes us all vulnerable, but I'll never walk away in fear again, because I believe love is the essence of life and the balance I searched for since childhood. Love gives us hope, drives our passion and brings joy to our lives—With love we endure.

Jim walked out of my life, but he left behind something no one can ever take away from me. He triggered confidence and strength I needed to obliterate walls that had held my soul and dreams captive for decades, and the courage to let go of fear, embrace life and open my heart to love. I spent fifty years as a Wingless Butterfly, torn and broken, unable to feel passion—until I met Jim. He helped me heal my wings so I could finally fly.

Part IV: New Beginnings

One discovers that destiny can be diverted, that one does not have to remain in bondage to the first wax imprint made on childhood sensibilities. Once the deforming mirror has been smashed, there is a possibility of wholeness. There is a possibility of joy.
Anais Nin

    My flashbacks faded as visions of my past intersected with my present, and my new journals now reflect an incredible new life. Secrets and lies from my childhood held me captive for decades. They influenced my self-worth and decisions, but by allowing my history to imprison me with abstract limits, I empowered others to steal my happiness. When I bent my life around others, my life became about them — and each time, I lost another part of me. I was lucky though. I finally realized no person could fill the emptiness within my heart. I thank God the strong woman trapped inside waited patiently to pursue her dreams. My past, and those I encountered will always be a part of me. My experiences molded my character, but they don't define who I am or the path of my destiny.

    I believe we are all part of one single and divine spirit. As different as each individual may seem on the outside, we love, hurt, and bleed the same. Each of us has a unique story lurking somewhere inside, but too many try to fill emptiness with relationships. The one thing I am absolutely sure of is if we can shatter the broken reflection in the mirror of our past, we can heal — only then can we find true happiness.

Everyone Has Baggage:

A few weeks ago, EJ, my childhood friend, contacted me through Facebook. Her note caught me off guard since she was one of the girls who, somewhere between baby dolls and boys, teased and ridiculed me with no explanation. In her email she mentioned a recent visit with her mother.

"...I couldn't remember why we weren't friends in high school." Her tone displayed an air of innocence. "But my mom said,

"Casi was so pretty and was a model, so you all were jealous of her and not very nice to her as you got older...

"Yikes Casi, was I really? I have no recollection of that."

When I read her words my inner child screamed to write back: "Yes! Yes, EJ, how could you not remember? It took years to overcome the damage to my self-worth." Instead I simply wrote: "...I don't recall much of those days. A lot was going on in my life back then..."

It didn't make sense to dredge up the past. EJ, Missy, and the other girls may have reinforced my broken self-image, but they didn't create it. Yes, they ridiculed me, but I don't believe they teased with innate malice. More likely they struggled with their own insecurities and their actions reflected a need to bolster their own elusive self-esteem.

That's how baggage evolves, and everyone has it. If they say they don't, they're lying. Short of a lobotomy, it's impossible to avoid carrying the affects of the past with you in some capacity, but the difference lies in how you deal with it, and the key is perception. I discovered first hand that my perception of events was not the only righteous, significant point of view. Things aren't always black or white and when I took the time to see events through the eyes of others, my world looked dramatically different.

Take Zack for instance. When I considered Zack's past, his betrayal made more sense. Not that some transcendental revelation excused his secrets and lies, but I began to understand his motives. Growing up the image of a perfect child damaged his self-worth as much as growing up invisible disturbs others. At first the limelight inflated his ego, but over time he was terrified of slipping off the pedestal he'd been neatly placed upon. He realized his decisions created a domino affect on his family, but couldn't control the balancing act he generated between Cheri and me; the high became as addictive as heroin or cocaine. Zack's affair showed me, upfront and personally, that I could get so wrapped up in my own stuff, my frame of reference could skew the very instrument that guided all of my choices and decisions. That *ah-ha-moment* triggered a metamorphosis in my life.

If you take nothing else from the pages of this book, take this:

Life is now.

The past fades into a stockpile of old memories. Hopes and dreams create a glimpse of what could be, but now is where we live, and choices we make now determine our destiny.

I now try to live in the moments of my life, enjoying where I am now without clinging to what I no longer have. It just feels better. Now is where I find happiness. I don't live in the moment so exclusively that I disregard the future like Jim did, but I try to remember it is the journey, not the destination that shapes my life.

Playing The Victim:

Eleanor Roosevelt once said: *"No one can make you feel inferior without your consent."* For fifty years, I drifted mindlessly through the fog of my own perception in search of acceptance and unconditional love, unaware that what I truly longed for was the strong arms of my *father* to hold, protect and love me. The mist clouded my vision and influenced my choices. I looked to others to fill emptiness within my soul, but no one could make up for the bottomless cavern I didn't realize existed.

All of my feelings were valid. I was conceived in rape. My mother fled with Brie and me, presumably to escape the pedophiliac hands of my biological *father* and the repercussions of her volatile marriage. She spent her life hiding the truth from my sister and me, leaving us feeling abandoned, disposable and unlovable. Secrets covered by lies haunted me for twenty-three years and thirty-three years later, I still battled collateral damage. High school classmates contributed to my feelings of inequality with rejection. I married two men who lead double lives, was played, used, lied to, and repeatedly betrayed. The recipient of unwarranted fury and rage, I was emotionally and physically abused. I lost myself in oblivions of fear and anxiety. When diagnosed infertile, I was probed, tested and medicated. I lost my business and savings to a failing economy, and when my dad died part of my world died with him. Yes, like everyone, I have a past.

My life sounds traumatic and I guess it was, but I'm not alone or unique. We all have a history. Unfortunately, there's no instruction manual handed to us at birth, or a guide to the pitfalls in life. Maybe someday I'll write "Life For Dummies" but for now, I'll simply pass along my hard-learned lessons. Holding on to a broken past kept me a victim, and the best way I found to break free was to consciously make choices to open new doors and close others. The more difficult step by far was closing past doors and letting go, not just of people or relationships, but of anger, fear and grief as well--to basically destroy my all my protective defenses and live in the present.

The walls I built were meant to shield me from pain, but instead they trapped me in psychological bondage. Of course, like most people, I rationalized my actions. I defended my struggle even when I wanted to change. The *emotional me* felt hurt and abandoned while the *intellectual me* validated the pain with proof from my past. It felt easier to play the defenseless, injured little girl. But as a victim I was only a fractured image of the real me. Playing a victim kept my wounds from healing--and open wounds fester.

True Beauty:

One night, not long ago, I felt a little down so I treated myself to dinner. I sat down at a bar and ordered a drink while I scanned the menu. Not being one to strike up a conversation with strangers I quietly sat lost in my own thoughts, and ate my dinner in solitude. When I asked for the bill, the bartender told me the check was paid. My first thought was to look around for some man trying to hit on me, but the bartender said not to bother. The man who paid for my dinner had already left.

I must have appeared confused because he explained further.

"It was simply a random act of kindness."

Stunned, I scanned the restaurant again. I mean, I did things like that, but I never expected anyone to pay it forward for me. I wanted to thank the kind stranger, tell him he made me feel better, less alone, but a sudden realization washed over me. I didn't have to thank him, and that was the point. Even though I didn't see the man I knew he was extraordinary.

The moment puberty changed my body I was a *pretty girl*. Not that I felt pretty, but many people formed opinions of me based on my appearance, without taking the time to discover who I was on the inside. The lost and broken little girl who tried to please everyone found her road to acceptance through the superficial opinions of others. Over time I began to believe my looks were the only significant quality I possessed. But looks fade, and my already poor self-image deteriorated when pregnancy stretched my stomach and wrinkles etched age in my face.

When I recognized the meaning of true beauty, the gleam shown bright within me. Writing my story unraveled more than my past. The search put my life in perspective and I discovered that self-worth mutates when attached to a nebulous idea or a fleeting image. Who I am—who we all are—is defined within each of us. I am significant not through my appearance, what I own, or what I accomplish, but rather in who I am, how I live, how much I love, and how I touch the lives of others.

My greatest gifts manifested when I performed random acts of kindness to total strangers never expecting anything in return. The gifts came back to me in ways I never imagined.

The Price of Anger:

Anger shattered my life, so this section may be a bit philosophical, but please stay with me. I've come to understand that emotions are the driving force behind thoughts and behavior. Love, fear, passion--all influence choices and spontaneous decisions, but when the emotion of anger enters the mix, the outcome rarely takes a positive spin. I've seen first hand that consequences of rage cause far more damage than their source. Fury consumes the soul and leaves little room for anything else.

Case in point, Zack's anger grew more intense over time, fed by guilt attached to his affair. His violent outbursts reflected resentment he felt toward himself, but the boys and I felt the impact of his wrath.

Jack's isolation triggered uncontrollable fury that festered inside him for decades. While he wanted and needed love, the acid of his rage and bitterness destroyed every relationship he entered.

When anger spins out of control, a violent tornado looms, leaving a trail of collateral damage and tragedy in its wake. America mourned the Columbine and Virginia Tech massacres, and Hitler's obsession drew hate, power, and rage to an unconscionable level almost wiping out an entire nation. Road rage, domestic violence, child abuse, rape, and murder capture front-page headlines nearly every day. More recently, terrorism under the guise of holy war drives Radical Islamic terrorists, ISIS, and lone-wolf violence that rip our world apart. And if physical carnage isn't barbaric enough, emotional violence follows behind in epidemic proportions. Psychological pain imprisons victims in muted captivity, walking wounded, unnoticed until their suffering explodes through silence to chaos.

Anger seeps into lives of young children through bullies who tease and torment to hold their own kind of power over innocent victims causing life long damage and sometimes-tragic consequences. No matter the venue, anger devours love, hope, and happiness.

We live in a stressful world where the effects of anger run rampant. Political positions incite disagreements as varying perspectives find an arena for battle. Religious beliefs wage century-old wars. Anger, like every emotion, remains part of the human experience and no one is immune.

But anger, in balance, provides strength to overcome adversity. The very emotion that creates fury and rage also gives birth to resilience, courage and grit. The problem is figuring out how to use the emotion positively and defusing harmful facets.

In my experience, people who exhibit uncontrollable outbursts of anger, usually harbor deep-seated rage rooted in their past. Like Zack and Jack, they are so angry inside that the emotion is out of balance and always on the verge of eruption. It doesn't take much pressure for a seething pot to boil over. They react, not respond, and here is the difference: reaction is a knee-jerk reflex, while response is a process of thought and choice.

The key to controlling anger occurs through balance. When my internal storm threatens, I calm the storm without hurting others. How? I work out, run, write or vent-- whatever releases pressure in a positive way. If everyone would find a healthy outlet to blow off excess steam, perhaps the impact would roll like a wave across the world.

What Good is Forgiveness?

People ask me how I forgive those who caused me so much pain. The answer is simple. I try to view events through their eyes. For the most part, the men in my life were as broken inside as I was, drawn to each other like magnets, we existed in codependent relationships until our pasts collided.

Everyone gets hurt at some point in life, and most could build a great case against the responsible party, but animosity entangles people in a destructive web that holds them in pain. William Arthur Ward once said: *"Forgiveness is the key that unlocks the handcuffs of hate."* When I remember that people generally act to benefit themselves rather than to hurt others, it's easier to forgive. Anger and resentment blurred my vision, but compassion and forgiveness dissipated the mist, and it wasn't enough to just say the words, I needed to live them.

Life is far too short to waste even one day living in anger and resentment. Forgiveness is simply a choice. As much as I wanted to scream to the world "Look what they did to me," I found that forgiveness just feels better. When I chose to forgive, I drained my soul of a cancer--now love can grow and thrive.

Disabling Fear:

Panic disorder not only showed me my inner strength, it taught me how my attitude, positive or negative, created a self-fulfilling prophecy. I programmed my own mind with self-doubt that hid in the hard drive of my mind for most of my life. Fear and insecurity kept me struggling in silence believing I was somehow different, my anxiety greater or my fear worse and I justified internal protective walls.

Fear is a tough enemy to fight, but the battle opens a whole new world. I lost sight of the fact that everyone faces hurt, fear, loss, and disappointment. The courage to fight back waned at times but I want to note that there's not much difference between a courageous person and a coward. A coward is crippled by fear. Courageous people feel fear too. They simply choose to move forward in spite of it. Courage is another choice—a decision not an attribute. When I lived a life afraid of shadows, I ran away in fear. Instead, I chose to run toward my dreams.

Why Trust?

For me, trust flitted in and out like an elusive butterfly. Secrets and lies created a vacuum that sucked trust from every relationship I entered. When betrayal bruised my heart, my deepest fears of rejection and abandonment, tightened its grip. Trusting anyone, even myself, left me too vulnerable, but traitorous walls I built to keep everyone out only served to imprison my own heart.

I spent decades locked within a self-induced tomb, terrified to trust, but fear of unrequited love piercing my soul inflicting a mortal wound didn't simply lock up my heart, it paralyzed my passion for life as well. Jim broke though the fortress and weakened my defenses. When I finally let myself trust again, hot swirls of passion rushed through me. Not sexual passion, but passion for life, the drive that encourages the spirit to soar. It wasn't lust, I felt lust plenty of times over the years--and it wasn't infatuation, the childlike captivation that dulls sensibility. I opened floodgates of life-sustaining passion, rekindled my spirit and felt a sense of hope and energy.

When I locked out trust, my faith suffered, especially faith in myself. Trust creates a foundation every relationship--friends, family, business, allies and love--needs for survival. Like a house built on the edge of a crumbling cliff, any relationship forged without trust can't endure.

As hard as you may try to sustain a structure without a foundation, eventually it will crumble and fall. I know how hard it is to trust after having been repeatedly hurt, but if I let past betrayals keep me from love, fear wins. True love can't exist without trust, and I won't deny myself the most amazing gift in life. To truly give and receive love, both partners have to completely invest in the other, break down barriers and become vulnerable, and that requires trust.

Taking Responsibility:

Many might say I let people off too easily, they should be held accountable for their behavior. True, it wasn't okay for people to use or abuse me, but I made choices. I could have chosen to walk away at any time. Like everyone else, I am responsible for my own decisions. I fight my own demons and survive the best way I can, in a sometimes-relentless world, but I don't believe vengeance ever helps anyone.

There are always two people in every relationship, two points of view and two sides to the equation. Taking responsibility means being honest with others, but it also requires honesty with one's self. In my experience, that's the more difficult task. When I didn't see the truth, I made the worst decisions.

I consider myself honest and go out of my way to protect others from hurt. While my intentions were genuine throughout my life, my Pollyanna attitude imposed a whiplash effect I didn't realize. Whenever I dated someone, even if I knew he wasn't right for me, I avoided ending the relationship. Typically, I began to distance myself until he broke up with me. I rationalized my actions were to protect him from being hurt—until my *tell-it like-it-is* friend Allie set me straight.

"So, you're going to the party at Cocktail Cove tomorrow night, right?" Allie probed, and I knew exactly where she headed.

"I'd love to, but I promised Cole I'd have dinner with him."

"I thought you were going to break things off with him, Casi. You've told me so many times you just don't feel chemistry with him. Why do you keep seeing him?"

"I'm trying to break it off." I felt my own nostrils flare. "He's just such a nice man and I don't want to hurt him."

"You know Casi, when you waste your time with a guy you know you won't end up with, it keeps you from meeting someone else who could be perfect for you."

"I know you're right. I'm just trying to let him down easily."

"Hmm." Her sarcastic tone stung. She turned away, but I knew Allie, and she had more to say.

"Okay Allie, spit it out."

"Think about it—and be honest, Casi. It's hard to tell someone you're just not into them. You, girlfriend, are a coward." She paused a moment and watched my reaction to her straightforward remark before continuing. "Look at it this way. You're not just wasting *your* time; you're wasting *his* too. As long as he thinks he has a chance with you, he'll hang in there. You're giving him false hope—and honestly, what I think you're really doing is stringing him along as a backup, in case you don't find real love. Either way Casi, you're lying to him—isn't that the same quality you despised in men you dated?"

I never looked at my behavior that way but, as usual, Allie's words jolted like a wake-up call. I convinced myself I was protecting Cole's feelings, but my pattern actually hurt him. I'm sure I acted the same way with other men too. It wasn't fair to them, but the sad part was, I lied to myself as much as the men I dated. Unintentional lies of course, and they were all part of my *stuff*. When I was honest with myself, I realized I was in fact holding on to Cole as a backup plan, and I hated emulating the insincerity I saw in others. Children learn what they live and I guess adults do too.

I went out with Cole that night and had an honest chat with him. It was another milestone for me, the start of a healthier life. But breaking hearts is never easy, especially when I needed to break up with someone I was really into--like Ryan. The attraction between us tipped the scales with undeniable chemistry.

I truly wished a future hid in the cards somewhere, but red flags blinded me. I knew his interest was purely physical and I'm glad I was the one to break things off. Damn, dismissing that passion took a lot of resolve, but I felt so incredible about letting go instead of hanging on to false hope and ending up with another broken heart.

That's when I knew I'd changed. It's impossible to grasp ahold of the future while securely holding onto old baggage. I play an integral role in each relationship I choose to enter and take responsibility for my decisions and how they affect my life. Even if my past relationships were with men who intentionally used me, my perception of what happened was all that mattered. Perception controls reactions and guides decisions.

Pollyanna still lives somewhere inside of me, and pops her head out from time to time. Like Anne Frank, I choose to believe despite overwhelming evidence to the contrary, people are truly good at heart. Taking responsibility — being honest with myself as well as others--proved to be one of the hardest patterns to break. But my self-esteem soared when I flew on a trapeze for the first time without a safety net.

Can I Change?

It's been said that writers espouse wisdom on the very topic they need most. My life validates that statement. I believe I was destined to become a writer, if for nothing more than to write this book about recovery and self-empowerment. When I first sat down and put pen to paper I wrote, "*I am me. I can't change who or what I am any more than I can move the moon or touch the stars.*" Do people ever change the core of their being? Or does the core being hide below the surface behind a skewed mask created through time? The only constant in life is change. But views, feelings and abilities alter throughout each lifespan.

My perspective had me completely confused. I identified with memories and selective flashbacks that over the years became my frame of reference, but the foundation was built on lies.

A mouse in a maze, I simply reacted. When I got hurt, I learned to avoid similar situations, but in doing so, my world closed in on me. Fear of rejection kept me from pursuing my dreams, avoiding abandonment prevented me from trusting anyone, and the belief I was unlovable led me right into betraying arms. The patterns I set in place influenced all of my decisions. I got that, but cognitively understanding a problem doesn't make it miraculously disappear.

I always hated when someone would say to me: "Just pick yourself up by your bootstraps and get on with your life." How could they understand what I was going through? It's not easy to change. Little insecurities took a lifetime to grow and take root, and when I least expected it, they crept back into my mind and affected my judgment.

I couldn't escape my past. It was part of me, but when I finally understood that events in my life had skewed my vision and twisted my perspective, that single bit of knowledge led to an incredible transformation. I discovered infinite possibilities and I really liked me. That person deserved a chance to thrive without the influence of past beliefs. I consciously chose to let go of my past and believe in myself.

So, can we really change our destiny? My opinion is an unequivocal YES. If I can alter my direction despite my insecurities, I'm convinced anyone can. I reinvented myself and walked away from negative people who held me back. I surrounded myself with positive influences that constantly reminded me of my possibilities. Years of self-destruction won't disappear overnight. It takes time to untangle the web, but patience, persistence and belief that dreams can come true allows them to unfold. I am certain life is a self-fulfilling prophecy, and if I believe I deserve the best, I know I can achieve my dreams.

The Key to Happiness:

It took decades, but I finally understand the key to true happiness and successful relationships. When I look back on my life I see a crystal-clear reflection that empowers me to draw an exciting blueprint of my future.

I believe there is an innate passion within us all to not just survive, but to thrive. The moments in life are the essence of that passion. Regardless of what life throws at me, my spirit will never be extinguished. It may sleep within me, waiting patiently for a spark to re-ignite smoldering embers into a passionate flame again, but when passion burns the glow of its radiance warms my heart and touches the lives of those around me.

Neil Armstrong once said: *"I believe every human has a finite number of heartbeats. I don't intend to waste any of mine."* We've all been given a beautiful gift, but it's limited in duration. I wasted far too much time, lost in the pages of my story, and I let life just happen to me. Like Rip Van Winkle, I slept through years, waking to find much of my life behind me.

Don't waste a moment more of life. Don't wait until some specific event to find happiness. Don't let fear prevent you from pursuing your dreams. Don't pin your future on someone else's visions. Don't loose your own significance. Don't awaken after years to find you're at the end of the ride surrounded only by broken memories and regret. Just don't!

My life isn't centered on relationships now, except one I neglected forever--my relationship with myself. The worst abandonment of all was giving up on *me*. I became what I believed, powerless and adrift.

Like a ship without a destination, I wandered aimlessly through life with no goal or direction. It was easy to get lost when I had no idea where I was headed. Convinced all I needed to be happy was my knight in shining armor, I waited for someone else to rescue me and make me happy.

If a thousand perfect knights all lined up declaring undying love and devotion to me, my heart would not have healed. Encouragement, healing, and strength had to come from within. I gave up the dream of my knight some time ago, but I still believe in a love that will make my heart beat a little faster when he walks into the room, someone who will always feel passion when we kiss, and have a smile at the end of a hard day. I will never again settle for less than a passionate and loving mutual relationship based on honesty, respect and adoration.

Love was never meant to fill internal emptiness, to replace something lost, or to cover fears. It thrives when two people have individual hopes and dreams and common ones as well.

The Greatest Secret of All:

There's no doubt secrets dramatically affected my life and, though intriguing, they were not as profound as the significant secret always within my reach. One consistency throughout this manuscript captures the essence of my prescription for happiness. Multitudes of teachers, philosophers, theologians, scientists, and psychologists have touched on the secret throughout history. I'm quite sure everyone has heard it in some capacity but, like me, remained unaware of its life-changing message. It's not just an idea, it's a way of life and it changes everything.

Norman Vincent Peale described the secret beautifully when he said: *"Any fact facing us is not as important as our attitude toward it, for that determines our success or failure. The way you think about a fact may defeat you before you ever do anything about it. You are overcome by the fact because you think you are."* The secret condensed into simplicity:

You are what you believe.

Countless great minds discovered this incredibly simple secret to happiness and they can't all be wrong. Here are just a few examples:

* Bible--Proverbs 18:21 *Death and life are in the power of our tongue.*
* Norman Vincent Peale--*Change your thoughts and you change your world.*
* Earl Nightingale—*We become what we think about.*
* Buddha—*All we are is what we thought about*
* Marcus Aurelius—*A man's life is what his thoughts make of it.*
* Ralph Waldo Emerson—*A man is what he thinks about all day long.*

* Lance Armstrong—*Anything is possible, but you have to believe.*
* William James—*Human beings can alter their lives by altering their attitudes of mind.*
* Henry Ford—*Whether you believe you can or believe you can't, you are absolutely right.*
* Rhonda Byrne—*The law of attraction—we attract what we think about.*
* George Bernard Shaw—*People are always blaming their circumstances for what they are. I don't believe in circumstances. The people who get on in their world are the people who get up and look for the circumstances they want and if they can't find them, make them.*

***

As a Christian, I believe God doesn't make mistakes. He created me, so I have faith in that miracle. I may be the sum of my past decisions, but past choices don't have to determine my future. It took me decades to figure out, but the very fact I am alive validates my significance and I will never empower a position, person or possession to define me. Perception is the key to happiness in life and I hold the secret in my hands. My future is largely dependent upon my own decisions—the choices I make every day--and I'm convinced I can make a difference if I dare to live my dreams. Anything is possible as long as I have hope and believe.

Looking at the Future:

There's no denying I lived through a lot, but here's the thing, *bad things happen* — and they aren't selective. Life can dump on anyone at any time. No one controls what other people do or say, major occurrences in the world, or acts of nature, God, or the universe. I may not be able to change events that happen to my loved ones or me, but Andy Stanley reminded me that I *am* in control of at least part of my own destiny. I make choices for my financial future, education, career, and religious affiliation. I choose where I live, what I eat, how I treat my body, and the people with whom I walk through life. I also control my thoughts, reactions and perception — all of which form my attitude, so in the scheme of things, I really do control the direction of my life.

They say hindsight is 20-20 because when we look backwards, we see things we could have done better. As I wrote my memoir, my life unraveled and I saw my story unfold first hand. Not everyone literally does that, but the truth is we all write our stories every day. Andy Stanley's words will always be seared in my mind:

The choices we make write the pages of our lives and unlike a book, once written, they can't be edited. When you write your story remember you only get one draft so make it a masterpiece.

It's easy to flashback, but what if I flashed forward. Years from now when I look back on these moments, what will I see? I want to be proud of my decisions and the paths I took. I realize now my life is what I make of it, and like the old man, I choose to be happy. It took a leap of faith to believe in myself and dare to live my dreams, but it was well worth the risk.

It's a wonderful feeling to wake up each morning eager to start the day and to look forward to the future. I know life will be filled with unforeseen roadblocks, but now I look at them as challenges and meet them head-on. The new pages of my story reflect an exciting future, where each day I have a fresh chance to make my mark on the world--to grab hold and soar with eagles.

Finding True Love:

For most of my life I couldn't grasp the difference between being in love with someone and being in love with love. Now I realize when I looked for significance through someone else's validation, real love lay beyond my reach. I needed to learn to love and believe in myself before romantic love was attainable.

People ask me how my philosophy has worked over the years. Have I found true love? Well, I see men through different eyes now and I can spot players a mile away. I believe true love shouldn't be difficult to sustain nor should it hurt. A man worth crying over won't make me cry. I know the qualities I'm looking for in a man and I won't settle for less. The most important thing I learned is I'm happy on my own...No, I'm more than happy, I'm fabulous. I don't need someone to validate me to make me feel significant. I live my dreams without relying on anyone else and that makes me a better partner too.

No one knows what the future holds. As for the answer to the question, have I found true love? Well, all I can say is I'm living proof fairy tales really can come true.

Epilogue

Love comes to those who still hope even though they've been disappointed, who still believe even though they have been betrayed, and who still love even though they've been hurt.
Anonymous

I've changed a lot over the years. The knowledge of age is invaluable, I wish I had it in my youth, but it's hard to warn someone about the pitfalls of life. They listen but don't hear — until they are ready.

I met one of my new sisters and both of my aunts, so I have an amazing new branch to my family tree. I've rekindled friendships from long ago. **Nash** and **Adam** email me from time to time, as do **Kendall, Kirsten** and **Sandy**. **Drema** and **Bobby** live on the other side of Atlanta and we try to get together when we can.

I looked for **Brad** after my divorce and, after a lengthy search, came across his email address. Hoping to get a second chance to connect somehow, I wrote him a note unsure if he would even remember me. I was excited to receive a return email:

Casi,
Thank you for remembering me... How could I forget the girl with the same last name as me? We had a lot of fun together. I especially remember my trip to see you and your family in Virginia. I am doing well. I have been divorced for about six years. I have three boys, Bradley 28, Thomas 26, and Ryan 25. After I stopped coaching football at the University in 1983, I went to work for an investment-banking firm, and have stayed in the industry for the past 25 years. Last October I met a fantastic woman and we are now making plans to get married. Please give Drema and Bob my regards.
Take care,
Brad

I have to admit my heart sunk a bit when I read the third paragraph. He was getting married, but all things happen for a reason and I knew reaching out to Brad brought me full circle back to the moment I imprisoned my heart. I'd like to think a part of me still lives in his.

Jim finally reunited with his beautiful daughter after missing five years of her life. We are friends and he wants me to write a novel based on his saga. **Jack** found love and drifted out of my life, but I hope he finds a way to heal someday.

Josh earned his master's degree and works as the Dean of Students at a prominent Christian school. He still coaches basketball and swimming. He married **Lacie** on July 10th, 2009 and has a beautiful family. My grandchildren are the lights of my life, and Josh and Lacie's loving relationship inspires hope to everyone they meet — including me.

Jace has yet to find true love, but he has come a long way. He went back to school, worked in production and recording for a while and found his future in finance. He still has a remarkable stage presence. Like his brother, Jace is a talented writer and has written many songs, particularly when he was struggling with his identity. He has always had so many special gifts and I am thankful he finally discovered how special he is.

Zack will always be the father of my children and a part of my life. He and **Cheri** are still married and live a few miles from me. When Cheri and I purged our hearts, Zack's lies were exposed, but our intent was not malicious or vindictive. We truly wanted to be free to move forward and, in the process, found we had much in common. I wish them the best and honestly hope they discover the love and trust that Zack and I could never find.

Brie lives in denial about our biological *father* and still has no memory of her childhood. Like me, her relationships were tainted by the secrets of our past. Steve has been good for her—but I think her life is on autopilot. She was a beautiful, talented and spirited young woman once, but her self-image misguided her. I often wonder what wonderful things she may have accomplished had she loved herself enough to pursue her dreams. Maybe she will some day.

Nicole, Brie's oldest daughter, has struggled with her weight for most of her life and her health is a constant battle. She still fights to let go of her childhood trauma, but her three boys provide strength and motivation. Since the year she lived with me, I've thought of her as the daughter I never had. I hope this manuscript will reach out to Nicole—and the millions of women who have been abused, rejected, abandoned and betrayed, to give them hope and show them they are not alone. Believe Nicole.

Kathleen, Brie's youngest daughter, spent years fighting drug and alcohol abuse and experienced repeated failed relationships, but after years of struggling with inner fears, she finally pulled herself free. She reconnected with a man she knew from high school, has two beautiful children and is determined to follow her heart.

Though **Alex was** my half brother and not the child of my biological *father*, he didn't escape collateral damage. He earned a Master of Theology and became a Baptist pastor, but divorce forced him out of the ministry. He searched for his own new beginnings for years.

After Dad's death, Alex and I became much closer. We worked together trading the market that Jack and I had such trouble negotiating. Sadly, Alex passed away in February of 2016 and he took another part of me with him. He was an amazing man.

Dad turned 82 in January of 2009. My rock, my strength, he taught me so many invaluable lessons. He had energy for life that inspired me. Daddy fought lung cancer with the strength typical of everything he did, with a positive spirit and unending passion that kept him strong to the end of his days. He loved life and lived it well, but lost his battle on November 11, 2009. Daddy was my hero. He saved my life when he married my mom and will always live on in my heart.

As for me, I still believe in happy endings. My life didn't follow the course I would have set for myself, but my story isn't over yet. There are so many pages left to write and there will be no ending until the day I draw my last breath. I may never unfold all the secrets and lies of my past, but the point is, the details of my past don't determine who I am. What is important is *today* — right *now*. I enjoy each day and realize the choices I make *now* chart the course of my destiny.

I live my passion. My new time travel romantic suspense series, Lake Lanier Mysteries, is selling strong. Book one, Beneath The Lake, continues to earn 5-star reviews on Amazon and my publisher negotiated a movie contract that we recently signed. Now that will be fun and I can't wait. Book two, Beyond The Mist, will be released next month and book three, Between The Shadows, will follow next year. I have volumes of books lurking inside, so watch out world.

Maybe my latent yearnings sparked my muse to write romance. For years I wondered how my life might have differed had I taken an alternate course, but we can't turn back time. But I can ask the question "What if?" and inspire others to live their dreams through my writing. My passion lives in my fiction books: time travel, romantic suspense, and ethereal stories with twist endings and a sprinkle of magic; and in my nonfiction like Wingless Butterfly and inspirational manuscripts.

I now let my heart decide my future instead of the cynical voice of my inner fears. And the lingering question, *did I find true love?* I kissed a lot of frogs before I found my heart's desire. Promises of love burned and died when a noose of control flirted with my newfound strength. But deep within the ashen rubble embers flickered until the dawn of a new day. And an eternal gift lingered. I discovered what I really wanted, what worked for me. A knight in shinning armor offering love lives only in fairytales. But happiness runs eternal. True love lies in the heart, but also in the mind, in character, respect, communication, loyalty and laughter, through good times and through bad...not in drama, ultimatums, pushing, or promises. Happiness is choosing to love despite differences, imperfections and expectations while accepting ourselves, and others as the unique and miraculous individuals we all are.

The man of my dreams...sometimes you find your heart's desire was in your own back yard all along. My life circled back to **Mark**. When we first met, I was broken and emotionally unavailable. But Mark waited patiently, popping into my life and out again until my childhood wounds healed. Finally our hearts and lives aligned; so yes, I found my happily ever after.

In many ways, I'm glad my past happened exactly as it did, because it made me who I am today. I'm finally the woman I was meant to be, strong and confident with the passion and courage to follow my dreams. It's a great feeling to love life and look forward to every day. I never want to lose that enthusiasm again. I'm convinced more than ever that fairy tales can come true. Like the Princess in Disney's *Aladdin*, I'm in--

"*A whole new world, a dazzling place I never knew – and like a shooting star I've come so far, I can't go back to where I used to be.*"

I believe each of us has a mystical purpose on Earth. We are all significant. So live your life with passion. Fill each day with laughter and love. Enjoy the simple things--the soft glow of a sunset, the intricate design of a snowflake, a starry night--and appreciate every wonderful moment. You write the pages of your story each new day, so live your dreams and create your own amazing Happily Ever After.

The greatest thing about dreams is they don't expire. They can lay dormant for years and when you pull them out and dust them off, they shine like new.
Casi McLean

Note From a Friend:

A friend is one to whom you can pour out the contents of your heart, chaff and grain alike, knowing that the gentlest of hands will take and sift it, keep what is worth keeping and with a breath of kindness, blow the rest away.

Arabian Proverb

Divine intervention or destiny, I can't help but feel something guided me to complete this book. Wingless Butterfly isn't just my life story, a commentary or advice about relationships. I bared my soul for the world to see to reach out to the millions of women and men who live their lives as I did, broken and defeated, with a damaged self-image that limits them.

I never thought I would thank God for the fear and pain of my past, but without that journey I would not have discovered my strength, passion and purpose. The Starfish Story and Butterfly Effect from Chapter Ten inspire me daily to believe that not only can one person make a difference; they can create a perpetual motion to move like a wave throughout the world.

I've sifted through the chaff and grain of my life and kept what was relevant to my journey. I hope you take what is significant to you and carry the inspiration within your heart long after my words fade into memories.

If you can let go of past pain, believe in yourself, and follow your dreams--you'll find true happiness.
Casi McLean

My friend and best selling author, Haywood Smith, quoted: "The smoothest, and most convincing liar of all is memory." So, with that caveat in mind, I affirm that every detail depicted in this book is true, barring hallucinations, dreams, or self-induced fantasies. Some segments came from the recollections of family and friends, but most came from the events as I remember them. Names were changed to protect the innocent--but protection of the guilty is purely coincidental.

Acknowledgements

In everyone's life, at some time, our inner fire goes out. It is then burst into flame by an encounter with another human being. We should all be thankful for those people who rekindle the inner spirit.
Albert Schweitzer

The above quote by Albert Schweitzer captures the essence of gratitude I feel for the multitude of souls who inspired and encouraged me throughout my journey. They helped me heal the broken child within, fight through the imprisoning cocoon suffocating my heart, and find wings to fly. Numerous others, like ghostly whispers from the past, served as a constant source of strength and insight, especially those quotes sprinkled throughout these pages: Albert Schweitzer, Randy Paush, William Arthur Ward, Robert Heinlein, Eleanor Roosevelt, Franklin D. Roosevelt, Albert Einstein, Aristotle, Charles Sanford, Marcus Aurelius, Ben Stein, Henry Ford, Patrick Overton, Charles Popplestone, William Shakespeare, Barbara Kingsolver, Dorothy Dix, Anais Nin, Allan K. Chalmers, Ruth E. Renkei, Kenny Rogers, Ruth Barrick Golden, Rose Lane, Maxwell Maltz, Rhonda Byrne, George Bernard Shaw, William James, Lance Armstrong, Ralph Waldo Emerson, Buddha, Earl Nightingale, Norman Vincent Peale, Dale Carnegie, Plato, Neil Armstrong and several quotes of unknown origin.

Others rekindled smoldering embers that now fuel a passionate flame inside of me: Words of wisdom from The Holy Bible, Andy Stanley, Anne Frank, Charles Swindoll, Eckhart Tolle and Paul Simon. To Lou Owensby, Ann Seagrave, and Faison Covington, a special thanks for the wonderful broadcast that reached out to me on a cold Thanksgiving eve in 1982. You helped me conquer the most daunting enemy of all--myself.

My deepest thanks to friends and family who supported and encouraged me: Michael Young who displayed passion for living dreams, which fueled my self-confidence. My Aunt Ginny who told me things my mother never could, Tracy Franklin who forced me to see the truth--even when I didn't want to, Sprague Theobald who pulled me out of my cocoon to see a strong women in the mirror, Durstin Wilson who lead me to NPCC, and Chris Dejaegher, Susan Brown Addis and Leslie Chastain who supported me through years of transformation.

To my closest high school girlfriends: Hilary Johnson, who helped edit Wingless Butterfly and provided a life-long friendship, and Barb Perine Hymas, Bev Snowden and Dale Dillon Lips for beta reading my first drafts. My deepest appreciation and love to my family for endless support: especially my sister Patricia, who stood beside me through our search for the truth, and my brother Al, who not only encouraged me to reach for the stars, he truly believed I could reach them. My heart breaks that he now lives among those stars, but I know he watches over me. My children, who inspired me with courage to move forward when I felt the world crashing in on me and encouraged me to tell my story despite airing their lives to the world. My eternal love and thanks to my mother who spent her life trying to protect me and my dad, my rock, my hero, who was my source of endless inspiration.

I treasure the multitude of positive and inspiring people who wrote books, spoke at seminars, and demonstrated motivating visions that broke through walls around my heart, especially: John Ortberg, John and Stasi Eldredge, Mac Anderson, Joan Brady, Peggy Anderson, Sebastian Schabowski and Steve Harvey. Special thanks to Atlanta Writer's Club and my wonderful critique group who painstakingly coaxed and prodded me through rough waters: Barbara Conner, Ron Vigil, Mary Anna Bryan, Farrar Atkinson, Michael Brown, and Margie Kersey, and my amazing author friends: Jedwin Smith, Haywood Smith, Frank Cox, Lauretta Hannon, and Patty Callahan Henry.

And special thanks to Jamie, my amazing cover artist!

www.ingramcontent.com/pod-product-compliance
Lightning Source LLC
LaVergne TN
LVHW051514070426
835507LV00023B/3107